POLICING BLACK BODIES

POLICING BLACK BODIES

How Black Lives Are Surveilled and How to Work for Change

**Angela J. Hattery
and
Earl Smith**

ROWMAN & LITTLEFIELD
Lanham • Boulder • New York • London

Published by Rowman & Littlefield
A wholly owned subsidiary of
The Rowman & Littlefield Publishing Group, Inc.
4501 Forbes Boulevard, Suite 200, Lanham, Maryland 20706
https://rowman.com

Unit A, Whitacre Mews, 26-34 Stannary Street, London SE11 4AB,
United Kingdom

British Library Cataloguing in Publication Information Available

Library of Congress Cataloging-in-Publication Data Available

ISBN 978-1-4422-7695-6 (cloth : alk. paper)
ISBN 978-1-4422-7696-3 (electronic)

♾ ™ The paper used in this publication meets the minimum requirements of
American National Standard for Information Sciences Permanence of Paper for
Printed Library Materials, ANSI/NISO Z39.48-1992.

Printed in the United States of America

We dedicate this book to our friend, Darryl Hunt, who, tragically, took his own life on March 13, 2016. He was locked up for nearly twenty years for a crime he didn't commit. He died just ten years after his exoneration. We will never truly know the rage that continued to police you even after your release, and we wish you the eternal peace that was denied you on this earth.

To Earl: This was, in many ways, the most challenging and exciting project we have ever worked on. All of the conversations we've had as we walked to and from the gym, as we watched our TV explode with protests or the news of yet another unarmed Black man killed by the police. Sometimes it is simply too much to hold, and this book, as difficult as it has been to write, provided a way to "hold" the pain and to offer up a perspective that I hope will help others to be more critical, to see the truth of policing Black bodies. In everything we do . . . I couldn't do it without you.

To Angela: Done. This one, while it may have been the hardest, is a story that needed telling. The date on the cover may be 2018 but across all our work, it began way back when. Thank you for letting me be a part of this project!

To Travis, Emma, Porter, and Daniel: Use your many privileges to lift up others and to create a more equitable and free society for yourselves and for everyone around you. Your life will only be richer when you do.

CONTENTS

PREFACE

This book has been incredibly difficult to write, perhaps the most difficult book we have ever written. We wrote it to shed light on issues that were finally getting the media attention they deserved but which we felt were being shortchanged in terms of analysis. We also hoped to bring to light issues that are just as tragic but receive less media attention, like the school-to-prison pipeline and the wrongfully convicted. We also wrote this book for ourselves. Like many authors, writing is the strategy we use to make sense of the world around us, much like art and music are for others.

We have been to Money, Mississippi, and stood outside the store where Emmett Till was accused of the wolf whistle that ended his short life. We have visited the courthouse in Sumner, Mississippi, where an all-white jury took less than thirty minutes to decide the fate of the men who murdered young Till and allowed them to walk free. We have worked with exonerees and written about their experiences along with dozens of other men and women who are trying to make a life outside prison after spending years, often decades, locked in a cage.

After years of working on these issues, we decided to write this book in the spring of 2016, after Trayvon Martin and Mike Brown were murdered, but before Philando Castile was shot and killed at point-blank range, around the time that Freddie Gray was given the police van ride that ended his life. It was, and still is, difficult to imagine a time when the violence, the policing of Black bodies, will stop. We have trouble imagining when it will slow down. Some days we do research for the book or revise chapters, only to have our work interrupted by a news alert that another unarmed Black man has been killed by the police or another police officer who has killed an unarmed Black man is being acquitted, not held responsible. Why? Because they are simply acting on behalf of the state.

Sometimes it's simply too much to hold in.

But what happens if we don't have the strength to hold the pain and the courage to write about it?

We had no other choice. To write. To teach about these issues in our classroom. To protest and struggle the only ways we know how. To bring our expertise to bear in the hopes that our work will inspire and aid those who work in other spaces, in police departments and welfare offices and schools and prisons and innocence projects, those who march and those who visit their loved ones in prison, and those who vote. The issues we interrogate here are among the most pressing of our time. The United States will be defined by them. How do you want your society to be? What legacy do you want to leave your children and grandchildren? These are the questions we ask and the challenges we raise in this book.

Our perspectives on the issues are herein.

ACKNOWLEDGMENTS

Every book we write is influenced by others who contribute their ideas, critiques, and support. We are especially grateful to our editor at Rowman & Littlefield, Sarah Stanton, who believed in yet another one of our ideas and helped us to shape the manuscript and move the book through the process so that it can get to the reading public and inspire thoughtful analysis and probably some critique.

We are grateful to Nancy Xiong, David Corwin, and Mary Ann Vega in the Women and Gender Studies Program at George Mason University, who supported us by allowing us to focus on this book for two summers while they kept the Women and Gender Studies Center open and the program flourishing.

We would like to thank Om Arvind, Spenser Rush, and Sarah Said, undergraduate research assistants at George Mason University, who assisted us with research and created all of the amazing data visualizations that we include in the book. They also contributed their talents to preparing ancillary materials that can be used by instructors and book clubs who adopt the book. The artwork *Revolutionary Gaze*, which appears in chapter 8, was created by our talented colleague and very dear friend Suzanne Scott Constantine. Thank you, Suzanne, for allowing us to include your social justice art in our book.

A special thank-you to Danielle Rudes, who invited us to be part of the "Together Alone" project and conduct interviews with men and women incarcerated in solitary confinement. The experiences they graciously shared with us informed our work.

Thank you to so many scholars who contributed to the development of the ideas and arguments we put forth in this book; their work is cited. We give a special shout-out to three professors who went above and beyond the call of duty: Wendi Manuel-Scott, Tim McGettigan, and Darron Smith, all of whom took the time, near the end of the spring 2017 semester when they were busy with their own work, to offer thoughtful, engaged, and often critical reviews. We are indebted to Peter Wagoner, executive director of the Prison Policy Initiative, for his careful read and thoughtful suggestions on chapter 5 and our discussion of prison industries. Without them, this book would not be as precise and insightful as it is.

Finally, our biggest debt of gratitude goes to all of the folks who let us into their lives so that we could learn more about what it's like to be incarcerated, about the challenges that go with being incarcerated for decades for crimes they did not commit, and about the violence that many women endure that often lands them in prison. Thank you to all of the women we interviewed in Winston-Salem, North Carolina, and Rochester, Minnesota, and to the incarcerated people we interviewed in a state prison in rural Pennsylvania. A special thank-you to Kirk Bloodsworth, Darryl Hunt, and Mark Rabil for allowing us to spend time with you, work with you, and be with you in the struggle. We are grateful for your friendship.

As with any book, we are grateful for the input of others, but any errors remain our responsibility.

I

SETTING THE STAGE

There are fundamentally two ways you can experience the police in America: as the people you call when there's a problem, the nice man in uniform who pats a toddler's head and has an easy smile for the old lady as she buys her coffee. For others, the police are the people who are called on them. They are the ominous knock on the door, the sudden flashlight in the face, the barked orders. Depending on who you are, the sight of an officer can produce either a warm sense of safety and contentment or a plummeting feeling of terror.

I've really felt the latter only once, at the 2000 Republican National Convention. I was twenty-one years old. . . . [My girlfriend Kate] and I began to make our way through the multilayered security check-points. . . . I suddenly remembered that I happened to have about thirty dollars' worth of marijuana stuffed into my eyeglass case in a side pocket of my travel bag.

I felt a pulsing in my temples as I watched an officer open the main pocket of my bag and search. Then he opened the second pocket and finally the side pocket with my eyeglass case. He reached in and was about to put it back in when he stopped and gave it a shake, realizing there was something inside . . .

"I think the cops just found weed in my bag," I whispered to Kate. . . . "What? Why'd you bring weed?" And at that very moment . . . the police officer who'd found the drugs put my bag on a table and looked at me, as if to say Go ahead and take it.

Luckily for me, the harrowing encounter is the closest I've come to the criminal justice system. But over the past several years, I've spent a lot of time on the ground reporting both on criminal justice and on the growing social movement to change how it operates.

On a warm October day on the Westside of Baltimore, I stood interviewing Dayvon Love in the parking lot of a public school where he once coached debate.

One night his life almost changed. "I was seventeen years old . . . and that night I was catching a bus to go to New York to see a friend." . . . On his way to the bus station in the wee hours of the morning, Love and his father were pulled over by police. "They say I match the description of someone who stole a woman's purse."

They took Love out of the car and had him stand in the middle of the street. . . . Luckily, I had the presence of mind to think, "We had just stopped at the ATM to get the money I needed for my ticket." . . . Love happened to have the receipt from the ATM; the time stamp corroborated his story. "And luckily, they let me get away, but that easily could have went in an entirely different way."

By "entirely different way," Love meant being swept into the vortex of a penal system that captures more than half the black men his age in his neighborhood. By "entirely different way," he meant an adulthood marked by prison, probation, and dismal job prospects rather than debate coaching and activism.

Fair to say that Dayvon and I, in our ways, both dodged a bullet. . . . Out of those two brushes with the law, we both ended up with the same outcome: a clean record and a sigh of relief. But it took vastly different degrees of effort and ingenuity to get there.

—Chris Hayes, *A Colony in a Nation*[1]

We wrote this book to make people uncomfortable, to disrupt stereotypes about Black bodies and to debunk myths and poke at deeply held ideological beliefs, to expose the machine of racism. This book is meant to invoke discussion and controversy. Everyone who reads this book will likely find something they disagree with. And that is OK. What we hope to do is to get people thinking about these issues in ways that they haven't thought about them before: as systemic, as deliberate. Policing Black bodies is not something a few bad police officers do to a few unfortunate Black people. Policing Black bodies is as deeply rooted in American history, culture, and ideology as democracy and "The Star-Spangled Banner." And, in exposing the systematic and deliberate nature of policing Black bodies, some people will be made uncomfortable—they will be required to stretch intellectually, ideologically, and perhaps even viscerally. And it is in that stretching, in that questioning of our deeply held values and beliefs, that radical change is possible.

For many folks living in the second decade of the twenty-first century, names like Trayvon Martin, Michael Brown, Eric Garner, Tamir Rice, and Freddie Gray are not only familiar but will likely remain indelibly marked on our collective consciousness; all are lives that ended too soon, all are lives ended by violence, all were unarmed Black men killed by police officers or those acting in that capacity.

We credit the Black Lives Matter (BLM) movement[2] for bringing national attention to specific tensions between the police and Black communities across the United States and, most important, to the police killings of unarmed Black men and women as well as the overincarceration of Black bodies, mostly young Black men.

The BLM movement receives the most media attention when it helps to organize marches and protests, often when yet another unarmed Black man is murdered by the police. And certainly the BLM movement was in the spotlight when members challenged Hillary Clinton and Bernie Sanders during the 2016 presidential election. That being said, what receives less media attention, and therefore may be less familiar to folks, is the fact that the BLM movement is a call for racial justice for all Black lives, including transgender, queer, and undocumented folks. Much like our own approach, according to the official #BlackLivesMatter website (blacklivesmatter.com),

> When we say Black Lives Matter, we are broadening the conversation around state violence to include all of the ways in which Black people are intentionally left powerless at the hands of the state. We are talking about the ways in which Black lives are deprived of our basic human rights and dignity.

Like many people who care about racial injustice, we were and continue to be inspired by the continued attention that BLM activists and others have brought to bear on the state of Black lives and the indignities Black bodies continue to experience not just at the hands of law enforcement and the criminal justice system but in every aspect of life. Our own work benefits from the work of BLM activists, including Nekima Levy-Pounds in Minnesota, whom we had the pleasure to bring to our campus in the spring of 2016.

We decided to write this book for three reasons. First, as we watched the BLM movement gain prominence on national TV and as we watched the protests in Baltimore in the spring of 2015 and the trial of the police officers[3] who murdered Freddie Gray unfold before our eyes, we began to connect what we were seeing with some of our other research on mass incarceration, the prison-industrial complex and, most important, exoneration. We were struck by the fact that in all of the conversations on social media, blogs, and news outlets, no one was connecting all of these phenomena together; the focus remained narrowly on police killings and mass incarceration. Our book is an attempt to reveal the interconnected nature of all of the various ways in which the criminal (in)justice system continues to police Black bodies.

Second, though the BLM movement is actually focused on systems of oppression and exploitation ranging from poverty to underresourced schools to global militarization and global warming, the news coverage that the BLM movement receives is focused almost exclusively on what are presented as acute rather than chronic problems. This diverts our attention toward seeking the indictment of an officer who has shot and killed an unarmed Black man or toward passing laws that would require police officers to wear body cameras or toward demanding full transparency in police investigations. And all of these things are critically important and in need of attention. What our book does differently is interrogate the chronic and interlocking nature of the problem in two ways. First, as noted above, by pointing to the vast array of ways in which Black bodies are policed, including through mass incarceration, the prison-industrial complex, and the school-to-prison pipeline. And, second, by providing a historical context in which to locate the more recent tragedies that are being experienced by Black people at the hands of police officers and other members of the law enforcement and corrections communities.

Third, we wrote this book in order to provide a framework for analyzing unfolding tragedies, particularly those highlighted by the BLM movement, especially the police killings of unarmed Black men, by interrogating these events through the lens of two theoretical frameworks: (1) intersectional theory and (2) the theory of color-blind racism. When the experiences of Black bodies are analyzed through these theoretical lenses, not only will the interconnected nature of these various forms of policing of Black bodies be illuminated, but the *deliberate* nature of the policing of Black bodies will be exposed.[4] Only when we can see both aspects of these tragedies—their interconnected nature and their deliberateness—will we be able to engage strategies that offer some hope for reducing the policing of Black bodies, and by extension Black communities, and the senseless loss that is felt when yet another Black man is killed or incarcerated for the rest of his life.

The BLM social movement has brought a great deal of attention to the policing of Black bodies, yet the contentious relationship between police and the Black community is nothing new,[5] nor is it limited to those tragedies we see in the news, specifically the murder of Trayvon Martin, which birthed the BLM movement. Indeed, police have been "policing" the Black community from the very moment Black people arrived on this continent.

The system of *chattel* slavery that enslaved millions and millions of people of African descent for the first 250 years of U.S. history is the story of policing Black bodies. The very definition of people of African descent as "chattel" sets the system of slavery in the United States apart from all other forms of slavery past or present, and it sets the table for race relations today and particularly the story of policing Black bodies. Defining enslaved Africans brought to the United States as chattel, in the same category as livestock, meant that human beings could be (and were) bought and sold, often on an auction block, routinely ripping apart families. The status of a chattel slave, unlike any other category of slave past or present, meant that the status was biological and thus could not be shed—one could not buy or work one's way out of slavery—and the status was inherited. In 1787, the Constitutional Congress of the newly forming United States enacted the Three-Fifths Compromise, which dictated that enslaved people would be counted as three-fifths of a human. The Three-Fifths Compromise, along with the definition of enslaved people of African descent as chattel, provided the ideological justification for the ultimate in policing Black bodies, both literally and symbolically.

Slave owners employed policing tactics in order to restrict the movement of their property, enslaved men and women, including when they attempted to run away. But they also controlled literally every aspect of the enslaved body, deciding what work the enslaved person would do, what the enslaved person would eat and how much, and even if and when the enslaved girl or woman would have a child, which was accomplished both by raping enslaved women and by forcing enslaved men and women to engage in sexual intercourse for the singular purpose of increasing property for the slave owners at the exclusion of the enslaved people's "right" to enjoy raising a family.

David Blackmon, author of *Slavery by Another Name*, traces the development of a set of policies and practices that allowed the southern plantation economy to continue on the backs of exploited, often "free" Black labor. In an interview with Bill Moyers, he notes "that the southern economy and, in a way, the American economy was addicted to slavery, was addicted to forced labor. And the South could not resurrect itself." Thus, after the formal end of slavery in 1865, Black Codes were quickly put into place to restrict the movement of the newly freed, formerly enslaved people. Blacks were subjected, for example, to curfews and could be arrested for merely hanging out and enjoying their freedom or "loitering." And, whereas Black Codes became a tool for the literal policing of Black bodies, Jim Crow segregation, which lasted another one hundred years after the formal end of slavery, was a set of tools and strategies coordinated to provide both literal and symbolic policing of Black bodies, controlling where Blacks could live, which schools they could attend, and even the days of the week they were allowed to swim in the community pool, if they were allowed to swim at all. The maintenance of a nation's integrity requires constant vigilance.

In his 1997 book *Worse than Slavery*, David Oshinsky writes about the origins of "plantation prisons" that popped up across the Deep South shortly after the Civil War, including Angola in Louisiana and Parchman in Mississippi. Prisons like Angola and Parchman were constructed *explicitly* to continue to enslave Blacks and exploit their labor in a deeply rooted agricultural economy. Oshinsky notes that there were laws that allowed the police to arrest Black men for status offenses, like loitering, and incarcerate them, specifically at plantation prisons, during planting and harvesting seasons when the demand for this "free" Black labor increased dramatically. These same men were released, *conveniently*, after the planting or harvesting seasons ended, their labor extracted at no cost, because the state no longer wanted to pay to house and feed them.

Prisons didn't just make money by extracting the "free labor" of incarcerated men, but they also "loaned out" inmates to local businesses for a fee, a system referred to as convict leasing. Inmates might be loaned out for manual labor in local businesses, or they might be sent to forced labor camps or sentenced to chain gangs where they were forced to do dangerous, highly intensive physical labor under conditions similar to the work camps we typically associate with Russia and China. There were forced labor camps in places like rural Georgia, where incarcerated Blacks worked in turpentine camps and lumber camps where they were chained to machines, whipped, and provided meager rations, just like they had been on the plantations of the antebellum South. In North Carolina, inmates in chain gangs were forced to build roads. They were "housed" in train cars that were used to transport livestock and circus animals, they had limited toileting, and they were fed meager rations.

At the end of the Civil War and at the time of the Emancipation Proclamation, most Blacks in the United States lived in the South, its economy, as noted by Blackmon, deeply embedded in agriculture. As a result, most Blacks who were emancipated continued to farm, often as sharecroppers on the same plantations where they had been enslaved. Not eager to give over even a fraction of their wealth to freed Blacks nor to pay them fairly for their labor, many white plantation owners set up complex systems, including sharecropping loans and company stores, that quickly led to freed Blacks being deeply indebted to the plantation owner. The debt peonage system allowed the police to arrest Blacks who were over a certain debt limit and return them to the plantation owner, where they were enslaved and required to work until their debt was paid off. As Blackmon argues, less than a generation after Emancipation, Blacks in the South were once again engaged in slave labor. And though all of this may seem like ancient history, plantation prisons like Parchman continue to rely on incarcerated labor to produce all of the food consumed by inmates. Parchman also continues to participate in the convict lease system. On a walk or drive through the downtown of many Delta towns, one can see inmates from Parchman cutting grass for municipalities or cleaning the windows of local businesses. All of this begs the question of whether Blacks have been truly emancipated more than 150 years after the official end of slavery.

Though some readers might take offense to the comparison between slavery and the plantation prison system, the Thirteenth Amendment to the Constitution of the United States that "freed the slaves" retained a clause that allowed for the confinement and exploitation of incarcerated people. It reads, in part,

> Neither slavery nor involuntary servitude, *except as a punishment for crime whereof the party shall have been duly convicted*, shall exist

within the United States, or any place subject to their jurisdiction [emphasis ours].

Today, as we argue strongly in this book, the labor of inmates continues to be exploited vis-à-vis the prison-industrial complex (PIC), a system in which inmates are engaged in every kind of labor from agricultural to factory work to high-end electronics and computer monitoring, for which they receive very little compensation. The profits of their labor are reaped by states and private multinational corporations, as noted by Maria Gottschalk in her recent (2016) report on prison reform.

Expanding on the argument made by Michelle Alexander in her 2010 book *The New Jim Crow*, we demonstrate herein the link between mass incarceration and the prison-industrial complex. The huge profits made off incarceration—both the act of incarcerating people and the profits associated with prison labor—require that prisons continue to be populated, beds must be filled and labor must be harnessed.

Much like the Black Codes of the nineteenth century, the Black community continues to find itself the target of racist drug laws, policies like "stop and frisk," racial profiling in traffic stops, and disproportionately harsh sentences for all kinds of crimes from simple drug possession to capital murder, all of which contribute to the system of mass incarceration and the continued expansion of the prison-industrial complex, conveniently populated disproportionately by Black bodies.

POLICING THE BLACK BODY

We use the term "policing" to mean not only the literal use of police force to control the behavior of Black people—by arrest, incarceration, murder, and so forth—but also to mean the *control, regulation, and surveilling* of Black bodies: how Black people are allowed to "be," where Black people are allowed to go and when, and what choices Black people are allowed to make. What do we mean by symbolic policing? Black bodies are policed in a variety of ways that do not involve either law enforcement or the criminal justice system. For example, for most of the history of the United States, Blacks have been relegated to living in segregated communities regardless of their social class standing or ability to purchase a home in a more affluent neighborhood. This sort of "policing" restricts the access many Blacks have to the benefits of living in middle-class neighborhoods, including lower crime rates, better public schools, and cleaner, safer housing. Policing Black bodies also means surveilling Black bodies, defining what hair styles are "acceptable" in various work places or when and how Black people are allowed to express their discontent. Colin Kaepernick, a quarterback for the San Francisco 49ers, found that his Black body was policed when beginning in 2016 he elected to express his concern for the welfare of Black people by refusing to stand during the playing of the National Anthem. By conceptualizing policing more broadly, we are able to identify more clearly the myriad ways in which Black bodies are controlled by a variety of systems that restrict Black people, Black families, and Black communities from equal access to the opportunity structure while allowing white people, white families, and white communities nearly limitless opportunities to get an education, get a good job, buy a house, and live safely.

THEORETICAL FRAMEWORKS

One way to think about the system of racism that exists and persists in the United States is as a machine. The machine of racism has deep roots, it is embedded in our Constitution, in our laws and practices, so deeply that even when we attempt to revise those policies or practices, all we are really doing is tweaking a piece of the machine rather than dismantling the machine entirely and replacing it with something new and better. Let's say, for example, that the machine of racial domination is like a car. When the car was first built it ran on gasoline, but as the economy shifted and gasoline was more costly, and as our beliefs about gasoline changed—it became a "dirty" fuel, people became concerned about climate change and carbon emissions—car manufacturers tinkered with the car so that it could be powered by rechargeable batteries. The car itself didn't change. It still continued to drive down the road moving people from place to place. The only thing that changed was the type of fuel used to power it.

When we decided to write this book, we wanted to bring two important lenses for thinking about race more generally, and policing Black bodies in particular, to what has otherwise been a discussion that is both atheoretical and lacking in critical analysis. We engage two theoretical paradigms in order to interrogate the policing of Black bodies in the post-Obama era, intersectionality and the theory of color-blind racism.

Intersectional theory, which is rooted in critical race theory, provides a frame for understanding *power* and *privilege* as well as the intersecting nature of multiple systems of exploitation and oppression that operate at the structural level. Why do Blacks, and Black men in particular, comprise the majority of the incarcerated population? Why is one of the least common crimes—the rape and murder of white women by Black men—the most common source of wrongful convictions and exonerations? And how can we explain the pattern of police killings of unarmed Black men? These are exactly the types of questions that an intersectional framework is best suited to address and illuminate, questions that involve individual identity or positionality as well as structures of oppression.

Black feminist theorists like bell hooks and Patricia Hill Collins illustrate the concept of intersectionality with the image of a matrix. Hill Collins calls this the matrix of domination.[6] The matrix is composed of various systems of domination—racial domination, patriarchy, class domination (capitalism), heteronormative domination, ableism, religious superiority—woven together in a mutually reinforcing structure.

Joan Acker aptly describes the concept of the matrix using what she terms "inequality regimes."[7] Each regime or system stands alone and is simultaneously mutually reinforcing of the other systems. Writing about the rise of the robber baron class during the industrialization of the United States, Acker notes that three systems—capitalism, slavery, and patriarchy—all facilitated the rapid and massive accumulation of both power and wealth among families like the Rockefellers, Browns, Carnegies, and Gettys. We summarize her argument here. The system of capitalism rests on the ability of those with access to resources—those who own factories, land, and natural resources—to accumulate vast wealth by transforming these resources into commodities that are then sold on the free market. In the nineteenth-century United States, unlike any other industrializing nation at the time, concomitant with the economic system of capitalism was the system of chattel slavery. Some, though not all, of the vast wealth accumulated during the early years of the industrial revolution in the United States was the result of transforming resources into commodities via the use of enslaved labor. In an ironic twist, some of John Brown's ships, which were built in part by using enslaved labor, were used in the slave trade to bring even more Africans to the United States to be enslaved on plantations across the mid-Atlantic and Deep South. Quite simply, the owner of the company amasses tremendous wealth by not paying for the labor needed to transform the resources into commodities.

Simultaneously, the system of patriarchy required a rigid division of labor by gender, what many refer to as the public/private split. Within this rigid division of labor and space, women were restricted to the private sphere, where they were responsible for caring for the home and the family, while men were allowed to enter the public sphere where they could work for wages. In the case of the robber barons, with a wife at home to take care of the children and the home, he was able to devote all of his time to running a company and making money. Quite simply, great wealth was amassed by men like John Brown, the shipbuilder whose family founded Brown University, not only because he worked hard, made good decisions, and responded with flexibility to a changing market, but because he used enslaved labor and because he had a wife who took care of all the other tasks that were demanded by his family. John Brown probably did work hard. But when we analyze his massive accumulation of wealth without acknowledging the institutional privileges he had access to, we give him too much credit and we fail to see the ways that the massive wealth he accumulated was the result of the oppression of others around him because of his involvement in the institution of slavery.[8]

So perhaps John Brown was just lucky, his individual positionality allowed him to benefit from the individual positionality of others around him. To rest with that conclusion is to stop the analysis at the individual level. Structural oppression is revealed when we examine patterns. John Brown did not simply decide, as an individual, to own slaves or to require his wife to stay at home and take care of the family. John Brown's experience is part of a larger pattern of relationships that were, and still are, dictated by race, gender, and social class as well as other systems of power and oppression. All women who were married, and most who were not, were relegated to the private sphere. Most white men living in certain regions of the United States during certain time periods, and who could afford to, owned slaves. And the patterns were never reversed: there were no instances of Blacks who owned white slaves, nor were there any examples of women who ran large companies while their husbands stayed at home caring for the family. Structural systems, not individual decisions, positioned people in the matrix of domination in specific and deliberate ways that constrained or enabled their opportunities.

Another way to think about intersectionality is through the illustration of the birdcage that was developed by feminist theorist Marilyn Frye:

> Consider a birdcage. If you look very closely at just one wire in the cage, you cannot see the other wires. If your conception of what is before you is determined by this myopic focus, you could look at that one wire, up and down the length of it, and be unable to see why a bird would not just fly around the wire any time it wanted to go some-where. Furthermore, even if, one day at a time, you myopically in-spected each wire, you still could not see why a bird would have trouble going past the wires to get anywhere. There is no physical property of any one wire, nothing that the closest scrutiny could dis-cover, that will reveal how a bird could be inhibited or harmed by it except in the most accidental way. It is only when you step back, stop looking at the wires one by one, microscopically, and take a macro-scopic view of the whole cage, that you can see why the bird does not go anywhere; and then you will see it in a moment. It will require no great subtlety of mental powers. It is perfectly obvious that the bird is surrounded by a network of systematically related barriers, no one of which would be the least hindrance to its flight, but which, by their relations to each other, are as confining as the solid walls of a dun-geon.[9]

The beauty of the birdcage that Marilyn Frye describes is that it cages the bird whether the bird can see it or not. Indeed its power is in our percep-tion that the bird, if it were just clever enough, could escape the cage and fly away, free to pursue its dreams and reach its potential. The solution, then, is to teach the bird to escape the cage, our focus diverted conven-iently away from the cage itself, which, were it dismantled, wouldn't require anything of the bird other than to fly away. The birdcage is much like the systems of policing that constrain the Black body and prevent it from living freely and accessing the American Dream. And, like Marilyn Frye's birdcage, we in the United States are far more comfortable talking about what Black people can do to avoid having their bodies policed—not acting like thugs, not marching in the streets to protest yet another police shooting of an unarmed Black man, or not "refusing" to comply when they are pulled over on a traffic stop—than we are talking about who built the police cage in the first place, why it was built, and what the impact of the cage is on the lived realities of Blacks and whites living in the United States.

Another way to think about intersectionality is to think about a spiderweb (which is kind of like a matrix). The spiderweb is both an individual web and a structural web. The outer edges of the spider web are looser, the silky lines are farther apart, and there is more space between the lines; consequently it is much harder for a fly or other insect to get caught in the outer parts of the web. For people with many privileges, they exist in a part of the web that is loose, where they can access opportunities and not get "stuck," where there are few silky lines constraining them. In contrast, for those occupying the center of the web, where the silky lines are close together, it is easier (and people are more likely) to get caught, to be unable to disentangle themselves from the web and access the opportunities that lie outside the web.

Moving beyond the particulars of individual social location or positionality, when we examine the web looking for patterns, we see that people with the most privileges—white, heterosexual, Christian, college-educated, able-bodied, men—are clustered around the edges of the web, where the silk strands are loose, where one is less likely to be stuck, and where one can more easily access opportunities. As we move in closer to the center of the web, we see more and more women, Black and Brown people, sexual minorities—including lesbian, gay, bisexual, transgender, and queer (LGBTQ) people—poor people, and people with disabilities. And those clustered in the center of the web are those with multiple marginalized identities: for example, queer Black women.

If racism and other systems of oppression were merely individual and not structural, we might expect some clustering of groups of people in different parts of the web. But in fact the type of clustering we see is indicative of systematic patterns that have existed for centuries, which produce differential access to the opportunity structure over generations and thus the accumulation, among particular individuals and specific communities, of advantage and disadvantage.

Black feminists such as Hill Collins were among the first to deconstruct the matrix as a relational system of privilege and oppression; any resource, including access to the opportunity structure, is finite. Hence, for every opportunity one person or group is afforded, another person or group is denied that same opportunity. In other words, individuals and groups are in constant competition for scarce and desirable resources,

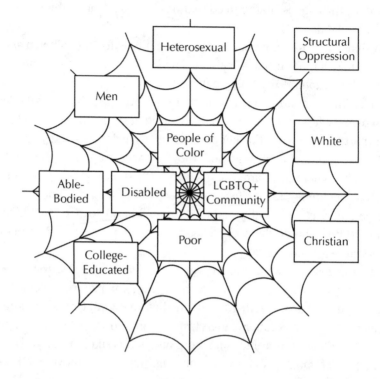

The Spiderweb of Intersectionality

including admission to college, buying a home in a nice neighborhood, or being hired into a well-paying job with good benefits. When institutions, including admissions offices, human resources, and mortgage lenders, discriminate by race, gender, or other social factors, over time the systematic distribution of privilege and oppression leads to one of the most insidious outcomes of systematic oppression: the accumulation of advantage and disadvantage. As planters in the South accumulated land and people as property, formerly enslaved people accumulated debt. And the patterns were exacerbated over time such that today the vast wealth of the southern plantation economy is concentrated in the hands of a few white planters and their families, and the vast majority of Blacks continue to live in extreme poverty, often still indebted as a result of the exploitative practices of sharecropping and debt peonage that their parents, grandparents, and great-grandparents were forced to endure.

In her latest text, published in 2016, Patricia Hill Collins, along with her coauthor Sirma Bilge, extended the concept of intersectionality as an analytical tool beyond the concept of the matrix of domination. They argue that in order to utilize intersectionality to understand contemporary social issues, we must understand that intersectionality is composed of several core ideas: relationality, social context, power, inequality, and social justice. In other words, when examining any phenomenon, we must focus our attention on the social context in which it exists, the ways in which inequality is structured and distributed, which groups put the current structures in place (power), and how they benefit from the current structures (relationality). Lastly, intersectionality is not merely an analytical tool; it is a call to action (social justice). Once the matrix, the birdcage, the spiderweb are revealed, what are those with power going to do about it? There are at least two choices: we can do nothing and allow social inequality not merely to exist but to expand, or we can identify strategies that will result in the dismantling of the structures that create social inequality and work toward relations that are more equitable.

Hill Collins reminds us that intersectionality is relational. In 1952, Frantz Fanon[10] wrote about the relational context of slavery: there can be no slave without a master, but there can also be no master without the slave. Oppression does not exist in a vacuum; every act of oppression benefits someone. Every benefit is the direct result of an extraction or exploitation. The plantation owner's wealth is created by the exploitation of the enslaved person's labor. Dozens of multinational corporations, including Victoria's Secret and McDonald's, increase their profits by exploiting the labor of incarcerated Black bodies. White, wealthy politicians fill up the seats in Congress, making policy that reduces access to food stamps, student loan debt relief, and health care, in part because of the felony disenfranchisement of Black voters. An intersectional framework therefore advances our understanding of the experiences of Black people, Black families, and Black communities because it illuminates not only the oppression experienced by Black people but also the privileges that are simultaneously accruing to whites—individuals, families, and the broader white community. Quite frankly, white people and white communities would lose not only wealth but also the power and control to dictate the terms of literally every aspect of the lives of those living in the United States—from policing practices to college admissions to voting restrictions to mortgage lending—if the system of racial domination were toppled and racial equality became the law of the land. White people and white communities have a vested interest in maintaining the racialized order that the United States was founded and built on.

OPPRESSION IS A NECESSARY CONDITION OF PRIVILEGE

One critique of our arguments contained in this book will likely be that not all white people are bad, that some white people also experience oppression, that these problems are more about class than race, and that the overwhelming vote cast by white people that elected a Black president not once but twice is evidence that the United States is now a postracial society.

This is where the perspective of the theory of color-blind racism is useful for understanding the ways in which good people can still be co-opted into "bad" behavior—in other words, how white people with very low levels of individual racism continue to participate in a racist system despite their best efforts not to do so.

In the late 1990s, Eduardo Bonilla-Silva emerged as one of the first scholars to write about the concept of color-blind racism. Color-blind racism, according to Bonilla-Silva, is the notion of what whites are expressing when they say, "I don't see race." We make a similar argument to Bonilla-Silva's in our book *African American Families: Myths and Realities*, in which we carefully debunk the argument that whites make in the post-Obama era that the United States is a postracial society by citing data on the continuing race gaps in education, work, income, and wealth, as well as incarceration. But when white people argue that they don't see race, what they really mean is that they refuse to see the system of racial domination that privileges them and oppresses everyone else.

Bonilla-Silva, like intersectional scholars, is also careful to point to the structural nature of racism. He writes,

> Racism is above anything, about practices and behaviors that produce a racial structure—a network of social relations at social, political, economic, and ideological levels that shapes the life chances of the various races. This structure is responsible for the production and reproduction of systemic racial advantages for some (the dominant racial group) and disadvantages for others (the subordinated races). Thus, racism as a form of social organization places subjects in common

social locations. As subjects face similar experiences, they develop a consciousness, a sense of "us" versus "them." This is why I stated in my *American Sociological Review*[11] piece that "(a)fter the process of attaching meaning to a 'people' is instituted, race becomes a real category of group association and identity." In this sense, racism and races have a material foundation. Races are indeed invented social categories, but they are socially real and reenacted in the everyday life in encounters in all sorts of situations and spaces. . . . The mutability and even instability of the category "race" is not unique to this category as all social categories (e.g., gender, class, etc.) are socially rather than biologically real; hence, they all are subject to change. To be clear, although race is a socially produced classification scheme (e.g., who is Black, white, Indian, or anything changes over time and varies from society to society), races are meaningful categories because as W. I. Thomas and Dorothy Thomas[12] stated a long time ago, they are "real in their consequences."[13]

Policing Black bodies is about more than individual people policing, incarcerating, and surveilling Black bodies; it is the deliberate and intentional creation of a set of structures whose primary purpose is the control of the distribution of resources and opportunities. Color-blind racism is built on the understanding that though these structures may exist, they are not racialized. They were not designed specifically to police Black bodies; Black bodies just happen to have gotten ensnared in the spiderweb or locked in the birdcage. And this is perhaps the most dangerous aspect of color-blind racism.

Tricia Rose[14] argues that color-blind racism is insidious not only because it focuses our attention on the individual rather than the structure, but also because it renders invisible the collective nature of color-blind racism. As Rose says, "We are all deeply implicated, differently implicated, but implicated." Color-blind racism not only allows but in fact *requires* us to ignore patterns of racial inequality, in this case the systemic and structural apparatuses that are deeply rooted and entrenched in the history of the United States, from our slaveholding centuries to the U.S. Constitution, which allow for the enslavement of incarcerated bodies and prevent us from seeing the residual impact of these structures well into the twenty-first century.

Ferguson didn't just happen.

Black men didn't just start committing more crime and start getting locked up or shot in the back.

Black women didn't just start experiencing the criminalization of their pregnant bodies.

When we honestly examine the history of race in the United States and the four-hundred-plus-year history of policing Black bodies, we realize that none of this is new and none of this is unexpected.

"The machine [colonialism] is not a thinking machine, nor a body endowed with reasoning faculties. It is violence in its natural state, and it will only yield when confronted with greater violence."[15]

What is unique is the role that color-blind racism plays in preventing us from naming it and thus analyzing it and fighting against it.

As Tricia Rose argues, color-blind racism is appealing because it reinforces the values Americans hold so deeply and with immense pride: meritocracy and egalitarianism. Color-blind racism allows us, invites us, supports us in believing that structural racism has been eliminated, first by the Thirteenth Amendment and the end of formalized slavery and next by the historic Supreme Court decision *Brown v. Board of Education* in 1954, the Civil Rights Act of 1964, and countless other decisions and laws that had the *appearance* of removing the structural barriers that blocked Black people's access to the American Dream. In reality, though each of these decisions brought about some positive change, none of them uprooted or dismantled the system of racial domination that is as much a part of the fabric of American life as apple pie and "The Star-Spangled Banner."

Color-blind racism is particularly appealing to whites because it allows them to overestimate the impact of these decisions and changes in American jurisprudence. White people feel good when they see Black children and white children playing together. Many white people felt damn good voting for the nation's first Black president. But the danger in this good feeling is that it renders invisible the structural inequalities that will continue to play out more or less as they always have, regardless of our intent and regardless of a Black president sitting in the White House. We invite you to examine the data on the accomplishments of the Obama administration as these apply to dismantling the systems of oppression. As confirmed by the National Urban League report (2016) titled *Locked Out*, which details the impact of the Obama administration as it relates to Black Americans,[16] inequalities, including poor schools, poverty, mortgage foreclosures, and incarceration, continue to be the defining experiences of Black America, and rather than getting better, on some of these measures Blacks are actually doing worse.

Color-blind racism prevents us from pointing a finger at the structure; rather it allows us, even requires us, to attribute success and failure to the individual. So, when the majority of white kids grow up and go to college, get good jobs, and buy houses in middle-class neighborhoods, we will pat them on the back. Their parents raised them well. They took advantage of the opportunities in front of them. They made good decisions. And all of that may in fact be true.

But when Black kids grow up and barely graduate from high school, and those who do are deemed not "college ready," or when they try to go to college but aren't successful—in the words of the late United States Supreme Court justice Antonin Scalia, arguing in the *Fisher v. University of Texas* case, Blacks should attend "a less-advanced school, a slower-track school"—and they leave without a diploma but with a truckload of student debt, or when they buy a house they can't really afford and default on the loan and have the house foreclosed on, we will express discontent that they didn't take advantage of the opportunities in front of them, that it's a shame they were raised by a single mom who couldn't parent them well, and we will blame them for falling in with a "bad crowd." And some of this may be true.

But the point is this: most if not all of the white kids had a chance, they live in a system that was designed for them, while many of the Black kids frankly never had a chance, not because they were raised by single moms or made bad choices, but because the system was designed for them to struggle and for many of them to fail.

How, one might ask, after all of the changes in policies and laws and practices that overturned racist structures would we construct a system designed for some people to succeed and others to struggle and fail? That's not meritocracy. That's not equal opportunity. That's not egalitarian.

Exactly. It's not, because the system of racial domination was intentionally built to sequester opportunities—to get an education, to get a good job, to buy a home—for whites and to deny access to these same opportunities to Blacks. And this system has never been dismantled. No policy or Supreme Court decision was ever intended to dismantle it.

That's the thing about color-blind racism: it allows us to *believe* that the system of racism has been successfully dismantled, pulled apart piece by piece, with each piece discarded, never to be resurrected again. Color-blind racism allows us to believe that the system of racial domination was not only dismantled but in fact replaced by a system based on equality of opportunity, the fundamental principle on which our country was founded.

But in fact the system of racial inequality was never dismantled nor replaced, and the system that remains is one that is built for the success of white people—OK, not all white people, perhaps not poor white people,[17] but white people. And it was designed for Black people to struggle and often to fail. OK, not all Black people—not Tiger Woods or Barack Obama or Oprah Winfrey, all of whom did struggle, however.

The race machine we described at the beginning of the chapter has been tweaked, much like the car. The historic decision in *Brown v. Board* banned racial segregation in school, at least in public schools. But because Blacks and whites continued to live in their same segregated neighborhoods, legal segregation (du jure) was soon replaced by de facto segregation. Faced with data on the results of de facto segregation in their own communities, whites, even those with progressive racial attitudes, began to express a preference for "neighborhood" schools. Whites were fond of saying that they didn't see any reason why Blacks and whites couldn't go to school together; it just made sense to them that students should be able to walk to school—to their "neighborhood" school. Today, in the post-Obama era, public schools are as segregated as they were in 1954. As recently as 2016, a federal judge had to order a school district in the Mississippi Delta to desegregate its middle and high schools, capping a legal battle that has dragged on for more than five decades.[18]

Color-blind racism allows us to explain this away as choice or preference—wanting children to walk to school—rather than as the perpetuation of educational inequality. We all feel better. All except for the Black students who continue to attend underresourced schools with low graduation rates and almost no preparation for college, and the racial gap in education is as wide as ever. The car may be running on an electric battery charge, but it's still the same car.

And, sadly, as we noted in our 2014 book *African American Families: Myths and Realities*, the machine of racism will continue to churn regardless of who is driving it. Much like a car on autopilot, electing the first

Black president, Barack Obama, has done little to change the structural racism that continues to persist and police Black bodies.

Baltimore, which experienced severe riots during the spring of 2015, has a Black mayor, a Black police chief, a Black congressman, and even a Black prosecutor. And yet Black residents of Baltimore face some of the deepest poverty and some of the worst schools, and they fear for their lives residing in a city with one of the highest per capita homicide rates, a city where police officers, Black and white, killed Freddie Gray and none were held accountable by the law. As we will argue throughout the book, changing leadership is important for many, many reasons, but we need to guard against being lulled into a state of complacency if we believe that electing Black officials, even a Black president, signals that we have entered a postracial America. It will take much more than changing drivers for the machine of racism to be fully dismantled.

The race machine is a system that puts a seemingly endless set of barriers—like roadblocks—in the pathway of Blacks, such that those who do succeed generally have to work much harder as they climb over the barriers on their way to the American Dream. And of course most don't succeed, not because they didn't want to or try hard, but because at the end of the day they simply couldn't overcome all of the barriers that lay in their path.

The problem, of course, is that for the most part Americans never talk about the barriers, the obstacles. We assume a level playing field. And thus, when we witness different outcomes, we blame Blacks for not working hard or saving or making good choices, and we applaud whites' work ethic and ability to defer gratification.

This gap, between what we believe and what we do, continues in postracial America, and it is one of the most powerful tools in maintaining the system of racial oppression precisely because of our failure to acknowledge it.

This book examines the ways in which a variety of practices, from mass incarceration to sexual abuse to the school-to-prison pipeline, serve to police Black bodies. Our book is unique in that it relies on a range of methods to construct the analysis, including ethnography, interviews, and secondary analysis of data. We begin by focusing on riots, social protests that have been taking place for hundreds of years and that are almost always sparked by racial antagonisms ranging from the brutality of slavery to Jim Crow segregation to police killings of unarmed Black men (chapter 2). We then move on to discuss several aspects of incarceration, including mass incarceration (chapter 3), the school-to-prison pipeline (chapter 4), and the prison-industrial complex (chapter 5). Chapter 6 is devoted to a wide-ranging discussion of the ways in which Black *women's* bodies are policed, followed by chapter 7, an examination of the policing of trans bodies. Chapters 8 and 9 are organized around analysis of data that we have compiled and analyzed: police killings of unarmed Black men and exonerations, respectively. The final chapter is reserved for applying the theoretical lenses to each of the various substantive issues we explore and for theorizing recommendations for moving forward.

2

URBAN RIOTS AND PROTEST, OR A LOGICAL RESPONSE TO POLICING BLACK BODIES

I read the governor in the *New York Times* today and he was saying in the paper that—[the week of the riots in Baltimore]—he was saying "violence will not be tolerated." . . .

I have a problem when you begin the clock with the violence on Tuesday [April 21, 2015, two days after the death of Freddie Gray]. Because the fact of the matter is that the lives of black people in this city, the lives of black people in this country have been violent for a long time. Violence is how enslavement actually happened. People will think of enslavement as like a summer camp, where you just have to work, where you just go and someone gives you food and lodging, but enslavement is violence. . . . Jim Crow was enforced through violence. . . . You didn't politely ask somebody not to show up and vote. You stood in front of voting booths with guns. . . . And the state backed this; it was state-backed violence. . . . And incarceration is . . . a very nice word, for what actually happens when they cart you off and take you to jail for long periods of time. Jails are violent. . . . And . . . this mirrors the kind of violence that I saw in my neighborhood as a young man in West Baltimore.

—Ta-Nehisi Coates, "The Clock Didn't Start with the Riots"[1]

Just like many people living in America, and we assume abroad, beginning in the spring of 2012 and continuing up through the writing of this book, we were transfixed as we watched on our TV as protest after protest unfolded in the aftermath of the shootings of unarmed Black men, beginning with Trayvon Martin in Sanford, Florida, through to Freddie Gray in Baltimore and Philando Castile in St. Paul, Minnesota. The protests shared many things in common, including the "triggers," of which there are typically two: (1) the announcement of the police murder of yet another unarmed Black man and (2) the aftermath of the criminal case when the police officers who killed unarmed Black men are not indicted or, in the rare case they go to trial, are acquitted. Yet as we sat and watched protest after protest unfold on our TV over the previous four years, we realized that there were several things missing among the comments by protesters and analysts, specifically an examination of the patterns that characterize most protests, an analysis that put the protests into a historical context, and a frank and honest discussion of the underlying root causes of the protest, for which the police shooting of yet another unarmed Black man or the failure to indict or in any way hold the police officer who killed the unarmed Black man accountable was simply the trigger, the match that reignited the flame. There was rarely if ever a discussion of both the importance of each individual protest and the fact that each one is yet another in a very long line of protests that have marked the relationship between the policing of Black bodies and Black bodies themselves. This was, along with our observation that other forms of policing of Black bodies were and remain absent from social commentary, among our main reasons for writing this book.

Though it is true that not all protests have been, as in Sanford, Florida; Ferguson, Missouri; Baltimore; Chicago; and Minneapolis, a response to the police killing of an unarmed Black man, a phenomenon to which we devote an entire chapter, all protests and social actions taken by Black activists have been a response to or a call for changes in the ways in which Black bodies are policed.

For example, in 1898, Blacks in Wilmington, North Carolina, protested after the southern Democrats took over the North Carolina legislature in a move that many Blacks perceived as a strategy that would turn back Reconstruction policies from which they had benefited.

In 1921, the deadliest of all riots took place in Tulsa, Oklahoma. It is estimated that fifty whites and upward of three hundred Blacks were killed. The Tulsa riot was sparked by the arrest of a Black man, Dick Rowland, who was accused of raping a white woman in an office building.[2] Though the larger urban areas in which riots occur, including New

York and Los Angeles, remain largely unchanged after protests, unfortunately, many neighborhoods and cities in which major riots occur, including Watts and Harlem, never fully recover, least of all for the Black folks who live there. And this is clearly the case for the Greenwood section of Tulsa. According to the late historian Dr. John Hope Franklin[3] in his testimony before the House Judiciary Committee, Subcommittee on the Constitution, Civil Rights, and Civil Liberties, titled "Tulsa Still Hasn't Faced the Truth about the Race Riot of 1921," the 1921 riot had a devastating social, political, and economic impact on the Black community in Tulsa that lasted for decades. Both homes and businesses were destroyed, and little if any responsibility was assigned to the perpetrators.

> Prior to the riot, the black community in Tulsa had been economically prosperous, not to mention spiritually and physically cohesive and strong. The riot was economically devastating, and given the lack of assistance and almost absolute segregation that existed for decades after the riot, people were not able to recover economically. The combination of circumstances that existed after the riot made it impossible for blacks in Tulsa to live as upstanding and fearless citizens even if they initially tried to do so. People did not just lose their homes and businesses, they seemed eventually to lose part of their dreams and their will, at least as a group.[4]

Throughout the 1950s and early 1960s, Black people engaged in complex and well-orchestrated public and private strategies in an effort to effectively dismantle Jim Crow segregation and its consummate inequalities and advance civil rights for all. Many readers will be familiar with marches in the streets of Birmingham or Selma, protestors often being sprayed by fire hoses and threatened by police dogs, or sit-ins at lunch counters in places like Greensboro, North Carolina, or Nashville, Tennessee. One of the most powerful strategies was the famous yearlong Montgomery bus boycott that led to the desegregation of buses. Blacks and whites also participated, often side by side, in summer teach-ins and voter registration drives, as well as in Freedom Summer, riding interstate buses in an attempt to get laws passed that would integrate interstate transportation. These periods of intense struggle for social change and greater equality, both nearing the end of Reconstruction and during the civil rights movement, reflect what is in many ways the story of the most recent riots, including Ferguson and Baltimore: the fight for racial equality, the right to control one's body and one's movement, and the right not to be shot and killed or beaten nearly to death just because you are a Black man.

Urban protests and their relationship to policing Black bodies have a long history in the United States, but a complex analysis that underscores how protests are the outcome of police brutality, poverty, income inequality, unequal schooling, and poor job security—or no job at all—is rarely conducted. It is these relationships that we will unpack, deconstruct, and explicate here.

Riots occur when people are ignored and when they have exhausted the mainstream pathways toward resolution of their long-standing problems, including racist police practices like racial profiling, stop and frisk, and police killings of unarmed Black men.

Riots are an important strategy in social movements, both in the United States and internationally. The Boston Tea Party was a riot of sorts. Many of the social actions during the civil rights movement, from the March on Washington to the march from Selma to the children's march in Birmingham, are examples of the ways in which the Black community mobilized to draw attention to the inequalities being perpetrated on their communities as well as to seek social-justice-oriented solutions to the problems they faced.

Because the purpose of this book is to provide a way to understand a variety of different ways in which Black bodies are policed and the interconnectedness among them, it is impossible to devote time and space to every occurrence, be it the sentencing of juveniles to life without the possibility of parole, police shootings of unarmed Black men, or those who finally get their freedom after serving decades in prison for crimes they did not commit. In each chapter, including this one, beginning with our discussion of race riots, we choose exemplars to illustrate the key points. We choose cases that are both unique and that illustrate a particularly pernicious aspect of the policing of Black bodies as well as those that are ordinary, those that occur and reoccur day in and day out in a state that is, we argue, addicted to incarceration. After careful deliberation, with the goals of this book in mind, we selected the following riots to take as our focus for more pointed analysis:

Chicago (1919)
Harlem, New York (1964)
Watts, Los Angeles (1965)

Newark, New Jersey (1967)
Washington, D.C. (1968)
Los Angeles (1992)
Ferguson, Missouri (2014)
Baltimore (2015)

These riots were selected specifically because they all involved responses by the Black community to various forms of policing, including housing segregation, a lack of economic opportunities, and brutal police practices. Though invisible in the contemporary discussion of the latest riots, be it in Sanford, Florida; Baltimore; Ferguson, Missouri; or Chicago, these same elements, coupled with long-standing tensions between the police and the Black community, are present in each of these riots across more than a century. And though each individual protest has a unique trigger, which we will explore, what is perhaps more interesting is the consistent and persistent policing of Black bodies that forms the basis of the distrust in the Black community, which when presented with a trigger erupts into violence.

The Chicago riots of 1919 took place between July 27 and August 2. Approximately fifteen whites and twenty-eight Black people were killed, and another five hundred or more were injured. The Chicago of 1919 was a deeply segregated city. As part of the "Great Migration," southern Blacks were moving northward in droves in part because they were being recruited there by industries seeking to bolster the depleted labor force lost to World War I. For many Blacks, jobs were not the only draw; so was the promise of life outside the constraints of Jim Crow segregation. Among the many destinations in the North, Chicago was one of the most popular. The city had hosted the World's Fair in 1893; it was known for agricultural processing, as detailed in Upton Sinclair's famous book *The Jungle*, which wove together the narratives of stockyard workers, many of whom were immigrants from Eastern Europe; and by the post–World War I era, Chicago was among the leading manufacturing hubs for steel and automobiles.

In his 1991 book *The Promised Land: The Great Black Migration and How It Changed America*, Nicholas Lemann chronicles the movement of Blacks from Mississippi to Chicago, most famously noting that he could trace an individual, a family who left the town of Canton or Clarksdale, Mississippi, down to the exact block they were living on in Chicago—

noting that between 1910 and 1934 the city's Black population grew by 500 percent, from 44,000 to 234,000.

Blacks migrating to Chicago came for work, building economic stability and expanded social opportunities from which they were systematically blocked in the rural South, in part because of racial segregation and in part because by the early twentieth century, the South remained primarily rural, relying on agriculture as its primary economic driver and continuing to resist industrialization and unionization in particular. Lemann's portrait is stark: he describes the despair that engulfed many rural Blacks on the eve of World War I and the lengths to which they were willing to go to exit this existence on no more than the word and a promise of those who had gone before them and moved north.

Yet the North did not in fact provide the racial freedom that many if not most Blacks, especially those "early" migrants who made the journey north in the late nineteenth and early twentieth centuries, expected.

Jim Crow segregation may not have been officially the law of the land in Chicago, but policies that required absolute, 100 percent housing segregation produced the same result. In her 2011 book, *Reimagining Equality: Stories of Gender, Race and Finding Home*, Anita Hill exposes the very policies that produced a segregated Chicago, which many northern whites may truly believe never happened in the "North." The Home Owners Loan Corporation, or HOLC, put a policy into place that gave preference to making mortgages on homes purchased in "homogenous" neighborhoods. In Chicago, the Chicago Real Estate Board modeled a "variation" clause after the policies of the HOLC that explicitly prohibited the sale of property in certain Chicago neighborhoods to Blacks. In order to deal with the fact that many households in these neighborhoods employed Blacks as domestics, gardeners, and chauffeurs, exceptions in the variation clause allowed Blacks to *live* in these neighborhoods but not purchase homes there, as long as living in these communities was a prerequisite for their employment.

Though Chicagoans at the time, and now, would likely say that Chicago did not practice Jim Crow segregation, in fact, Chicago was then and remains now one of the most racially segregated cities in the United States. Census maps and tools such as dissimilarity indices provide powerful mechanisms for exploring the degree to which various states and metro locations are racially segregated. These data are useful not only because they enable us to document segregation but also because they are more accurate than simply asking residents to describe the racial composition of their neighborhoods. Whites, in particular, regularly underestimate the level of social segregation in their communities. In Chicago, 87 percent of Blacks live in racially segregated, all-Black neighborhoods. In other words, 87 percent of Blacks would have to move in order for them to live in racially integrated neighborhoods. Only 6 to 7 percent of Blacks and whites have any *regular* contact with one another.

Today the Black community in Chicago is further segregated by social class. Affluent Blacks like the Obamas, and before his death Muhammad Ali, own homes in the famous South Side community of Hyde Park, which sits along the shores of Lake Michigan and houses the famous University of Chicago and the Museum of Science and Technology. Poor Blacks live both south and west of the Chicago "Loop" in housing projects and communities, including Lawndale, which is featured prominently in sociologist William Julius Wilson's work on poverty.

Deep racial segregation that countered the expectations of Blacks who migrated north was not the only context for the riots of 1919. An additional factor was the discontent of the Black community following the arrival of Black soldiers who had defended their country during World War I and returned home to resume their lives only to find that the jobs they had left behind were no longer available to them. Southern Black men and immigrants were now holding down these well-paying jobs, and rising tensions ensued. The spark that ignited the fire came from an incident surrounding recreational swimming.

This same confluence of factors existed in other cities across the United States and riots erupted in cities as far apart as Chicago; Washington, D.C.; Omaha; Knoxville; Elaine, Arkansas; and Harlem. Across these race riots, hundreds of Blacks were killed, and property was destroyed. Historians refer to 1919 as the "Red Summer." We focus on Chicago because the number of deaths was high, and the damage to property was the most extensive.

Between July 2, 1919, and August 2, 1919, there was "race" trouble in Chicago. A variation of the triggers of several other protests we discuss here, the race riots in Chicago in 1919 were sparked by an incident that many Blacks believed they had left behind in the Deep South. Eugene Williams, a seventeen-year-old Black youth, was swimming in Lake Michigan. Unbeknownst to him, the lake had a racial dividing line (Twenty-Ninth Street), and as he was swimming he crossed over into what was known by custom as the "white" swimming area. There was no actual marker or set of buoys indicating the line. Rather people, especially Blacks, were supposed to just "know" where it was. Williams's body was policed, much like Trayvon Martin's would be more than eighty years later, for crossing a racial divide—in short, for acting as a free person.

Several white men who were standing nearby threw rocks at him. Several of the rocks hit Eugene, he lost his grip on a railroad tie he was holding on to, and he drowned.[5] While accounts vary, it is clear from the work of Spear and the coverage in the *New York Times* that young Williams was doing nothing more than swimming and was accosted by white men who did not want him coming close to the "white" part of the segregated lake. We do have to stop and wonder how on earth it seemed at all reasonable to segregate the second-largest freshwater lake in the United States. But, as with most aspects of racism in the United States, there are rarely any rational or reasonable explanations. The machine of racism is not a "thinking" machine; it is violence in its natural state.

William Stauber, the white man who threw the fatal rock, was never arrested or charged with the murder.[6]

Word spread quickly that the police did not apprehend the men who participated in the murder of young Eugene Williams. Coupled with the heat of summer and high unemployment among Black men, especially those who had returned from the war, tensions quickly exploded into a full-blown race riot. The Chicago police along with the Illinois National Guard were called in to quell the riot. The events lasted close to a week, and before it all finally came to an end, a total of fifteen whites and twenty-eight Blacks were dead. Another five hundred Chicagoans were injured.

Examining records after the riot, it is clear that the root causes were never addressed. Despite having a hard time renting office space because of deeply entrenched segregation in Chicago, the multiracial commission, appointed by Governor Frank O. Lowden, spent a lot of time and ultimately came up with several legitimate recommendations that at the time made sense. They did report ignoring some recommendations from the white community, including one suggestion that all Blacks living in Chicago be "sent back" to Africa. Never mind the fact that Blacks living in Chicago had likely never been to Africa.

We summarize several of the commission's recommendations here and point interested readers to the book detailing the report that was published by the University of Chicago Press.

Despite some good work done by the commission, their approach and the tone of the report laid the blame at the feet of the Black community. For example, despite that fact that the riot started when a white man threw a rock that killed a Black youth, among the recommendations that came from the commission was a focus on Blacks needing to "clean up their act."

Despite the victim-blaming tone, the commission recommended policy changes that would address some of the most pressing issues facing Blacks in Chicago. One of the first recommendations that came out of the commission was that Blacks be treated as humans. We are struck by this recommendation because it seems so straightforward, and yet the fact that it was actually articulated underscores the conditions under which Blacks were living; the very conditions had been burning like embers and were ignited by the murder of Williams. This recommendation was almost as if to say, more than eighty years ago, that Black Lives Matter.

The remaining recommendations focused on housing, work, schooling, interpersonal relations, and so forth. Specifically, the commission called for Blacks to be admitted into unions, that Blacks be able to live in decent housing, and that Blacks be guaranteed wages equal to whites. It is insightful that the recommendations for accommodations of Blacks are so progressive at this time in the early 1920s. One reason for this might be the diverse makeup of the commission, which included Robert S. Abbott, editor of the *Chicago Defender*, an influential Black newspaper at the time. Despite including influential members of the Black community and a reasonable set of recommendations, from the very beginning it was clear that the commission lacked the "teeth" or muscle to make meaningful change happen. Is it any wonder, then, that tensions in the Black community in Chicago run deep and that when other actions by whites dehumanize Black people, such as the 1968 Democratic Convention that refused to seat Fanny Lou Hamer and the Freedom Democratic Party of Mississippi or more recently the shooting of Laquan McDonald in 2014, they retrigger protests by Black leaders and the Black community? Chicago is not unique in this regard. In most of the cases we will examine in this book, the triggers—the police shooting of an unarmed Black man, resistance to school integration, or refusing to allow Blacks to buy homes in white neighborhoods or selling them predatory mortgages—are just that, triggers that reignite a long history of the policing of Black bodies, literal, geographic, and symbolic.

Unlike the Chicago riots, the Harlem riot took place in a time and place of greater Black optimism, and it was a specific reaction to police brutality. On July 16, 1964, fifteen-year-old James Powell, a ninth-grade student who was in Harlem attending summer school, was killed in front of his fellow students. The shooter, white New York policeman Lieutenant Thomas Gilligan, was investigated but never tried or held accountable for the murder. Powell's murder sparked the 1964 "Harlem" riots that lasted for a week, from July 16 to 22.[7]

By the time the riot was over, in addition to Powell, one other person was dead, 118 were injured, and approximately 450 people were arrested. The New York Police Department estimated property damage to be between $500,000 and $1,000,000. As far as we are aware, there were no commissions convened, but it is clear that Harlem would never be the same.[8]

As noted, there were race riots in Harlem during the Red Summer (1919) and in 1935. We examine the 1964 Harlem riot because it is considered by historians to be the first "modern" race riot. With growing optimism, Blacks of the 1960s had reasons to be hopeful, even if not entirely optimistic, as the federal government in response to demands by the Black community and resistance by the white community began to step in. Much of the civil rights movement of the 1950s and 1960s had been focused on protesting Jim Crow policies that policed Black bodies. The struggle for civil rights, which is still being fought as we approach the third decade of the twenty-first century, can be characterized as a series of wins and losses, gains and setbacks, always in tension. As important as the landmark 1954 *Brown v. Board* U.S. Supreme Court school desegregation decision was in validating Blacks' experiences in inferior schools and their right to the same educational opportunities as whites, it did not, in fact, deliver. White families actively and passively resisted school desegregation and integration across the South. And though most are familiar with the strong and sometimes violent resistance by whites such as in Little Rock, Arkansas, other communities across more moderate southern states such as Virginia and North Carolina engaged in more subversive actions and passed laws that rendered *Brown* unenforceable. For example, in places like Prince Edward County, Virginia, whites resisted school integration by simply refusing to send their children to school. For an entire year. White parents would rather stunt their own children's education than allow them to sit next to Black children in school. Across Mississippi, white parents collaborated with churches to found private schools or what came to be known as "seg academies." Because these schools did not accept public funding, they were not required to comply with *Brown*. Today in Mississippi, public schools are colloquially referred to as "Black public schools," and schools are as segregated as they were in 1954.

The signing of the Civil Rights Act of 1964 and the Voting Rights Act of 1965 had similar results. Though they were opportunities or moments of optimism, whites have been fighting, mostly successfully, to make these federal laws essentially unenforceable, most recently through color-blind racist strategies such as redrawing congressional districts (gerrymandering) and felony disenfranchisement.

By the early 1960s, Harlem, New York, had grown to be home to hundreds of thousands of Black residents. In fact, this neighborhood in the borough of Manhattan was home to the largest concentration of Blacks in the United States at that time and remained so up through the early 1970s. Along with this concentration of Blacks in a single New York community, Harlem became an epicenter, perhaps the greatest at the time, of Black culture, including history, literature, music, dance, politics, and social activism.[9]

Charles Brooks speaks of a "mystique" about Harlem:

> There's a mystique that surrounds Harlem—with its rich historical tradition, literature, music, dance, politics and social activism. Consequently, Harlem is referred to as the "Black Mecca," the capital of black America, and arguably the most recognized black community in the country.

Though perhaps not on par with Greater Manhattan, Harlem had its own hustle and bustle—a rhythm, one could even say, a style that was a carryover from the era between 1921 and 1931 that was termed the "New Negro Movement" or the Harlem Renaissance.[10] At that time, literature, art, music, and theater were a thriving part of Harlem.

Among others, film, television, and Broadway star Ossie Davis got his start there, and the preeminent Black intellectual W. E. B. Du Bois lived in Harlem and published from his offices there. Black activists such as

Marcus Garvey were influential, as was the West Indian orator Hubert Harrison. Often missing from discussions of this cultural renaissance were Harlem sports, which in fact were an important part of the social life of Blacks living in and visiting Harlem. The Rens played basketball in Harlem, and several Negro League baseball teams played there as well. We should not forget boxing, which was one of the country's biggest sports and very popular among Harlem Blacks.

The riot of 1964 and the two preceding it left an indelible mark on Harlem, though it remains a cultural center for Black life. Jeffrey Stewart noted that "the first modern race riot . . . symbolized that the optimism and hopefulness that had fueled the Harlem Renaissance was dead."[11]

The history of racialized policing coupled with the race riots of 1919, 1935, and the 1960s are deeply woven into the fabric of life for Blacks living in New York. Like Chicago and the other cities we choose as our case studies, the relationship between police and the Black community remains tense, not only in Harlem but in all of New York City's boroughs and neighborhoods, in which Blacks are now able to live, work, and go to school. This tension was reignited under then-mayor Rudy Giuliani, who blessed the implementation of New York's stop-and-frisk laws, which, among other things, laid the groundwork for more recent tragedies, including the murder in July 2014 of Eric Garner, who was killed by police officers on the sidewalk in Staten Island. His death launched the "I Can't Breathe" social media campaign.

In apparent retaliation, in December 2014 Ismaaiyl Abdullah Brinsley shot and killed two on-duty New York City police officers as they sat in their car in the Bedford-Stuyvesant neighborhood of the New York City borough of Brooklyn. In so many cities like Chicago, New York, and Baltimore, the long history of tension between the police and the Black community remains unresolved, much like the embers of a long-burning fire that are reignited by the next act of violence or police brutality. As we have noted, this is part of the reason we decided to explore race riots in this book, to connect the dots for the reader. The protests of the second decade of the twenty-first century in Chicago, Baltimore, New York, and Ferguson didn't just happen. They are simply another moment in the four-hundred-plus-year racial history of the United States. A history marked by policing Black bodies and Black resistance.

Perhaps the most well-known riot of the 1960s took place in Los Angeles, California, in the summer of 1965, which flooded into American living rooms via television sets in a way no previous riot had. While not high-definition (HD) TV yet—in fact, not even color TV (!)—Americans could watch the six o'clock news and see, whether up close from other parts of California or from afar in Portland, Maine, that something was going on in American society, and it was troubling. The Watts riots, which lasted six days, resulted in more than $40 million worth of property damage. Over the course of the week, the protesting caused severe damage to property and human life. Estimates have it that fourteen thousand California National Guard troops were mobilized, and the rioting claimed thirty-four lives, injuring another one thousand, and four thousand people were arrested before order was restored on August 17. It was both the largest and costliest urban rebellion of the 1960s.

The riot began on August 11 in the predominantly Black community of South Central Los Angeles when a young Black man by the name of Marquette Frye was stopped by a white California highway patrolman named Lee Minikus. He was then forcibly arrested for drinking while driving. He was intoxicated.

Though the specific conditions are different in Chicago and Harlem and Watts, we observe similar patterns of oppression that were laid bare for all to see over the course of the Watts riots. Like the migrations to Chicago and Harlem, Blacks migrated west, to Southern California, looking for employment and a way to escape the harsh realities of Jim Crow. Southern California is unique in that the number of Blacks moving there was significantly smaller, and the population even today is less than 10 percent Black, but the exclusion that Blacks faced from safe, affordable housing, employment, and security of person was no different. And the Watts riots exposed this, both for Blacks who may have continued to believe that California was a panacea and for whites who by and large believed that racial injustices were limited to Dixie.

The governor at the time, Edmund G. Brown, ordered an investigation, which revealed that the riot was in large part a result of the long-standing grievances of the residents of the Watts community, including their growing discontentment with high unemployment rates, substandard housing, and inadequate schools. Yet, despite these insights, the leadership throughout the state and specifically in Watts did nothing. The socioeconomic conditions and despair of the Watts neighborhood persisted. Only after the protests, the community was left with the devastation created by the rioting, including damaged property, burned-out buildings, and the like. In many ways, Watts has never recovered.

On August 17, 1965, nearing the end of the riots, Martin Luther King Jr. arrived in Watts. King told those gathered,

> The violence was environmental and not racial. The economic depriva-
> tion, social isolation, inadequate housing, and general despair of thou-
> sands of Negroes teeming in Northern and Western ghettos are the
> ready seeds which give birth to tragic expressions of violence.

He continued, noting that the riots were just the "beginning of a stirring of those people in our society who have been by passed by the progress of the past decade."[12]

In pointing to structural inequalities as the cause of the Watts riots, Reverend King hit the nail on the head. The protests, in and of them-selves, illuminated all of these structural inequalities, including poverty, unemployment, and underresourced schools, and provided an outlet for pent-up frustrations, ill hope, lack of access to the opportunity structure, and an overwhelming sense that society cares little about its citizens who occupy the underclass.

Similar to the response to the riots in Chicago—and coming just four-teen months after the sweeping Civil Rights Act of 1964—Governor Brown appointed a commission that produced the McCone Commission Report. The eight-member commission was headed by John A. McCone, former head of the Central Intelligence Agency. The report the commis-sion produced identified the basic ingredients of the rebellion but fell short of offering solutions to the deep causes. Just like the commission that followed the Chicago riots of 1919, after one hundred days of site visits and several interviews with Black residents, the report issued its main finding, which simply confirmed what Black residents already knew: that Watts suffered from problems of police malpractice, lack of jobs, poor housing, economic exploitation, and inadequate educational opportunities.[13]

We cannot overstate this point. Though all of the protests we examine here are triggered by an act of policing Black bodies, the literal policing by arresting or shooting an unarmed Black man or the symbolic policing in Chicago in which a Black youth was murdered for failing to mind the color line, the protests are a reaction to much more than the triggering event. In every single case, the riots are a response to the inhumane conditions in which Black residents are forced to live, segregated into the poorest housing stock and the most underresourced schools and away from economic opportunity. As Erik Olin Wright argues, they are "cordoned off." The riot is not only an act in protest of these conditions but a mechanism for drawing attention to these conditions and a call for social action.

The dissonance between President Johnson's "Great Society" programs and the urban unrest of the 1960s was, to be sure, perplexing. How could some of the most powerful government legislation that funded programming in urban America, giving states and cities resources to end Jim Crow segregation and its practices not quell this growing unrest? The Watts riots were the first to test the theories that social programming could and would placate Black people and encourage them to strive toward a more accommodationist approach to daily life. As the riots reveal, the predictions of the theory did not hold up. Truth be told, we should not be surprised by this finding, most obviously because the Great Society programs, which were focused on building community centers to keep kids off the streets, did little if anything to address the deeply entrenched residual effects of Jim Crow segregation, including housing segregation, a lack of good jobs, and underresourced schools. In her 2016 book *From the War on Poverty to the War on Crime*, Elizabeth Hinton describes the situation when the root causes of riots—poverty, unemployment, and equal access to education—are not addressed:

> The long-term impact of the federal government's decision to manage urban problems by divesting from the War on Poverty and expanding the War on Crime was evident . . . in the flames that literally consumed the nation's cities from within. If large-scale urban civil disobedience was a relic of the 1960s, the American cities that constituted the battlegrounds of the crime war continued to burn during the 1970s.[14]

The Newark riot of 1967 took place in Newark, New Jersey, between July 12 and July 17. The riot was sparked, as so many are, by an incident of police brutality. A Black cab driver was arrested for a minor offense and was apparently beaten and hauled off to jail. Several civil rights leaders asked permission to see John Smith, the cab driver, and when they arrived at his jail cell, it was clear he had been severely beaten. The civil rights leaders asked that Smith be taken to a hospital. By midnight his fellow cab drivers, using their cab radios, spread the word of the arrest, the beating, and that Smith was now in the hospital.

Much like we have seen in other protests, crowds soon gathered, and bricks and Molotov cocktails were thrown at the jail. New Jersey governor Richard J. Hughes ordered in the National Guard, and when they arrived they were three thousand strong.

This did not stop the protesters. Across the weeklong riots, approximately twenty-six Black people were killed, another 750 people were injured, and over 1,000 people were jailed. The assessment of property damage exceeded $10 million. While we are not comparing one riot against any other riot, we have to pause and ask, why didn't the Newark police simply lock up the cab driver John Smith, get his story with his attorney present, and find out why he was "tailgating" in the first place, the minor offense for which he was pulled over? In the language of the twenty-first century, Smith was racially profiled, an issue we will unpack in the next chapter and throughout the book. Sadly, as was the case with so many of the other protests we examine in this chapter, by all measures, Newark was a city already in decline, having seen high-paying jobs in manufacturing leave, and unemployment was on the rise, as was white flight. Many argue that the 1967 riot was a major turning point in Newark's reputation, reinforcing widely held beliefs that Newark was a dangerous, poverty-ridden, increasingly Black urban landscape. Those who could get out did, never to return.

On Thursday, April 4, 1968, the day Martin Luther King Jr. was murdered in Memphis, Tennessee, Blacks led by Stokely Carmichael in Washington, D.C., began to gather on U Street for a march. Carmichael urged the crowd to go door to door and request that shop owners close in honor of King's death. He also urged them to go home and get guns.

What Carmichael failed to anticipate was that President Johnson was not about to let the city burn. The protesters reached within two blocks of the White House before they retreated, and in response Johnson unleashed civilian and military police forces that had never been seen in civil disturbances before. On Friday, April 5, Johnson dispatched 13,600 federal troops, including 1,750 federalized District of Columbia National Guard troops, to assist the overwhelmed D.C. city police force. Marines mounted machine guns on the steps of the Capitol building, and army troops deployed from the Third Infantry guarded the White House.

At the end of the day, twelve people had been killed, 1,097 were injured, and over 6,100 people were arrested.

Despite the death, injury, and destruction, there is rarely if ever any commentary or reference to the D.C. riots. Why? Perhaps because President Johnson's swift and powerful combined military and civilian police response to the onslaught contained the protesters in ways that were more "successful" than in Watts and Newark. But perhaps a more significant contributing factor to the lack of attention historically to the D.C. riots is the fact that after the murder of Martin Luther King Jr., riots broke out in over one hundred cities across the country, including in the nation's capitol, and as a result, coverage of and attention to the D.C. protests was diffused. [15] Or perhaps white Americans did not want to see the realities of life for Black citizens in the nation's capitol.

The nation's capitol, Washington, D.C., one of the most segregated cities in America, with 66 percent of Blacks living in communities that are predominantly Black, is home to the United States government. In and around the White House are some of our most treasured and popular tourist destinations, including the National Mall, statues of great presidents, and museums, and in the southeast ward of the city are vast housing projects populated primarily by Blacks. Most Blacks who live in D.C. reside in the southeast, with the exception of the small number of Blacks of higher social-class status who live in other parts of the city or even in the affluent surrounding suburbs of Northern Virginia and Maryland. Supreme Court justice Clarence Thomas, for example, lives in our home community of Fairfax, Virginia. And the Obamas, who lived on Pennsylvania Avenue in the White House until January 2017, moved just a few miles away to the tony section of D.C., Kalorama, just houses away from the home selected by Ivanka Trump and Jared Kushner when they moved to D.C. to join the White House staff. Seeing the Black faces in the White House or picking up the dry cleaning in Fairfax at the same shop Thomas frequents, it is often easy to forget that the vast majority of Blacks living in the nation's capitol live in some of the most distressed, economically depressed, violent neighborhoods in the United States. One measure of this is the fact that in 2016, of Black students attending public high school in D.C., only 4 percent scored well enough to be considered "college ready" overall, and only 10 percent were "college ready" in math and 25 percent in English upon graduation. [16] Underresourced schools remain a key indicator of poverty and instability in Black communities, be they rural or urban.

Rodney King was severely beaten by the Los Angeles police on March 3, 1991. The trial of the police officers, which was held in the overwhelmingly white community of Simi Valley in the spring of 1992, returned an acquittal of all the officers involved. This verdict, along with the release of the George Holiday video that brought the beating of Rodney King into the living rooms of Americans from coast to coast, was the spark that ignited some of the worst rioting in United States history.

Then-president George H. W. Bush would later comment that

> viewed from outside the trial, it was hard to understand how the verdict could possibly square with the video. Those civil rights leaders with whom I met were stunned. And so was I and so was Barbara and so were my kids. [17]

The Los Angeles riots showcased some of the worst of the pent-up frustration that builds over time, especially with respect to relations between the Black community and the police. While the Rodney King beating that was caught on tape may have been the catalyst that sparked the Los Angeles riots, the conditions in South Central Los Angeles were arguably what caused them, just as they had in Watts in 1965, nearly thirty years prior. There was a lack of job opportunities, crushing poverty, housing that was barely habitable, and of course long-standing tensions with the police, all of which had been going on for decades and contributed significantly to both the Watts and the Los Angeles riots.

The Los Angeles riots resulted in 54 deaths, 2,383 injuries, more than 7,000 fires, damage to 3,100 businesses, and nearly $1 billion in financial losses. It was costly on all fronts.

As with many of the other riots we analyze here, there was an investigation, this time headed by William H. Webster, former head of the CIA and FBI. The Webster Commission identified the same kinds of preexisting factors as identified by the other riot commission investigations across the country, with one exception: why was there no police presence during the protests? On video after video of the riots, we can see the looting of stores and many motorists being dragged from their vehicles, and yet we never see the police. Some eyewitnesses recounted that they, too, did not see a police presence. Thanks to the work of filmmaker Ezra Edelman, who directed the documentary on O. J. Simpson titled *OJ Made in America*, we have video footage of Los Angeles police officers commenting on the riots. Those who agreed to speak on camera described the situation as one in which they were well aware that the riots were going on; they were in fact just two blocks away. And yet they were explicitly ordered *not* to enter the riot zone and attempt to contain the protesters and limit the damage they wrought on the community. The Webster Report noted,

> This city is plagued by hostility, rage and resentment in many areas . . . where minorities and economically deprived citizens believe the LAPD did not treat them with respect or extend the same level of protection as elsewhere. It could happen again.

Our question remains, how much damage to property, and more important to human life, could have been prevented had the Los Angeles police actually protected the community they were charged to serve as they did during the riots in Washington, D.C.? Which lives matter?

The commission delivered to Mayor Tom Bradley, in a room full of attorneys and Police Chief Willie L. Williams, a report that cited budget problems and the lack of communication inside the police department as *causal factors* for the riot. Though acknowledging their importance, the report never cites directly the severe beating of Rodney King or the acquittal of the police officers as *causal factors* in the riots. Just as the death of Freddie Gray at the hands of the police was not the root cause of the protests in Baltimore, centuries of racist policies and practices were. Freddie Gray's death, like Michael Brown's, like Rodney King's, was simply the trigger, the catalyst.

Singled out for being massively underprepared for the riot was the former police chief Daryl F. Gates. Both authors of the report, William Webster and Hubert Williams, said that Gates lacked a specific plan for dealing with the riots. Gates, not known for backing away from confrontation, lashed back:

> Clearly that night we should have gone down there and shot a few people.
>
> In retrospect, that's exactly what we should have done. We should have blown a few heads off. And maybe your television cameras would have seen that and maybe that would have been broadcast and

maybe, just maybe, that would have stopped everything. I don't know. But certainly we had the legal right to do that.

Gates, in an interview, also said William Webster and Hubert Williams were "both . . . liars."[18]

When we ask what the larger impact has been in terms of "lessons learned" from all these protests across the history of the United States—including the Los Angeles riots—we have to come to the basic conclusion that in fact Black Lives Don't Matter, especially not poor Black lives. After decades of protest and commission after commission coming to the same conclusion, riots, though triggered by specific acts of violence, most often police violence, are in fact protests about human and civil rights. The trigger is a profound reminder to Black people and Black communities that Black lives don't matter, that Black lives can be policed, that the conditions under which many Blacks are forced to live—substandard housing, lack of economic opportunities, underresourced schools—are acceptable and not worth the time and money to address. Black protest, in the form of riots, has given us everything we need to know to innovate social justice responses, and if we would implement social change, we would likely prevent future riots. Perhaps the cost of riots—in terms of damage to property, human life, and policing costs—are deemed to be a small price to pay compared to the kind of radical social change that Black leaders have been calling for since Black people were first captured and smuggled, against their will, to this place we call America. The same conditions that sparked riots in the 1920s, 1960s, and 1990s hold true in the second decade of the twenty-first century.

Michael Brown, an eighteen-year-old Black youth, was shot and killed on August 9, 2014, by Darren Wilson, a white police officer, in Ferguson, Missouri. His body lay in the street—in the blistering heat—for approximately four hours. Many bystanders took photos of Brown's body lying in the street and streamed them online via Facebook and Twitter before they were picked up by mainstream media outlets and streamed through our TVs into our living rooms.[19]

Brown's friend Dorian Johnson, who was with him at the time of the shooting, recounts in several testimonies he gave that Brown was unarmed and that he was shot in the back. Hence the slogan "hands up don't shoot," which went viral on Twitter and became a rallying cry (and a hashtag) for those protesting in Ferguson, as well as the Black Lives

Matter movement and many other social actions that followed. The police officer, Darren Wilson, a white male, testified in his indictment that Brown not only lunged at him but that Brown had actually reached for his weapon. This is where the story gets both confusing and complex.

Regardless of who is to be believed, the facts show that not only is Brown dead, but just as important, he is unable to tell his side of the story. In the immediate aftermath of the shooting death of Michael Brown, Ferguson residents and others started to gather in front of the police station, and across the next several nights, citizens and the police clashed. Much looting also took place. On August 10, 2016, President Obama made a national call for peace.[20] For most of the entire period from the killing of Brown on August 9, 2014, to December 2, 2014, approximately a week after a hearing panel failed to indict Officer Wilson, protests raged in the city of Ferguson. All told, six police officers were injured, ten citizens were injured, and over 325 people were arrested. Additionally, several cars, including police vehicles, were burned. Businesses in the community where the riots took place were devastated, including many that were burned literally to the ground: the International Market, Qdoba, Rooster, Advanced Auto Parts, AutoZone, Ferguson Beauty World, Family Dollar, and Ferguson Market & Liquor, just to name a few.[21]

As was the case in so many riots that came before Ferguson, there was an investigation meant to uncover the root causes and triggers to the protest and to evaluate the police reaction to it. The U.S. Department of Justice report (March 2015), titled "Investigation of the Ferguson Police Department,"[22] details the findings of the investigation into the riots in Ferguson. The U.S. Justice Department report uncovered, in the words of the report, "a pattern or practice of unlawful conduct within the Ferguson Police Department that violates the First, Fourth, and Fourteenth Amendments to the United States Constitution, and federal statutory law."

These twenty-two words from the U.S. Justice Department report expose, quite succinctly, the explicit biases that existed and persist inside the Ferguson Police Department, policies and practices that violate three amendments to the United States Constitution. Policing Black bodies. What we found of particular interest is the section of the report that addressed the use of arrest warrants as a strategy for generating revenue for the police department.

Ferguson uses its police department in large part as a collection agency for its municipal court. Ferguson's municipal court issues arrest warrants at a rate that police officials have called, in internal emails, "staggering." According to the court's own figures, as of December 2014, over 16,000 people had outstanding arrest warrants that had been issued by the court. In fiscal year 2013 alone, the court issued warrants to approximately 9,007 people. Many of those individuals had warrants issued on multiple charges, as the 9,007 warrants applied to 32,975 different offenses. [23]

The U.S. Justice Department's one-hundred-plus-page report is scintillating and demonstrates just how deep the abuses were in the city of Ferguson, Missouri. The report uncovered racist e-mails targeting both President Barack Obama and First Lady Michelle Obama. Other e-mails pointed to the role of the police chief in approving increased patrols in the Black community in order to extract ridiculous fines for minor offenses such as traffic violations. This same police chief also had oversight of the municipal court judges. In one e-mail the chief brags about how much revenue he brings in.

The report makes quite clear that the primary role of warrants is not to protect public safety but rather to facilitate fine collection, thus in essence creating a sort of a "debtor class," a majority of whom, as we explore in the next chapter, will end up in jail simply because they cannot afford to pay the fines and fees attached to the warrants. Policing Black bodies.

Finally, and perhaps most damning, the U.S. Justice Department's report identifies the unlawful use of deadly force against Blacks—termed the "Ferguson effect." As more and more communities erupt into riots, often triggered by the murder of an unarmed Black man by the police, U.S. Justice Department investigations reveal that the use of deadly force against minority citizens takes place not just in Ferguson but across the United States. To date, there have been few effective recommendations given for curtailing these abuses.

The U.S. Justice Department's report on policing in Ferguson recommends many strategies to appropriately address these problems, including but not limited to a shift from policing in order to raise revenues to policing in partnership with the entire Ferguson community. And these recommendations can and should be applied in many communities nationwide. Additionally, the report recommends that the Ferguson police change the way they conduct vehicle stops and searches, issue citations and summonses, and make arrests.

It remains to be seen if these and other recommendations will work in a city torn apart by the murder of the young Black man named Michael Brown. We are not optimistic, for all the reasons we have explored in this chapter, but also because since the election of Donald Trump and the appointment of Jeff Sessions as U.S. attorney general, much of the hard work that has been done is being systematically undone. One of Jeff Sessions's first acts as attorney general, in April 2017, was to remove the requirement that police departments comply with the negotiated agreements, called consent decrees, that were made between the U.S. Justice Department and local police departments. Thus, in cities like Ferguson, despite a scathing report and recommendations by the U.S. Justice Department for meaningful changes, these negotiated agreements are no longer legally binding.

Although the investigations into Ferguson revealed many of the same underlying issues that were present in previous riots across dozens of cities, this is the first report that focused so precisely on policing practices. In the next several chapters, we examine data from a variety of sources that explicates these deeply engrained and widely utilized strategies that serve to police Black bodies and restrict Black movement, but also fill our jails and prisons with poor Black men and women, often for the simple fact that they cannot pay a fine from a mundane traffic stop. We will also explore and demonstrate the relationship between policing strategies and the police murders of unarmed Black men like Michael Brown and Freddie Gray.

"Charm City." On April 12, 2015, Freddie Carlos Gray Jr. was arrested for the possession of what was thought to be a switchblade knife. He was taken in a police van, and based on all accounts he was given "a rough ride." Gray died on April 19, 2015.[24] Across the span of the following week there was intense rioting. Thankfully there were no deaths to citizens as occurred in the Watts riots of 1965 and the Los Angeles riots of 1991.

In Baltimore, on the day of Freddie Gray's funeral, the CVS pharmacy was looted and set on fire, and shortly after the funeral a full-blown riot broke out. Approximately 145 vehicles were set on fire, 201 adults and 34 juveniles were arrested, and more than 500 National Guard personnel were called in to police the city. On national TV, in plain sight, we watched the rioters hurling stones, bottles, and firebombs at both the police and in some cases the media and even cutting the water hoses set out by the fire department should they be needed.

So, what happened in Baltimore? It depends on who you ask, but a careful sociological analysis reveals that what took place before and after the Freddie Gray murder is similar to what sparked the protests in other cities in the United States: persistent poverty; neglect; redlining, a practice that produced persistent housing segregation; high rates of unemployment; underresourced schools with low graduation rates; and abusive police practices.

One major contributor to the tension in West Baltimore was the housing market. The long history of racial segregation no doubt played a major role in the brew that led to the explosion. As a direct result of redlining and later predatory mortgage lending practices, Black residents were mostly living in neighborhoods characterized by destabilization, gentrification, deindustrialization, mass incarceration, foreclosures, and urban renewal. These practices have a long history in Baltimore and are systematic. [25] For example, in the case of Baltimore, the *deliberate* banking practices of Wells Fargo contributed to underlying tensions and frustrations. Wells Fargo made dozens of impossible-to-pay mortgages, as is evidenced by the $175 million housing discrimination suit that was settled and paid by Wells Fargo to both the city and individual residents of Baltimore. These deliberate and predatory lending practices led directly to high rates of foreclosure and the economic devastation of many Black neighborhoods in Baltimore. [26]

The other systematic factor that fueled the protesting seen on TV was police brutality, especially the treatment of Black bodies by the Baltimore police department. Baltimore police brutalize Black residents with impunity and have been doing so for a long time. According to the *Atlantic*, there is a culture of police brutality in Baltimore, which produces a deeply ingrained set of norms for behavior. These norms create expectations and beliefs and practices that transcend individual police officers and become deeply embedded in the underlying organizational structure of police units in the city. Decades come and go as do hundreds of individual officers, but the culture of police brutality remains the same. [27]

In Baltimore, a southern city, this culture has a long history.

Among many other things, what the riots in Baltimore did was expose every form of policing Black bodies. As a coda to the discussion of

Baltimore, though city prosecutor Marilyn Mosby secured indictments of each of the six officers involved in the murder of Freddie Gray, all were either acquitted in bench trials or had the charges dismissed. Publicly Mosby has argued that this is yet another example of the reach of the culture of the Baltimore Police Department, protecting their own above the public safety of the citizens of Baltimore.

Like all the other cities and riots we have analyzed in this chapter, Baltimore was and remains a city on slow boil, primed for the next trigger and its next explosion. Indicative of the mood of the city during the riots, the Orioles canceled a ball game. In the week following the riots, the Orioles played a game, but out of concern for the safety of the residents of Baltimore, it was closed to fans. It was surreal watching the broadcast of a Major League baseball game being played in a silent stadium. To add some levity and routine, the players themselves performed the seventh-inning stretch.

All of the protests addressed here are ultimately a demand by Black citizens about hopelessness, economic exclusion, joblessness, deep debt, housing insecurity, food deserts, racial profiling, and mass incarceration. All of these social and economic issues impact the way Black people feel about the reality of their access to the coveted American Dream and the steep uphill battle to achieve it. Policing Black bodies.

As riots unfold and images of burned-out stores being looted flood our television screens, and more recently our Facebook and Twitter feeds, commentators, almost always white, express shock and outrage that Blacks are destroying their own communities. And yet, as a direct result of slavery, Jim Crow segregation, and the dismantling of Black communities in the aftermath of the civil rights movement, the reality is that Blacks own very little in their *own* communities. Many cities with vibrant Black communities have only a handful of Black-owned restaurants or other businesses. In most cities, Blacks have homeownership rates that are significantly lower than whites. As many commentators mourned the burning of the CVS in Baltimore and loathed Blacks for burning their own neighborhoods as they rioted in protest after the murder of Freddie Gray, what was missing in the analysis was the fact that only 46 percent of Blacks in Baltimore own their own home. And in the communities where the riots took place, the typical homeowner is a slum landlord who exploits the poverty and desperation of the Black folks living there. [28]

The question before us remains, how do the riots of the twentieth and twenty-first centuries help us to better understand policing practices, especially mass incarceration, the shooting of unarmed Black men, and the school-to-prison pipeline?

3

MASS INCARCERATION

America imprisons a higher percentage of its citizens than any other country, free or unfree, anywhere in the world.

—Chris Hayes, *A Colony in a Nation*[1]

As long as Nina could remember, the prison system held uncles and cousins and grandfathers and always her father. Nina, like Toney and Lolli, was raised in the inner city; for all three, prison further demarcated the already insular social geography. Along with the baby showers of teenagers, they attended prisoners' going-away and coming-home parties. Drug dealing and arrests were common on the afternoons Nina spent playing on the sidewalk as she and her parents hung out with their friends. People would be hauled away, while others would unexpectedly reappear, angrier or subdued. Corrections officers escorted one handcuffed cousin to Nina's great-grandmother's funeral; her favorite uncle had to be unshackled in order to approach his dying grandmother's hospital bedside. *The prison system was part of the texture of family life.*[2]

We have both been inside prisons—never as incarcerated people, but as employees and as part of classes in which we were students or instructors. But nothing could have prepared us for our first visit to Parchman Farm, the Mississippi State Penitentiary. Like many prisons, one of its most striking attributes is that it is visible only to those who know to look for it.

The first time we saw Parchman we were driving north from Hattiesburg to Clarksdale as we mapped out a travel class we were preparing to teach on social inequality in the Deep South. Twenty students were soon to accompany us on a three-week, 2,500-mile journey that zigzagged through cities and rural communities across Alabama, Louisiana, and Mississippi to the places where civil rights battles were waged and continue to be fought, meeting with local activists in order to better understand the centuries-long impact of slavery and Jim Crow on local Black and white communities.

As we rolled along the highway, we noticed a brown road sign that simply said "Parchman" with an arrow pointing left. Intrigued, we decided to take the left. We drove for miles through cotton fields, and since it was summer, they were green and robust but not yet bursting with bolls. Just as we began to wonder if we had missed it, we saw a green sign that alerted drivers "not to pick up hitchhikers as inmates were working in the area." A few miles later we parked in a gravel lot that could accommodate no more than a few dozen cars and found ourselves at the crossroads of Mississippi state highways 49 and 32, staring at the gates of Parchman. For such a notorious prison, the entrance gate to Parchman is somewhat underwhelming. If we had driven past it going north or south on Highway 49 we might have missed it entirely. Yet, once inside the gate, the air feels heavier.

Parchman is a prison farm. It is not a behemoth of a prison like Attica that towers over the community, or Alcatraz that sits high atop a rock in the middle of the San Francisco Bay. The only structure really visible is the gatehouse. Parchman has no walls. Its security system is its vastness in the expanse of the Mississippi Delta, the poorest region in the United States. Parchman sits on a tract of land that covers eighteen thousand acres. All of the housing units are located deep within the expanse of the farm. On our first visit to Parchman, it was immediately clear that the secret to its low escape rate is both its size and the nearly 100 percent chance that prisoners will be disoriented as they are driven from unit to unit. Every time we visit Parchman, a routine part of our class on the Deep South, we are struck by how easy it is to lose sight and even the general direction of the gate. People are fond of saying that an inmate trying to escape could wander for days and never leave the prison grounds. All of the units are surrounded by razor wire, yet inmates roam seemingly freely around the grounds as they move from job to job or from their units to their work in the fields. It seems an impossible task to escape because you have no idea which way to run to get to the edge of the prison. Parchman is a working farm with cotton fields and catfish

The Gates of Parchman Farm (Mississippi State Penitentiary)

ponds and fields of beans and okra, and running through the fields to escape is not terribly efficient. If by some miracle an inmate were able to make it to the edge of the prison, he would be met by a two-lane road, nestled deep in the Delta, with no towns closer than twenty miles away and with no idea which way to go. And of course he'd be wearing his prison stripes, an easily recognizable uniform in the Mississippi Delta. Parchman's power is in its vastness and its invisibility. That is, except to the Black folk who live in the Mississippi Delta, for the possibility that they will either be incarcerated or visit family and friends at Parchman is so common that even young children in the local communities are threatened by their parents that they will end up in Parchman if they misbehave.

The invisibility of prisons, that they are kept away, out of sight and out of mind of the vast majority of Americans, both allows them to operate in ways that would offend many Americans and simultaneously leaves many Americans fascinated by them, at least through the lens of television and the popularity of shows like *Locked Up* and *Orange Is the New Black*, both of which tend to reinforce the stereotypes rather than the realities of prison life, rarely featuring, for example, the inmate whose primary offense is possessing some drugs and lacking the resources to pay fines or post bail. Our goal here is to paint a realistic picture of the state of mass incarceration in the contemporary United States and to dissect the impact on Black people, Black families, and Black communities.

WHAT'S THE DIFFERENCE BETWEEN JAILS AND PRISON, PAROLE AND PROBATION?

For most of us, the distinctions between jails and prisons or parole and probation are not that important. At the end of the day, whether one is locked up in jail or prison, one is locked up, and whether one is on parole or probation is only a matter of semantics. And for the most part this is true. Unless there is a specific reason to distinguish the type of facility in which one is detained, we will use the terms "jails" and "prisons" interchangeably. Jails function at the city and county level, both as a final stop for those serving short sentences but also as a feeder to state prisons. Thus high rates of incarceration in one local jurisdiction can shape state-level trends.[3]

One important distinction in the changing carceral landscape is the increasing role that private prisons are playing.

Private prisons are the new kid on the block when it comes to incarceration in the United States. Private prisons are owned by giant, multi-billion-dollar corporations that are in the business of making money off of locking people up. We will have a lengthy interrogation of private prisons in our chapter that focuses explicitly on the prison-industrial complex, but for the purposes of our discussion here, what is important is that though they house only a small fraction of all people incarcerated in the United States, about 10 percent, their share of the incarceration pie is growing. As states struggle with balancing their budgets, one commonly employed strategy has been to "downsize" their prison systems by consolidating and closing prisons. When they run out of bed space, they "outsource" incarceration by shipping some of their inmates off to private prisons and paying a fee to have them housed. Ultimately "outsourcing" is cheaper, and as a result we believe the private prison industry will become a major player in the overall system of incarceration in the United States. Additionally, the private prison industry raises ethical questions about making money by incarcerating people, especially if there is even the appearance that capitalism has an incentive to incarcerate. We argue that it does, and this need to incarcerate bodies in order to make private prisons profitable, is one of the drivers of mass incarceration.

All prisons, regardless of type, are what sociologist Erving Goffman termed "total institutions." Some of the features of a total institution include the assignment of a number or rank that replaces one's name, dress codes or uniforms, the inability to simply leave or quit the institution, and the absolute control of every aspect of daily life, including when and what to eat, when to shower, when to sleep, and how much access one has to luxury items such as a TV. The military, and basic training in particular, is another example of a total institution.

While writing this chapter, we had an experience that reinforced the total institutional nature of prisons. We wanted to share one of our books with an inmate who is currently incarcerated in Attica. We followed all the rules about sending books that were posted on the New York State Corrections website and confirmed by the inmate. Specifically the book had to be ordered and sent from a retailer (we could not simply send the book ourselves, even though it was one of our books), and the package had to come with a receipt. So, where did we purchase the book? Amazon, of course. And a short two days after purchasing the book on Amazon, a text message confirmed that the book had been delivered and signed for by "David." A few weeks later, a letter arrived from the inmate. The opening line of the letter read, "I know the book arrived, but they wouldn't let me have it." In a total institution, even the privilege of having a book is controlled. The story continued as we called Amazon to track down the book. The customer service representative confirmed that the book had been delivered. He admitted that this was not the first time he had heard that an inmate had been denied a shipment. As we lamented that all we wanted was to give the poor guy a book to read to ease the boredom of being locked up twenty-three hours a day, the customer service representative revealed that he understood. He had been in prison. After contacting Amazon, we called Attica and talked to the "counselor" assigned to the inmate. After learning who we were sending the book to, he responded that "[inmate name] ain't getting no book." We cannot emphasize enough the impact of a total institution on one's daily life. It is the ultimate in the policing of Black bodies.

* * *

A debate that has been raging for many decades is the treatment of people who are incarcerated. This is yet another way in which the United States seems to be out of step with the rest of the world, at least those postindustrial economies to which we regularly compare ourselves.

Inmates constantly complain about the quality of the water; even Johnny Cash sings about it on his album *At Folsom Prison*. Another point of constant tension is the quality of the food inmates are provided. Inmates at Parchman complain about being fed a processed meat that when heated in the microwave seems to come alive. They call it "wolf booty." They claim they can taste and feel the sand left on the unrinsed greens that are harvested from the Parchman farms. Because of allergies and dietary restrictions, there are almost no spices available for use in the prison kitchen. So the food, though it may jump, is bland. In the spring of 2017, the Milwaukee County jail came under scrutiny when inmates died from dehydration after being denied water for nearly a week while they served time in solitary confinement.

In contrast, most European countries take an approach to incarceration that seeks to limit the experience inside a prison to the removal of freedom of movement while retaining all other human rights, including access to health care, nutritious food, and a variety of opportunities to develop skills that can be applied to work and home life once the inmate is released back into society. A model for humane incarceration is the system in Norway. And what does Norway get for leading the world in human-rights-centered approaches to incarceration? Not the highest, but perhaps counterintuitively, one of the lowest recidivism rates in the world.

The comparison between the system of incarceration in the United States and in Norway is often cast as a debate about the purpose of prison. Is it punitive or rehabilitative? Rather than enter that debate, we pose a different question: would the same conditions exist in prisons in the United States if the population of inmates were of a different complexion? Locking people in literal cages, often in solitary confinement, even for decades, providing nonpotable water and inadequate nutrition, is yet another form of policing the body, of policing Black bodies—bodies that have no value, for which there is no rehabilitative hope, which require cordoning off from mainstream society, not so much for what they have done *but for who they are.*

Supervision outside the prison walls may not constitute a total institution, but that does not mean that it does not involve policing Black bodies. Parole and probation are both statuses in which someone convicted of a crime is not incarcerated but is under the supervision of the criminal justice system. In both cases, the individual is required to check in on some schedule with an officer of the court, usually a probation officer; they may be required to participate in a rehabilitation program, such as drug or alcohol treatment, sex offender treatment, and so forth; and in some cases the individual may have to wear an electronic monitor. Most important to note is that any violation of the terms of parole or probation will result in the individual being returned or sent back to jail or prison. As we unpack the factors that contribute to mass incarceration, we will see that parole and probation violations play an important role in keeping our jails and prisons filled to maximum capacity. And though neither parole nor probation rises to the level of the policing of the body performed in prison, the level of surveillance that probation and parole require, including phone calls to check in and random drug tests, is another way in which the Black body is policed by the criminal justice system.

WHAT DO THE NUMBERS TELL US?

According to the Bureau of Justice Statistics, 2.25 million American adults are incarcerated. Nearly twice as many Americans, 4.7 million, are on probation or parole. A total of 6.8 million American adults, or 2.8 percent of the population of the United States, are in some way "policed" by the criminal justice system. As we will explore in a subsequent chapter, mass incarceration is fed by a pipeline—fifty thousand juveniles are also currently incarcerated.

Two mainstream news reporters, Adam Gopnik and Chris Hayes, have both noted that the incarceration rate in the United States is *higher* than that under one of the world's most oppressive regimes: Stalin's gulag. Chris Hayes writes, "Americans under penal supervision, some have argued, even rivals the number of Russians in the gulag under Stalin."[4] The United States makes up 5 percent of the world population and 25 percent of the incarcerated population. And this doesn't even count the number of people on parole or probation. There is no other way to put it than to say that the United States is addicted to incarceration.

It is widely believed that David Garland in his book *Mass Imprisonment*, published in 2001, coined the term "mass incarceration." It is a useful term and has now become part of common parlance in households and on the mainstream news in discussions of incarceration in the United States and around the world.

Critics of the term "mass incarceration" argue that it implies that the bodies of racial and ethnic groups in the United States are equally incarcerated. The term inadvertently or perhaps deliberately passes over the fact that Black bodies (mostly men) are incarcerated at levels that are twice those of white men. Further, the term is more political than scientific. That is, it does not get close to the empirical underpinnings of large-scale incarceration. We use the term, but we use it with caution.

The term "mass incarceration" hides another phenomenon as well; it is important to remind ourselves that probation and parole, which control the lives of nearly three times as many people as those incarcerated, are often invisible, and this invisibility masks the number of people our incarceration nation snares in its claws. One might conclude that probation and parole are not so bad because folks serving time under supervision are at least not locked in a cage. And of course we would agree. That being said, the impact of any supervision, including probation and parole, is significant. Those under supervision have restrictions on where they can be physically and at what time; it limits their ability to travel, who they can spend time with, and so forth.

Maya Schenwar, whose investigation of house arrest appeared in *Mother Jones* in 2015,[5] describes the insidious nature of house arrest, a policy that is both sold to the American public as *prison reform* while simultaneously being in some ways more restrictive than jail or prison. She notes, for example, that many of the civil rights guaranteed to inmates, including a minimum number of calories provided per day, guaranteed time outside in the yard, and access to legal resources vis-à-vis the prison library, may in fact not be guaranteed for all, or even most, of those who are confined to house arrest. From a surveillance perspective, house arrest offers 24-7 monitoring, as Schenwar notes, without the blinking of a guard, and a nearly unlimited capacity for warrantless searches, including drug tests, all at very little cost to the American taxpayer. Not only is it much cheaper to incarcerate people in their own homes, which they pay to live in and maintain, but in most states, those under house arrest must pay for their own monitoring, typically $100 per week.

> Such a situation is certainly preferable to being caged in a prison cell. However, does [Marissa] Alexander's release—and that of others in her shoes—mean freedom? In reality, an ever-growing number of cages are proliferating around us, even if they assume forms that look nothing like our standard idea of a cage.

And, lest we be lulled into the comfort that house arrest allows those whose bodies are being policed to at least maintain their relationships with family and friends, in fact, the majority of people under house arrest report that it has negative consequences for their relationships. Their bodies are policed literally in front of their loved ones twenty-four hours a day. As one parent testified, "When it beeps, the kids worry about whether the probation officer is coming to take me to jail. The kids run for it when it beeps."[6]

So, how did we become, as Fareed Zakaria put it, "incarceration nation"? As we will demonstrate here, it is not by accident but instead a very deliberate set of policies and practices that are racialized and target low-income people, Black men in particular. If we focus only on the state of mass incarceration, we miss the critically important story of the process—the fact that the policies and practices that result in mass incarceration do so specifically by the targeting of Black bodies. Today, roughly one-third of all Black men will be incarcerated in their lifetimes, and nearly three-quarters (70 percent) of Black men without a high school diploma will be locked up. Many people argue that more Black men are in prison because they commit more crime. If we do nothing else in this chapter, it will be to debunk this myth. No system, applied equally to all people, would result in the portrait of the system of mass incarceration as it exists in the United States, a system in which one of every two inmates is a Black man. Of the 2.25 million prisoners, *nearly one million are Black men*. To put this number in context, there are approximately sixteen or seventeen million Black men living in the United States, and on any given day, one million of them are in prison.

As the quote that opens this chapter makes clear, incarceration has become part of the life course for many Black Americans, and for low-income Black Americans in particular. What does all of this mean for

Black people? What is the impact of mass incarceration on Black bodies, Black families, and Black communities?

HAS IT ALWAYS BEEN THIS WAY, OR HAVE THINGS CHANGED IN THE LAST CENTURY?

For the majority of the history of the United States, the incarcerated population was relatively flat, and white men outnumbered Black men by a nearly two-to-one ratio in jails and prisons. As the following graph demonstrates, beginning in 1980, the incarceration rate took a significant and very steep climb upward, so that within fifteen years, by 1995, the percentage of the American population that we were locking up quadrupled! And the incarceration rate has remained at this high level for the last twenty years.

Simultaneously with the steep rise in the percentage of Americans who are incarcerated came a dramatic shift in the race of the incarcerated population. In 1926 whites made up 78 percent of the incarcerated population, and Blacks comprised 21 percent. After a slow shifting in the racial composition of prisons, in 1980 the transition accelerated rapidly such that by 1986 whites had fallen to 65 percent of the incarcerated population and Blacks had more than doubled to 44 percent.[7] Not only did we become a nation addicted to incarceration, but we became, as Michelle Alexander describes, a nation with a new system of racial segregation: mass incarceration is the "new Jim Crow."

One might come to the conclusion that in 1980 Black people began, for some reason, committing more crimes and that the racialized shift in patterns of incarceration is simply a response to their behavior. And this is one of the central, dominant, and most dangerous myths about mass incarceration. This belief is nothing short of a quintessential example of color-blind racism.

In fact, a series of policies and practices, some that *specifically targeted Black Americans* and others that targeted the poor, who are disproportionately Black, changed the landscape of prisons both in terms of the number of people we imprison and the complexion of those we lock up. The United States became addicted to incarceration largely as a consequence of a move to incarcerate Black people—Black men in particular—and move them away from a capitalistic society that had no use for

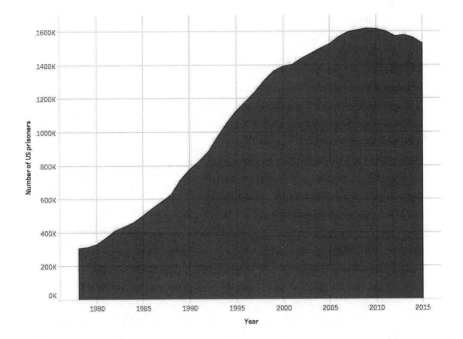

Prison Growth in the United States, 1925–Present
Note: **Chart shows the number of people per one hundred thousand national population at that time confined to state, local, and federal correctional facilities.**

them, a cordoning off if you will, a new Jim Crow, and a few whites, white men in particular, were merely the collateral damage of these racist and classist policies.

Specifically, the steep rise in the incarceration of Black men is driven primarily by two forces: overt racial discrimination and racialized policies, including the now infamous "War on Drugs."

One of the most efficient ways to address individual discrimination in decision making is the presence of rules. The gender wage gap disappears among minimum wage workers, for example. When the law prescribes a minimum wage, employers pay it to everyone who works for them, and gender discrimination in wages vanishes. As we shall see in our discussion of the school-to-prison pipeline, when schools have specific rules for the suspension or expulsion of students, there are very few racial differences.

In the pathway to incarceration, each moment, each decision, involves subjective, individual decision making, and this is precisely the type of process that is ripe for discrimination. So, for example, though the data reveal that Black and white drivers are pulled over at the same rate, Black drivers were more likely to be subjected to "forced search" of their cars and were more likely to have "force used against them" during a traffic stop. The relationship between racial profiling and racial disparities in incarceration is significant and clear. Part of the explanation for the higher rate of incarceration of Black bodies is a direct outcome of the higher probability that they will be searched, arrested, and charged with a crime.

For example, the controversial stop-and-frisk laws that allowed police in New York City to search anyone they reasonably believed to appear suspicious came under intense scrutiny when it was revealed, coming as no surprise to the Black community, that police were unfairly targeting Black and Hispanic New Yorkers, and as a result it was repealed in 2013.

Along with differences in traffic stops and arrests, there is also substantial evidence to support the argument that Black defendants receive stiffer sentences than their white counterparts who commit the same crime. Despite all the talk of sentencing guidelines—rules—judges hold significant power, free from scrutiny, when it comes to sentencing those convicted of crimes, and Black men and women pay the price. Among people convicted of drug felonies in state courts, whites were *less likely* than Blacks to be sent to prison. Specifically, a 2001 report by the U.S. Department of Justice that focused on sentencing in state courts found that only 33 percent of convicted white defendants received a prison sentence, whereas 51 percent of Black defendants were sent to prison.[8] In addition, in a review of forty methodologically sophisticated studies investigating the link between race and sentence severity, many of the studies, especially at the federal level, found evidence of *direct discrimination against minorities* that resulted in *significantly more severe sentences* for Black defendants than their white counterparts.[9] Therefore, we conclude, based on the data, that part of the explanation for differential rates in incarceration is racial disparities in sentencing. More Black men are in prison than their white counterparts because when convicted of the same crime, they are more likely to receive prison sentences, and these sentences are typically longer and more severe.

In the spring of 2017 we spent several days in a medium-security prison in rural Pennsylvania. The county where this prison is located is 94 percent white. According to the Prison Policy Institute, the incarcerated population of Pennsylvania, which mirrors that of the United States, is 46 percent Black. As we walked each day from the solitary confinement unit to the staff cafeteria, we passed through the yard while the 2,500 men incarcerated there were moving from their cell blocks to the "chow hall." A sea of Black men's bodies—all dressed in brown, marked with the letters PA DOC. As we moved through the local community, eating in local restaurants, checking in and out of the hotel where we stayed, our team of researchers included the only Black faces we saw. Policing Black bodies. Segregating Black bodies.

THE ROLE OF DRUG LAWS

In addition to exposing racism in the criminal justice system, which without a doubt accounts for some of the racial disparities in incarceration, any examination of mass incarceration and the overincarceration of Black men must include an interrogation of drug laws. There are several policies that have been put into place, beginning in 1980 and the infamous War on Drugs, that not only produced an astronomical increase in the number of Black men in prison but specifically *targeted* them for incarceration in an attempt to segregate them from the economic and social opportunities that would allow them to prosper and reach the middle class.

The number of people incarcerated for drug offenses increased exponentially between 1980 and 2014. Those incarcerated in state prisons and jails for drug offenses increased tenfold in this twenty-five-year period; in federal prisons, the number of people incarcerated for drug convictions increased by a factor of twenty. To put this into perspective, during this same period, the total population of the United States increased by a factor of only 1.5, from 200 million to 330 million. [10]

Similarly, the share of total incarcerations made up by drug convictions more than doubled, from comprising 21 percent of all sentences to 50 percent. In other words, in 1980 drug convictions comprised less than one-fourth of all incarcerations, and today they contribute more than half. So what, specifically, led to this disproportionate rise in the incarceration rate of drug offenders?

Let us be clear. The dramatic increase in the incarceration of bodies on drug possession charges is not a reaction to an increase in drug use. In fact, research by the White House Office of National Drug Control Poli-

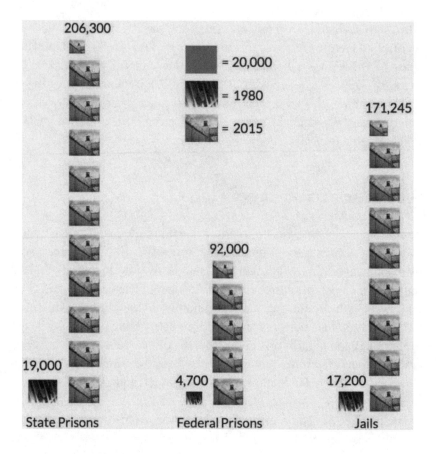

Number of People in Prisons and Jails for Drug Offenses, 1980 and 2015

cy,[11] which has collected data on drug use categorized by age beginning in 1975 to the present, shows overwhelmingly, in every age category, that drug use rose from 1975 to 1979 *and then dropped off significantly in the 1980s, 1990s, and early 2000s.* The evidence is overwhelmingly clear that the tenfold increase in drug convictions between 1980 and 2012 cannot be explained as a response to increased drug use but rather to changes in the criminalization of substances and changes in the policies designed to address drug possession.

THE WAR ON DRUGS

The "War on Drugs" officially began in 1972 with a formal announcement by President Richard Nixon. The War on Drugs intensified under the administration of President Ronald Reagan, who added the position of "drug czar" to the President's Executive Office. There has always been speculation that the War on Drugs targeted Blacks, but until the spring of 2016 there was no proof, so to speak. *Harper's* magazine contributor Dan Baum[12] was working on a book in which he was trying to answer the question, "How did the United States entangle itself in a policy of drug prohibition that has yielded so much misery and so few good results?" As part of his research he tracked down John Ehrlichman, who had been Nixon's domestic policy advisor, and asked him a set of questions about the impetus for the War on Drugs. Ehrlichman's response both surprised many of us in its honesty and confirmed long-held speculation about what was really behind the War on Drugs:

> "You want to know what this was really all about?" he asked with the bluntness of a man who, after public disgrace and a stretch in federal prison, had little left to protect. "The Nixon campaign in 1968, and the Nixon White House after that, had two enemies: the antiwar left and black people. You understand what I'm saying? We knew we couldn't make it illegal to be either against the war or blacks, but by getting the public to associate the hippies with marijuana and blacks with heroin, and then criminalizing both heavily, we could disrupt those communities. We could arrest their leaders, raid their homes, break up their meetings, and vilify them night after night on the evening news. Did we know we were lying about the drugs? Of course we did."

And the War on Drugs, though not necessarily successful in reducing drug use or eliminating illegal drug trafficking, did exactly what Ehrlichman admitted was the goal: to lock up Black people, to produce stereotypes about Black people, and to disrupt Black communities. The War on Drugs has had a devastating impact on the Black community, removing fathers and sons and spouses from their families, limiting the kinds of jobs these men can get when they return from prison, and excluding them from political representation through felony disenfranchisement laws. For an excellent film that traces a century of criminalizing drugs in order to police a variety of nonwhite bodies, we recommend the PBS documentary *The House You Live In*.

What Ehrlichman referred to as the "criminalization" of drugs, specifically marijuana and heroin, and later, under Ronald Reagan, crack and cocaine, produced four policies that are a direct cause of mass incarceration and have led unequivocally to the incarceration of one in every three Black men. The War on Drugs put into place stiffer sentencing guidelines that required (1) longer sentences, (2) mandatory minimums, (3) the recategorization of some drug offenses from misdemeanors to felonies, and (4) the institution of the "three strikes, you're out" policy. Each of these policies alone contributes to mass incarceration, but their power lies in their combination. Elizabeth Hinton notes, "As a result of these provisions combined, the average prison sentence increased 33 percent, from forty-six months in 1980 to sixty-one months in 1986."[13]

One of the most problematic outcomes of the War on Drugs policies is "mandatory minimums." Prior to 2010, the mandatory minimum sentence for possessing a mere five grams of crack cocaine was five years, *without the possibility of parole*. In 2010, under pressure from advocacy groups that presented clear data on the racial disparities of drug sentencing, President Obama signed the Fairness in Sentencing Act (21 U.S.C. 841), which increased the minimum possession from five to twenty-eight grams of crack, which now carries the mandatory five-year minimum sentence, without the possibility of parole. The mandatory minimum sentence *doubles to ten years* if a defendant has one prior felony drug offense. Though perhaps viewed as a step in the right direction, a mandatory five-year minimum sentence for *possession* of twenty-eight grams of crack is still absurd. Twenty-eight grams of crack is low-level drug possession and will do little to address racial disparities in drug sentencing. And, to add insult to injury, the Fairness in Sentencing Act is not retroactive. As a result, those individuals sentenced for possession of five grams of crack under the original mandatory minimums must serve their entire sentence. After the election of Donald Trump as president of the United States, his attorney general, Jeff Sessions, has announced that he has plans to turn back many of the mandatory minimum reforms gained under the Obama administration. As a result, mandatory minimums will continue to fuel the state of mass incarceration. Policing Black bodies.

As part of the 1986 Drug Abuse Act, small possession convictions, particularly of crack cocaine, were recategorized from misdemeanors to felonies. When combined with mandatory minimums and doubling sentences for a second possession offense, from five to ten years, the average defendant convicted of crack cocaine possession receives an eleven-year sentence. For drug possession. Not for murder or rape or child molesting. Child molesters are incarcerated, on average, for merely three years in prison. After release, the majority of child molesters reoffend within the first year. That is, they molest another child within the first year of getting out. This begs the question: how concerned are we about public safety, including the safety of our precious children, when we lock up Black men for possessing the equivalent of a handful of "sugar packets" of crack three times longer than a child molester?

Finally, the habitual felon law, often referred to as "three strikes, you're out," endorsed by then-president Bill Clinton, prescribes *life sentences* for convicts receiving a third felony conviction. As a direct result of recategorizing some drug *possession* offenses, including crack cocaine, from misdemeanors to felonies, the outcome has been that many inmates serving life sentences have been convicted of nothing more than three drug possession offenses; in effect, they are serving life sentences for untreated addiction.

The Peculiar Case of Crack Cocaine

One of the most important and decisive changes to drug policies that was implemented beginning in the 1980s, and that specifically targeted Black bodies, was distinguishing, in the law, between two forms of cocaine: crack (or rock) and powder. Crack is less pure than cocaine, and as a result it's cheaper. Dealers specifically targeted low-income communities to distribute the new drug, and the crack epidemic of the 1980s and early 1990s exploded, primarily in the Black community. In her groundbreaking book *Killing the Black Body*, Dorothy Roberts argues that "crack's apparent confinement to inner-city neighborhoods made it the perfect target for Reagan's ferocious War on Drugs and the media's disparagement of Black Americans. The media soon imbued crack with phenomenal qualities: it was instantly addicting, it intensified the sex drive, and it turned users into violent maniacs. While powdered cocaine was glamorized as a thrilling amusement of the rich and famous, crack was vilified for stripping its underclass users of every shred of human dignity."[14] Roberts's analysis confirms just what Ehrlichman described: racializing and criminalizing drugs in order to effect a war not on drugs but on Black bodies.

As part of the War on Drugs, federal drug policies were developed that established a distinction between crack and powder cocaine and set a 100-to-1 sentencing disparity between the two forms. Though this was revised by the Fairness Sentencing Act of 2010, this meant that possession of just five grams of crack cocaine (about a thimbleful) yielded a five-year mandatory minimum sentence; in contrast, a defendant must possess five hundred grams of powder cocaine to receive the same five-year sentence. Proponents of this ratio in sentencing argue that it is simple chemistry. Because it takes one hundred grams of cocaine (powder) to make one gram of crack, sentences ought to reflect differences in the amount of "high" that is derived from different amounts of cocaine when it is consumed in different forms—thus the 100:1 ratio that is employed in the sentencing guidelines. [15]

This would be equivalent to tying alcohol possession laws—for minors, for violations of open-container laws, and so forth—to the "proof" of the alcohol that is possessed; illegal possession of "three-two" beer (beer that is no more than 3.2 percent alcohol) would carry a lighter sentence than the illegal possession of eighty-proof vodka. Laws governing the possession of alcohol have never been applied differently with regard to the percent of alcohol in the beverage, and most Americans would probably find the idea preposterous. Similarly, the laws around the illegal possession of narcotic prescription drugs do not vary based on the number of milligrams of the drug per tablet. Yet this is just what the crack cocaine laws do. Policing Black bodies.

A second issue is the fact that the new drug policies treat crack differently than other banned substances, including powder cocaine. Simple possession of any quantity of any other substance by a first-time offender—including powder cocaine—is a misdemeanor offense punishable by a maximum of one year in prison (21 U.S.C. 844). In contrast, simple possession of crack by a first-time offender is a class C felony, carrying a mandatory five-year minimum sentence, and the offender carries a felony conviction on their record. Crack cocaine is the only drug for which there is a federal mandatory minimum sentence for mere possession.

This sentencing disparity, enacted in 1986 at the height of the War on Drugs, was rationalized by invoking the myth that crack cocaine was more dangerous than powder cocaine and that it was instantly addictive and caused violent behavior, just as Dorothy Roberts argued. Since then, copious amounts of scientific evidence and an analysis by the U.S. Sentencing Commission have shown that these assertions were not supported by sound data and were exaggerated or outright false.

The crack/powder disparity is a primary contributor to racial disparities in conviction and sentencing. In 2006, 82 percent of those sentenced under federal crack cocaine laws were Black, and only 8.8 percent were white—even though more than two-thirds of people who use crack cocaine are white. The U.S. Sentencing Commission has found that "sentences appear to be harsher and more severe for racial minorities than others as a result of this law. The current penalty structure results in a perception of unfairness and inconsistency." The "crack epidemic" is, quite simply, nothing more than a tool to police Black bodies, to effect a War on Black bodies that is deliberate and built on stereotypes and myths about drug use. It has, in many ways, accomplished just what Ehrlichman said it was intended to do.

IT'S ALL ABOUT THE MONEY

Money plays a significant role in the system of mass incarceration. It shapes everything from one's likelihood of being profiled or frisked to begin with to the type of lawyer one can afford to hire to plea-bargain the case down to a lesser charge or have it dismissed outright. And none of this is fair or equitable. That being said, the inequalities run much deeper than we originally understood.

Unique to the United States, law enforcement agencies are funded locally, not federally, as they are in most European nation-states. And one perhaps unintended consequence of the rapid growth in incarceration has been the rapid rise in the cost of policing Black bodies through surveillance, arrest, prosecution, and incarceration. Coupled with a growing sentiment, fueled in large part by the War on Drugs, the public increasingly felt that *the costs of policing Black bodies should be passed along to those same Black bodies*. And it all begins with bail.

Judges set bail, and typically a defendant must pay 10 percent of the bail in order to be released while they await trial. If the defendant is unable to pay or cannot secure a high-priced "loan" from a bail bondsman, they will be incarcerated in the local jail while awaiting trial. The

Council of Economic Advisors estimates that nearly one-third (30 percent) of inmates in local jails, or almost a quarter million people, are there awaiting trial, not yet convicted of any crime, simply because they cannot afford to pay for their release.

Courts also began to assess various fees that quite simply pass the costs of court proceedings on to defendants who are convicted. Even if the person convicted is not sentenced to jail time, if they are unable to pay the fees, they will be incarcerated in the local jail until the fees are paid. If the convicted person is sentenced to some confinement, the fee will follow them in the form of a bill. In most cases, the fees must be paid before the person is released from confinement. And though many inmates serve a decade or more in prison to satisfy their formal sentence, if their families are not able to pay the fees, they may see their term of confinement extended until the fees can be paid. How widespread is this? According to the Council of Economic Advisors, 20 percent of all incarcerated people are confined for their failure to pay court fees. And because Blacks are disproportionately likely to be poor, they are more likely to be incarcerated, not because they commit more crime but because they are unable to post bail or pay fines, something the Council of Economic Advisors terms a system of regressive taxation.

But it doesn't end there. The fees continue to accrue interest during the period of confinement. The Council of Economic Advisors reported on a study conducted in Washington State where the interest rate on fines and fees is 12 percent. Convicted drug felons unable to pay the typical $10 per month payment on the average fine ultimately paid $15,000 over a thirty-year period! So, how will the inmate who was unable to pay a fee prior to incarceration pay it during incarceration if they are not allowed to work? We will explore the work that inmates are able to do for pay in our discussion of the prison-industrial complex, but suffice it to say the wages they are paid are so meager that no amount of work, even over decades, would ever generate enough in wages to pay off the fees and fines. And, as we will demonstrate, in many prisons in which inmates are allowed to work, their pay is "docked" in order to pay fines and fees as well as the costs of their incarceration. In Pennsylvania, if an inmate owes a fee or a fine, the Department of Corrections "taxes" not only wages but commissary contributions, made by family and friends, at a rate of 20 percent. These policies create nothing more than a treadmill that low-income people convicted of crimes can never get off.

Forfeitures of assets during drug raids provide another powerful illustration of the confluence of factors that lead to long-term, perhaps lifetime, financial consequences for those caught in the drug snare while generating huge revenues for local law enforcement agencies. The forfeiture provision of the Comprehensive Criminal Control Act of 1986 allows law enforcement agencies to keep money, drugs, and other assets—for example, weapons—when they make a drug arrest.

> The legislation's forfeiture provision permitted local law enforcement to seize as much as 90 percent of cash and property from accused drug dealers, which brought federal governments, local police departments, and civilian whistle blowers lucrative returns from the assets of drug dealers and other criminals. . . . After the legislation passed, gross receipts of all seizures increased from $100 million to over $1 billion within three years. . . . As Vice President Bush said, "We can use the criminals' own property to help finance law enforcement."[16]

No other crime has such a provision. As a result, it is in the best interests of law enforcement agents to turn most of their attention to drug possession and trafficking crimes rather than all the other sorts of crime that threaten our public safety but do not allow for the opportunity to seize lucrative assets, including burglary, child sexual abuse, or rape—all of the policing energy focused on policing Black bodies possessing drugs.

And the forfeiture laws apply even if no conviction is obtained. "Even if a suspect was released and acquitted on all charges, his or her property would still be subject to forfeiture. Low-income citizens unable to secure adequate legal representation lost income, assets, and material goods that could never be recovered."[17]

The investigation conducted by the Department of Justice in the aftermath of the protests in Ferguson revealed a long-standing, widespread, but often invisible practice of using ticket quotas to fund local law enforcement agencies. Quite simply, officers were charged with writing a certain number of traffic tickets each shift in order to generate revenue for their departments. And the U.S. Department of Justice report on Ferguson revealed that "Black residents of Ferguson received speeding tickets at 'disproportionately high rates overall.'"[18] According to the Council of Economic Advisors report, in a high-profile example of this practice, a Department of Justice investigation of the Ferguson Police Department in Missouri showed that the town of Ferguson set revenue targets for criminal justice fines and fees of over $3 million in 2015, covering over 20 percent of the town's operating budget. [19]

The report goes on to reveal even more insidious practices that target Black bodies and police them in order to extract monetary resources.

> The model of cops as armed tax collectors didn't stop with simple traffic stops for speeding: the entire municipal court system was designed to function as a payday lending operation. Relatively small infractions quickly turned into massive debts. Many traffic citations required the ticketed person to make court appearances, but the local court would hold sessions only three to four times a month for just a few hours. Because of the limited hours, the court couldn't process everyone who came for their court date. Those left outside were cited for contempt for failing to appear. Not coming to court triggered another fine and failure to pay that fine counted as its own form of contempt, adding to the total. [20]

The report identifies one woman who ended up owing nearly $1,500 for a $151 parking ticket because of the payday lending apparatus operated by the municipal court in Ferguson. Policing Black bodies.

And, as the report revealed, Ferguson was not unique but was actually quite typical.

Not only will fines and fees continue to accumulate over time, but in a series of recent cases, the U.S. Supreme Court decided that officers may now search individuals without a warrant or probable cause if the individual has an outstanding fine, including for something as minor as an unpaid traffic ticket. In the case of *Utah v. Strieff*, Mr. Strieff was leaving a suspected drug house, and an officer followed him to a local convenience store where he initiated a "stop." The officer asked Mr. Strieff for his driver's license so that he could verify his identity, and when he ran his ID he discovered a warrant for an unpaid traffic ticket. Based on this, the officer searched Mr. Strieff and discovered a small amount of methamphetamine. Mr. Strieff was arrested and charged with felony drug possession. Mr. Strieff argued that the arrest was illegal because the search, without a warrant, violated the Fourth Amendment. Writing in the dissent, Justice Sonia Sotomayor argued,

The Court today holds that the discovery of a warrant for an unpaid parking ticket will forgive a police officer's violation of your Fourth Amendment rights. Do not be soothed by the opinion's technical language: This case allows the police to stop you on the street, demand your identification, and check it for outstanding traffic warrants—even if you are doing nothing wrong. If the officer discovers a warrant for a fine you forgot to pay, courts will now excuse his illegal stop and will admit into evidence anything he happens to find by searching you after arresting you on the warrant. Because the Fourth Amendment should prohibit, not permit, such misconduct, I dissent.

She went on to argue that unwarranted searches are humiliating and that they more often than not target Black bodies and other communities of color. Policing Black bodies.

The officer's control over you does not end with the stop. If the officer chooses, he may handcuff you and take you to jail for doing nothing more than speeding, jaywalking, or "driving [your] pickup truck . . . with [your] 3-year-old son and 5-year-old daughter . . . without [your] seatbelt fastened." . . . At the jail, he can fingerprint you, swab DNA from the inside of your mouth, and force you to "shower with a delousing agent" while you "lift [your] tongue, hold out [your] arms, turn around, and lift [your] genitals." . . . Even if you are innocent, you will now join the 65 million Americans with an arrest record and experience the "civil death" of discrimination by employers, landlords, and whoever else conducts a background check. . . . And, of course, if you fail to pay bail or appear for court, a judge will issue a warrant to render you "arrestable on sight" in the future. . . . This case involves a suspicionless stop, one in which the officer initiated this chain of events without justification. As the Justice Department notes, . . . many innocent people are subjected to the humiliations of these unconstitutional searches. The white defendant in this case shows that anyone's dignity can be violated in this manner. . . . But it is no secret that people of color are disproportionate victims of this type of scrutiny. . . . For generations, black and brown parents have given their children "the talk"—instructing them never to run down the street; always keep your hands where they can be seen; do not even think of talking back to a stranger—all out of fear of how an officer with a gun will react to them.

Although the protests in Ferguson were triggered by the police shooting of unarmed Black teen Mike Brown, the tensions between the Ferguson police department and the Black community in Ferguson had been brewing for years. And who wouldn't feel victimized by being targeted by the police, not because your community is committing more crime or posing a threat to public safety, but rather as a way to generate revenue for one's own policing? *Put plainly, the police department is policing Black bodies in order to extract the cost of policing Black bodies.* And, to add insult to injury, those who cannot pay the fines or fees levied will have their freedom denied through incarceration.

Why target the Black community? Because Black people are disproportionately poor, and law enforcement agencies can, quite simply, generate significantly more revenue when they police Black bodies and Black communities. For example, because poor Black folks are less likely to be able to hire a lawyer to have their tickets reduced, they will be more likely to be required to pay the entire fine. Because poor Black folks will be less likely to be able to pay the entire fine at once, they will be forced to pay the fine on an installment plan, which accrues interest and ultimately raises the total cost of the fine. The police department in Ferguson figured that out! More data from the U.S. Department of Justice report indicated that in 2013, in a city of just more than twenty-one thousand, which is 67 percent Black, police issued fifty-three thousand traffic tickets. That's more than two tickets per person, including children.

We remind the reader of the experience of Chris Hayes that opens the book. Many if not most middle- and upper-middle-class people have had the experience of talking an officer out of a ticket or showing up for the court date and promising not to speed again, only to be rewarded by having the fine reduced or dismissed. And if the charges are more serious, most middle- and upper-middle-class people are able to employ a lawyer to plea-bargain the charges down. Perhaps tens of thousands of middle- and upper-middle-class white teenagers have marijuana possession or underage drinking charges handled in just this way; they leave the encounter paying a fine and, most important, without a criminal record. Police officers target Black communities, especially low-income Black communities, because they can, because there is no consequence for doing so, even when they kill a young Black man, a subject we will explore in much more depth in a later chapter. And, because the fines tend to generate more fees, they generate more income for the local police department, the very regressive tax the Council of Economic Advisors report describes.

Fines and legal fees typically do not end once an inmate is released. It is incredibly common for individuals who are sentenced to probation, those who serve out a period of probation after a period of incarceration, and those who serve parole to have to pay fees while they are under the court's supervision. In many cases, the costs of court-ordered offender treatment programs, such as drug or alcohol interventions, sex offender treatment, or batterer intervention programs, are passed on to the offender. We worked with a batterer intervention program in Winston-Salem, North Carolina, and observed this practice in real time. Men convicted of intimate partner violence assault could often avoid jail time by agreeing to attend the batterer intervention program. Here's the catch: the program was twenty-five weeks/sessions at a cost of $25 per session, or a total "fine" of $625. Many participants indicated that they simply didn't have the $25 each week, and so they would skip their sessions. If attending a program was a condition of their probation, they could be locked up (again) simply for not being able to afford the costs of the conditions of their probation.

Most of us cannot imagine finding ourselves in this situation; the $25 per week fee seems a very small price to stay out of jail or prison. And yet, especially for those convicted of a felony, be it intimate partner violence or simply possessing twenty-eight grams of crack cocaine, they may not be able to find a job at all. Or they may not be able to find a job that allows them to pay rent, buy food, *and* afford a weekly fee.

In an interview about her 2017 book *Pound of Flesh*, Alexes Harris argues,

> Given that the vast majority of people who receive felony convictions in the U.S. are disproportionately of color and poor, with minimal employment and income prospects post-conviction, the practice of imposing financial penalties cements people to lives of poverty and reinforces existing inequalities. Legal debt matters because of the large number of people it affects, and for the pernicious impacts it has on their lives.[21]

GET A JOB! GET AN APARTMENT! THE BOX AND INVISIBLE INCARCERATION

Regardless of how one feels about crime and appropriate sanctions, the stark reality is that nearly three-quarters of a million people will return from prison to our communities each year. And there is simply no question that we are all safer if those returning are able to start a new life, turn over a new leaf, and become contributing citizens. Many Americans are fond of employing the ideology of "second chances." Yet the system of second chances is decidedly and deliberately stacked against people who have been convicted of a crime, even when they have served their time. Policing Black bodies extends far beyond the prison walls.

For the hundreds of thousands of Americans returning from prison to our communities each year, 70 percent or more will be returned to prison within three years of their release. Recidivism is a result of many factors, but contrary to popular belief, the least likely cause of recidivism is commission of another crime. In fact, the vast majority of recidivism is the result of three factors: failure to pay fines or fees; violating another aspect of parole or probation, for example, failing a drug test; or engaging in the illegitimate economy because routes to legitimate work are blocked. And of course in some cases these factors coalesce, as was the case for Jonathan Earl Brown.

> Jonathan Earl Brown . . . was trying to get his life back on track when he was released from a Ramsey County [Minnesota] workhouse early last year.
>
> But just four months into his probation, Brown was sent back to prison. His offense: failing to enter sex offender treatment that he could not afford.
>
> Brown was homeless, jobless and so destitute that his probation officer suggested he sell his blood to cover his $42 co-payment, court records show. . . . Chief Judge Edward Cleary said that preventing indigent sex offenders from obtaining treatment, due to lack of funds, sets them up for failure and undermines public safety.
>
> Requiring convicted sex offenders to pay for their own treatment is touted as a way to give them a financial incentive to do well in therapy and take responsibility for their crimes. Yet treatment programs are few in number and expensive; health insurers often won't cover individual therapy, forcing offenders to dig into their own pockets to pay for treatment ordered by the courts.[22]

A felony record makes it nearly impossible to permanently return to the "free world." A felony record prohibits one from accessing most social safety net programs, including welfare and public housing. A felony record also creates an enormous barrier to employment, and this is especially true for Black men. Though this has been widely known for years among the formerly incarcerated, their families, and people who work with them, Devah Pager[23] published the results of an experiment that demonstrated both the impact of a felony record on employment and the intersections between a felony conviction and race. Specifically, her experiment documented that when Black and white male "testers" applied for employment, white men were more likely, overall, to be offered a "callback" than Black men; white men without a felony were the most likely to be offered a "callback"; and, most disturbing, *white men with a felony were more likely to be offered a "callback" than Black men without a felony.* Only 3 percent of Black men posing as "testers with a felony record" were offered a callback. This study illustrates quite clearly the profound impact that a felony record has on the employment available to Black men.

Many of those advocating for and working with people with felonies as they attempt to successfully reenter the "free world" and become productive citizens argue for the removal of the "box," which people with felony convictions must check on every employment application. It is

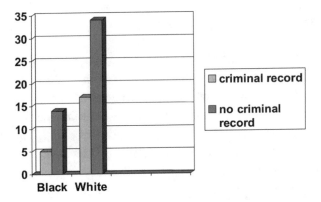

Male Applicants Receiving Callbacks, by Race and Felony Status (in Percentage)
Source: Devah Pager, "The Mark of a Criminal Record," *American Journal of Sociology* 108 (2003): 937–75.

also a common box on college applications; our own institution has such a box. Pager's research provides clear documentation that the box negatively impacts the probability that someone with a felony record will be able to secure gainful employment, and the impact is most severe for Black men with felony records.

Proponents of the box argue that employers should have the right to know if someone they are considering hiring has a felony; it's a matter of safety. Opponents argue that, as Pager's experiment demonstrates, the box results in immediate discrimination. And removing the box would not prevent employers from conducting background checks, which would reveal felonies. The difference is that background checks often take a few weeks, and formerly incarcerated people often report that if they get a chance to start a job and prove themselves, once their employer finds out about their felony record, they rarely fire them because they are able to look past the box and focus on their job performance. Given all of this evidence, we advocate for removing the box from employment and school applications while allowing employers and schools to continue to perform background checks. This approach would reduce the policing of Black bodies who have served their time and simply want an opportunity to become successful citizens while still ensuring the public safety of workplaces and the community.

In addition to the discrimination that people with a felony record face with potential employers, they also face bans on certain types of jobs and employment certificates as well as accessing social safety net programs. Debbie Mukamal's[24] work on these types of barriers to reentry details these bans. For the purposes of this discussion we provide some poignant examples.

Employers in most states can deny jobs to people who were arrested but *never convicted* of any crime. Employers in a growing number of professions are barred by state licensing agencies, for example, barber shops, from hiring people with a wide range of criminal convictions, even convictions that are unrelated to the job or license sought. This is exacerbated by the fact that some of the licensing bans apply to trades that inmates are taught in prison as part of rehabilitation programs. For example, many prisons offer inmates the chance to certify in barbering, but most states ban individuals with a felony record from holding a barber's license, even if the conviction is for a drug possession or other nonviolent offense. Clearly, there is a significant disconnect between the skills prisons invest in teaching inmates and the jobs they will be able to obtain once they reenter the "free world." This finding seriously calls into question the professed goal of many state corrections departments that they are focused on rehabilitation.

As part of the research we conducted for another book (*Prisoner Reentry and Social Capital: The Long Road to Reintegration*) published in 2010, we interviewed countless men who had spent a reasonable length of time in prison. Most of the men we interviewed had spent at least five years in prison, and some had spent upward of thirty years behind bars. These men talked at length about the various certification programs they had completed, partly as a way to fill time and partly as a way to prepare—they thought and were told—for their reentry.

Bill's experiences were echoed by many. Bill had spent his time in prison pursuing training and certifications in the trades: construction, electrical wiring, plumbing, and so forth. Well equipped with his certificates, when Bill was released from prison he immediately started applying for jobs in the construction industry. Potential employers were usually impressed with his credentials, but questions arose when they looked at his certificates and noticed that all were earned at places with names like Morrisville State Institutional Facility. When they inquired where *exactly* his certificates were earned, Bill had to admit that he had earned them as an inmate in a state prison. Suddenly the once enthusiastic potential employer no longer had a need to hire in Bill's areas of expertise. This simple but critical illustration was repeated perhaps hundreds of times by the men we interviewed. We can only surmise how frustrating it is to commit to the types of training these certificates require, all along believing they are your "ticket" to a better life after you reenter the "free world," only to find them discarded by potential employers who are more worried about the felonies and incarceration than the skills one acquired.

The barriers to reentry weren't always so high. In the first half of the twentieth century, men released from prison, even those with felony records, were usually able to find work in the local communities they returned to. They didn't face the kinds of bans we see today on licensure. They weren't necessarily prohibited from living in public housing, especially if they were moving in with family members, and they weren't necessarily barred from receiving social welfare. As a result, recidivism rates were significantly lower. Men who did their time had a legitimate second chance. But all of that changed.

Beginning in the late 1960s, as part of President Johnson's War on Poverty, social welfare programs and incarceration became inversely related; there seemed to be less interest in offering the poor and Blacks a "leg up" and more interest in criminalizing their behavior. Not only did the War on Poverty in some ways lay the groundwork for the War on Drugs, which ultimately *replaced* it, but it also set a new precedent with regard to social welfare programs and criminal behavior.

As part of the 1996 Temporary Assistance for Needy Families (TANF) reform and the changing drug laws of the 1980s and 1990s, a series of bans were imposed on returning citizens with felony records that prevent them from accessing many of the social programs that provide basic-level support. Proponents of these bans argue that they work as a crime deterrent by operating as an incentive to keep people out of the kinds of trouble that will result in a felony, especially involvement with drugs. Opponents of these bans argue that denying returning citizens, particularly individuals with *felony drug convictions*, access to social welfare programs that provide housing, income, and educational support amounts to stacking the deck against people who, without these support programs, will not be able to successfully reenter the "free world." In short, opponents argue that these bans contribute significantly to the revolving door that now characterizes prisons and contributes significantly to the state of mass incarceration.

Bans on social welfare programs vary from state to state. Our intent here is to paint a broad picture of the bans, and we encourage the interested reader to visit the website of the Legal Action Center (http://www.lac.org) and obtain their report for a more detailed understanding of the bans as they are imposed across the various states.

Most states (thirty-eight) impose a ban on the receipt of cash assistance (TANF) and food stamps for individuals with a felony drug conviction. Nearly half of these states (seventeen) impose a lifetime ban on cash assistance and food stamps. The changes in drug laws that we outlined above thus have lifetime consequences; the simple possession of twenty-eight grams of crack cocaine can result in a lifetime ban from cash assistance and food stamps for millions of Americans whose only real crime is an untreated addiction.

Interestingly, *no similar ban is imposed on individuals with felony convictions that are not drug related.* The ban does not extend, for example, to those convicted of felony rape, murder, or child molestation.

Blacks are disproportionately likely to be convicted of a drug felony (which carries the ban), whereas white men are disproportionately likely to be convicted of child molesting, serial rape, and school and other mass shootings, none of which carry the ban. Policing Black bodies.

Given the fact that individuals with a felony record face serious obstacles to employment, we ask the question, upon release from prison, struggling to find a job, facing a ban on cash assistance and food stamps, how will the reentering citizen eat?

The federal government also allows public housing authorities to use evidence of a criminal record in determining eligibility for public housing. The federal government imposes lifetime bans on eligibility for public housing on two groups: (1) those convicted of the production of methamphetamine and (2) those required to be registered for their lifetime on the state's sex offender registry. In addition, Debbie Mukamal's research on housing authority guidelines found that the majority of housing authorities do consider a person's criminal record when determining their eligibility for public housing. The most common bans were for felony drug convictions and violent offenses. Furthermore, her research noted that more than half (twenty-seven) of housing authorities "make decisions about eligibility for public housing based on *arrests that never led to a conviction.*" Because children are most likely to live with their mothers, *children* of mothers with a drug felony will be ineligible to live in public housing. As a direct result, this ban poses a serious threat to the safe housing of millions of Black children. A ban on public housing for people convicted of possessing a controlled substance—a drug felony—is a powerful tool in extending the control over Black bodies that Michelle Alexander describes as the new Jim Crow. Not only does mass incarceration become a mechanism for segregating Black bodies into a massive system of detention, but the power to segregate Black bodies with regard to housing extends well beyond prison walls, in many cases impacting not only the citizen returning with a felony record, but their family members as well. We cannot underestimate the power of this particular social welfare policy as a strategy for policing Black bodies, even, as is the case of children, those who are completely and totally innocent.

The War on Drugs and welfare reform also conspired and collaborated in restricting access to the coveted system of higher education assistance that had previously been available for inmates but was systematically dismantled by a key funding decision.[25] The Higher Education Act of

1998 makes students convicted of drug-related offenses ineligible for any grant, loan, or work-study assistance. This federal barrier cannot be lifted by states. *No other class of offense, including violent offenses, sex offenses, repeat offenses, or alcohol-related offenses, results in the automatic denial of federal financial aid eligibility.*

This single act completely dismantled the opportunities for inmates as well as returning citizens with drug felonies to pursue any postsecondary education. Research on wages, the racial and gender wage gaps, welfare to work, and recidivism all point to education as a key factor in eliminating inequality. Higher education leads to better jobs and higher wages, it keeps people out of poverty, and it is closely tied to reducing recidivism. This ban, then, stands as yet another barrier to the successful reentry and reintegration of people with drug felony convictions—but not rapists, murderers, or child molesters—back into their families and communities and contributes significantly to recidivism, a major contributor to mass incarceration.

Proponents of this law argue that it prevents drug users from using student loan monies to feed their drug habits. Opponents argue that it affects millions of incarcerated men and women and significantly reduces their possibilities for successful reentry. We wonder how many more times we need to pose the question, what exactly is the desired outcome of this law? And why does it target drug offenders and not violent offenders?

We already know that Black men are among the least likely to graduate from high school and complete any postsecondary education. With a third of Black men being incarcerated over their lifetimes, and *the majority being incarcerated for drug offenses*, there is no other conclusion we can come to than that this particular ban on access to higher education contributes to the anemic number of Black men with high school diplomas and post–high school education. Is this law yet another example of policing Black bodies? It's not such a far stretch to argue that in the post–*Brown v. Board* environment that renders racial segregation in schools unconstitutional, if this law effectively serves to deny Black people, and Black men in particular, access to further education, can it not be understood as an extension of the outcomes, if not the direct intent, of the laws *Brown* was seeking to overturn? This is yet another way that Jim Crow segregation extends beyond the prison walls and impacts the lives of millions of Black Americans for the rest of their lives.

Another outcome of the "reform" of drug laws in the 1980s and 1990s was a law that allowed the federal government to deny highway funds to any state that refused to impose a minimum six-month revocation on the driver's license of individuals convicted of a felony drug offense. And though thirty-two states have modified this law to offer "restrictive licenses" that allow citizens with drug felony convictions to travel to work, school, or treatment programs, eighteen states have not. Four states require that the license revocation last beyond six months. Clearly driving restrictions significantly impact a returning citizen's chances of getting and holding a job. In fact the literature on welfare notes that one of the keys, no pun intended, to a successful transition from welfare to work is having reliable transportation. This driving restriction is one more barrier facing those with drug felony convictions who are looking to turn their lives around. And though many of the men we interviewed for our book on reentry did not have the financial resources to purchase a vehicle, others noted that the lack of reliable public transportation, especially in the evening and on weekends, posed a significant barrier to their ability to hold and keep the kinds of jobs they were eligible for. Linwood, a Black man who was in his sixties when we interviewed him shortly after he was released from prison after serving nearly twenty years for felony drug possession convictions, talked enthusiastically about the job he had working in the kitchen at a local K&W restaurant.

After having cooked for many years in the cafeterias of several federal prisons, Linwood was thrilled at his good fortune at landing a job cooking at K&W while he watched so many other returning citizens struggle. What troubled Linwood was the fact that he lives in a halfway house in the downtown part of town, and the K&W where he works is more than ten miles away in the most outlying part of the northern "suburban" part of town. During the weekdays he can walk to the bus station and catch a bus—riding forty minutes or more—to his job. However, when he is assigned a shift that ends after 7 p.m. or on the weekends—which are the highest-traffic times for restaurants and thus the shifts when most of the workers are scheduled—Linwood struggles to find coworkers who are willing to pick him up or take him home because the public transportation he relies on during the week stops service before his evening shift ends. We wonder if Linwood and so many others like him will be able to sustain their employment despite barriers such as transportation. We know that their chance for successful reentry and thus the life chances of their families depend upon this success.

After decades of civil rights activism to ensure the right to vote for Black people, this right is being systematical eroded through felony disenfranchisement laws, leaving many Black people, Black families, and Black communities with no political power. According to the work of the Sentencing Project, one in thirteen Black citizens is disenfranchised, compared to only one in fifty-six non-Black citizens. Laws vary from state to state. In some states individuals with a felony record lose their right to vote forever. In other states, people with felonies can have their voting rights reinstated, but often this takes time and a trip to the courthouse, and of course there are associated fees. So, as a result, even in states that have provisions for felony reenfranchisement, very few people with felony records take the time or spend the money to have their voting rights restored. In low-income communities, where 50 to 70 percent of Black men have felony records, there may be few people who can vote. Entire Black communities have no political voice in choosing the next president let alone the next representative to the local city council or school board. Taxation without representation takes on a whole new meaning in low-income Black communities. Policing Black bodies.

We conclude this section by asking what chance families, and disproportionately Black families, have of surviving the incarceration of one of their members, mothers and fathers, when they face such serious barriers to reentering the "free world" and reintegrating into family life. Returning citizens face barriers to employment, including bans on licensure; bans on the receipt of cash assistance and food stamps; driving restrictions; bans on public housing; bans on obtaining funding for higher education; and political disenfranchisement. And though these bans vary from state to state, the one constant theme is that all of the barriers and bans are the *most severe for, or in some cases are even limited to, individuals with drug felony convictions.* And because such a high percentage of Black people are incarcerated for drug offenses, *the impact on Black families is nothing short of devastating.*

Our aim in this chapter was to pull back the curtain and reveal the real intent of the War on Drugs and shine a light on the real reasons that we have become a society addicted to incarceration. In fact, the playing field is not level; the criminal justice system is nothing like the figure of Lady Justice blindly holding the scales. Black bodies are targeted, deliberately, through a not so intricate web of policies and practices that result in the overincarceration of Black people, and Black men in particular, and the total blockage of any routes to a second chance. As Michelle Alexander so eloquently writes, mass incarceration is a tool for segregation and discrimination, just as the system of Jim Crow was. And, as Justice Sonia Sotomayor wrote in her dissent in *Utah v. Strieff*, stop-and-frisk policies, which target and police Black bodies, will continue to contribute to locking up Black people far away from mainstream culture and economic opportunity, thrusting them, their families, and their communities further into peril. She writes,

> By legitimizing the conduct that produces this double consciousness, this case tells everyone, white and black, guilty and innocent, that an officer can verify your legal status at any time. It says that your body is subject to invasion while courts excuse the violation of your rights. It implies that you are not a citizen of a democracy but the subject of a carceral state, just waiting to be cataloged. We must not pretend that the countless people who are routinely targeted by police are "isolated." They are the canaries in the coal mine whose deaths, civil and literal, warn us that no one can breathe in this atmosphere. . . . They are the ones who recognize that unlawful police stops corrode all our civil liberties and threaten all our lives. Until their voices matter too, our justice system will continue to be anything but.

Many people have said that the United States can only be described as a carceral state, that we are addicted to incarceration. And while the numbers certainly support this claim, it is not quite true. In fact, the United States was founded and built on a system of racial domination that is one of, if not the, most powerful forces shaping its evolution. Mass incarceration is not so much a story about being addicted to incarceration as it is a story about policing Black bodies. As Nixon said, he needed to wage a war on Black people, and the War on Drugs was designed to do just that. And it has. A million Black men are currently incarcerated, making up nearly half the incarcerated population. There is no plausible alternative explanation for this fact other than policing, indeed waging a war on, Black bodies.

And we agree with Michelle Alexander and U.S. Supreme Court justice Sonia Sotomayor, who argue that the real power of mass incarceration as a tool for policing Black bodies is not just the removal of Black bodies from society, but the extension of policing well beyond prison walls. Black families and Black communities suffer when one-third of all Black men will spend some time in jail or prison. Many others have noted this. But it goes much further than that. A system of barriers, including the felony box on job and college applications, the bans on food stamps and public housing, the bans on employment like barbering, and restricted driver's licenses, are all forms of policing Black bodies that extend beyond the prison wall, beyond time served. This policing of Black bodies, specifically targeting those with drug felonies, ensures that Black men's citizenship and human rights will be forever denied them. Possessing twenty-eight grams of crack returns nothing short of a life sentence. And it prevents Black men and their families and communities from participating in the democracy and economic prosperity that is reserved for white people.

And this process begins in elementary school.

4

SCHOOL-TO-PRISON PIPELINE

Kuntrell Jackson was barely 14 on the night of the incident that led to his arrest. He was walking with an older cousin and a friend when the boys began discussing the idea of robbing a video store. When they arrived at the store, the other two boys went in, but Kuntrell stayed outside by the door. One of the other boys shot the clerk, and then all three fled without taking any money.

Because Kuntrell had prior arrests for shoplifting and car theft he was tried as an adult and convicted of capital murder. The court imposed a sentence of mandatory life imprisonment without the possibility of parole.

Kuntrell Jackson's childhood was unstable and violent, according to court filings. When he was 6, his mother was incarcerated for shooting a neighbor. [1]

This chapter explores the disturbing trend known as the school-to-prison pipeline. Beginning with the disciplinary treatment of Black boys and girls in school through the use of juvenile detention for minor infractions, this chapter charts the pathway that many Black youth find themselves on, with jail or prison often their final stop. The vast majority of young men and women incarcerated were locked up for minor offenses that could and should have been dealt with by other agencies, including schools, but also mental health services, social workers, substance abuse programs, and counselors. Despite being incarcerated for what amounts to nothing more than disciplinary problems, once they are caught in the net of the system of incarceration, it is extremely difficult to chart a

different path; the school-to-prison pipeline plays a critical role in the growth and maintenance of the system of mass incarceration. Young men and women who are incarcerated are subjected to abuse—physical and sexual—that is unimaginable and which further facilitates the pipeline; they exit juvenile detention facilities often with significantly more wounds to heal than when they were first locked up. Perhaps most tragic are the cases of juveniles who are given life sentences without the possibility of parole—locked up before they are eighteen years old and sentenced to remain in prison until they die.

SEGREGATED AND UNEVENLY RESOURCED SCHOOLS: THE SOIL IN WHICH TO BUILD THE PIPELINE

In her recent book *The School-to-Prison Pipeline: Education, Discipline, and Racialized Double Standards*, Nancy Heitzeg argues that the school-to-prison pipeline is an outgrowth, perhaps inevitable, of the racialized system of education that continues to dominate the educational landscape in the United States. In our book *African American Families: Myths and Realities*, published in 2014, we demonstrated that despite the historic ruling in *Brown v. Board of Education*, schooling in the United States is not only segregated but decidedly unequal. Jonathan Kozol has spent the better part of the last twenty-plus years detailing racialized inequalities in education. His book *Savage Inequalities*, published in 1992, details the racial divide in education. Students attending majority-Black public schools, often bearing names like Martin Luther King Jr. Middle School—the irony of which was not lost on the students themselves—studied from hand-me-down textbooks that were often twenty or thirty years out of date. Students attending underresourced schools frequently experienced environmental threats to their safety, including sewage backing up in bathrooms, lead paint and asbestos yet to be removed from floors and ceilings, and inadequate heat and/or air conditioning. Children attending these schools are not allowed to go out for recess because the playground is dangerous: both because it desperately needs maintenance and because of the risk of gang violence, including gun violence. In his follow-up book, *Ordinary Resurrections*, originally published in 2000, Kozol details the lives of elementary school children in Mott Haven, New York, children who are more likely to have a parent in prison than to have visited one of the public museums in New York City. As Kozol so aptly demonstrates, inequalities begin from the very beginning.

The educational inequalities that we see today are deep, and they are both a result of the school-to-prison pipeline and a cause of it. Despite all good intentions, and we believe there were some, though they likely did not outweigh the resistance to integration, following the *Brown v. Board* decision, public schools reached the height of integration in the 1970s and 1980s. As a direct result of the "walk to school" movement that white parents launched in the mid-1990s, today, boys and girls living in the United States are more likely to attend a racially segregated school than their parents were. In fact, children today attend schools that are as racially segregated as their *grandparents* did. The average Black student today attends a school that is 96 percent Black. And, not surprising, as Kozol's important work reveals, the vast majority of Black segregated schools are severely underresourced.

Research by the Government Accountability Office (GAO)[2] published in 2016 revealed that 16 percent of all public schools were 75 to 100 percent Black and poor, with similar percentages of students attending these schools receiving free or reduced lunch. The most highly segregated school districts have the highest rates of Black students being suspended or expelled. Entering the school-to-prison pipeline.

Whereas Heitzig's focus is primarily on the movement to criminalize misbehavior in schools, failing to appropriately educate Black students, especially young Black men, is also a major contributor to the prison pipeline. Across the board, only 69 percent of Black youth graduate from high school, and the rate of graduation among Black young men is dismal: fewer than half (48 percent) earn a high school diploma. And of those who do graduate from high school, only 25 percent or so are deemed "college ready." Ultimately, fewer than 20 percent of Blacks successfully complete a college degree, compared to nearly 40 percent of whites.[3] This is important for a multitude of reasons, not least of which is the fact that as a result, unemployment and underemployment rates are significantly higher among Black men than among men of other racial and ethnic identities. Unemployment and underemployment often lead to "hustles" to make ends meet, which as we noted in our discussion on mass incarceration contributes to the overincarceration of Black men. In fact, based on a study conducted by the Brookings Institute in 2014, it is estimated that 70 percent of Black men without a high school diploma will be incarcerated in their lifetimes.[4]

As Nancy Heitzig argues, the seeds for the school-to-prison pipeline have been planted.

THE SCHOOL-TO-PRISON PIPELINE

The term "school-to-prison pipeline" is relatively new, and yet, as Elizabeth Hinton argues in her book *From the War on Poverty to the War on Crime: The Making of Mass Incarceration in America*, concerns about "Black youth" and the need to control their behavior first became institutionalized much earlier:

> Almost immediately after World War II, when the "teenager" emerged as a formidable political and cultural category, state and local governments began to enact delinquency policies that expanded the surveillance of black urban youth. Urban police departments from New York City to Houston started to increase patrol in targeted low-income

neighborhoods as a means to control unruly teens. Juvenile delinquency programs in Oakland, for instance, brought police officers into public schools to monitor and arrest youth identified as "troublemakers" by school and social services staff. The Oakland Police Department aggressively enforced misdemeanors—both on and off school grounds—just as it began to offer recreational programs for this same group of "troublesome" young residents. As a result of such anti-delinquency measures in Oakland, Houston, New York City and other urban centers with concentrations of African American youth, the number of young people under some form of criminal justice supervision nationwide grew 2.5 times between 1949 and 1957.[5]

Most recently, as significant attention has been brought to bear on the school-to-prison pipeline, researchers have turned their focus to analyzing data on suspensions, expulsions, and juvenile detention. Shaun Harper and Edward J. Smith, researchers at the University of Pennsylvania's Center for the Study of Race and Equity in Education, examined school suspensions and found that 55 percent of all suspensions nationwide occurred in just thirteen southern states, including Alabama, Arkansas, Florida, Georgia, Kentucky, Louisiana, Mississippi, North Carolina, South Carolina, Tennessee, Texas, Virginia, and West Virginia.

Digging deeper, their research revealed that across the board in these southern states, Black students were suspended or expelled at rates more than five times their representation in their schools. In other words, if Black students made up 10 percent of the student body, they accounted for 50 percent of the suspensions and expulsions. At the extreme, in nearly one thousand southern school districts, Black students accounted for the majority, 50–100 percent, of K–12 school suspensions and expulsions.

How can we interpret these findings? First of all, it is not surprising that the highest number of Black students suspended or expelled are in southern states, as this is where the majority of the Black population continues to live. That said, the power of the work of Smith and Harper is that it compares rates of suspension and expulsion to the actual representation of Black students in a school or school district. An intersectional analysis suggests that the racialized system of privileges and oppressions that has existed in the southern region of the United States since its inception remains very much alive and well today. Black and white students are treated differently. Black students are disciplined more harshly than their white counterparts for reasons that have to do with stereotypes and expectations of their behavior.

So, you may be saying, perhaps the Black kids were engaged in more serious misbehavior, and that accounts for their higher rates of suspension and expulsion. As we argued, one of the major causes of mass incarceration is racial disparities in arrest, conviction, and sentencing; each stage of the process involves discretion on the part of law enforcement and judicial officials. Across the board, Blacks are more likely to be arrested, convicted, and given harsher sentences, regardless of the type of crime committed. And Smith and Harper's research confirms these same patterns in school suspensions and expulsion. But perhaps most interesting and convincing is research conducted by the Public Policy Research Institute,[6] which revealed that there are very few racial differences in suspensions and expulsions in schools with *written disciplinary policies*. Racial disparities are most present, then, in schools and school districts in which administrators have *discretion* with regard to suspension and expulsion, a finding that reinforces our argument that racial bias is largely at the root of the racial disparities that exist in the criminal justice system more broadly and that Smith and Harper report in their examination of school suspensions. And, again, not surprisingly these disparities are the most pronounced in the southern region of the United States. Policing Black bodies.

Racial disparities in suspension and expulsion are concerning enough on their own, but what makes them even more troubling is the fact that suspension and expulsion are often a precursor to experiences with the juvenile justice system. Students who are suspended multiple times or expelled are significantly more likely to enter the juvenile justice system.[7] Is it just a coincidence that other than New York and California, southern states have the highest rates of incarceration nationally? Given the rise of plantation prisons in the post–Civil War era, a system that was designed both to replace enslaved labor in a labor-intensive agricultural economy and police and detain Black bodies, the fact that both mass incarceration and high rates of school suspension and expulsion coexist in the South is no surprise. In fact, it's predictable. The school-to-prison pipeline is clearly a mechanism for cordoning off or segregating Black people, in this case boys and young men.

Heitzeg provides the following definition and explanation of the school-to-prison pipeline:

For nearly two decades, scholars, educators, and activists have identified and decried the emergence of this school-to-prison pipeline. Most immediately, the pipeline is a consequence of the "criminalization of school discipline" via zero-tolerance policies. It is characterized by schools that rely on suspensions, expulsions, and arrests for minor infractions, and which have police and/or security officers (School Resource Officer, or SRO) present for the enforcement. While these policies were motivated in part by the perceived need to increase "safety" and "security," the zero-tolerance policies and police in schools have instead increased the risks of criminalization for segments of the student body, particularly students of color. This pattern of "push out" has become so pronounced that scholars, child advocates, and community activists now refer to it as the "school-to-prison pipeline," the "school to jailhouse track," or as younger and younger students are targeted, "the cradle to prison track."[8]

So, not only do Black students fail to graduate, which is a major predictor of the likelihood that they will eventually be incarcerated, but school officials, lacking the resources they need to address the demands of a needy student population—school counselors, social workers, adequate feeding programs—turn to discipline rather than educational and social work strategies for dealing with behavioral issues.

In the spring of 2016, police in Murfreesboro, Tennessee,[9] sparked a national debate on the overpolicing of students. Despite protests by officers, ten Black children, some as young as nine years old, were arrested at their elementary school and removed in handcuffs. They were accused of participating in a neighborhood bullying incident that had transpired several weeks earlier. And, though we do not condone bullying, even police officers at the scene argued for alternative strategies for handling the situation rather than arrest and detention. Smith and Harper's research found that Black students in Murfreesboro were 1.3 times more likely to be suspended and expelled than their white counterparts.

Not far from where we live, in Prince William County, Virginia, in the spring of 2016 a middle school boy, who is Black, was handcuffed, arrested, and charged with larceny for allegedly stealing a sixty-five-cent carton of milk. He was suspended and is required to appear in juvenile court. At the time we were finalizing the information for this book, in the summer of 2017, this case is set to go to trial. The ridiculousness continues: as it turns out, this young man qualifies for free school lunch. We wonder how he could have stolen something he was supposed to have for free.[10] Black boys' bodies are policed in school and out of school as the result of criminalizing otherwise minor acts of deviance.

WHAT THE DATA TELL US

According to the U.S. Department of Justice,[11] in 2013 there were approximately fifty-four thousand juveniles incarcerated in juvenile detention centers, youth facilities, and adult prisons. Fourteen percent of incarcerated juveniles are female. Sixteen- and seventeen-year-olds are the vast majority of incarcerated youth, but it is important to note that youth as young as twelve years old are incarcerated, making up 1 percent of all youth in jail or prison. Of all young people, Black youth are the most likely to be incarcerated, followed by Native Americans and Hispanics, with whites and Asians having the lowest rate of juvenile incarceration. According to research by the Sentencing Project, Black boys and girls are five times more likely than their white peers to be incarcerated. Of the 54,000 youth incarcerated in 2013, the latest year for which data are available, 21,600 (40 percent) were Black. Put another way, Black youth make up 13 percent of the U.S. population but 40 percent of the population confined in juvenile detention facilities. *The majority of juveniles are incarcerated for property crimes, including arson, vandalism and burglary. A very small number of juveniles are incarcerated for violent offenses like rape and murder.*

Racial disparities in sentencing, which vary by type of crime committed, are in part to blame for the disproportionate incarceration rates for Black boys and girls. According to research conducted by the Sentencing Project,[12] Black youth were *269 times* more likely to be arrested for violating curfew laws and 2.5 times more likely to be arrested for property crimes, but perhaps most troubling is the data on drug arrests. First and foremost, Black and white youth report using drugs at similar rates. Second, prior to 1980, Black and white youth were arrested for drug use at about the same rate, 1 in 300. Most troubling, after the War on Drugs began in 1980, as we and others have documented with regard to adults, *the rate of arrest for drug use by Black youth went up 350 percent while the rate of arrest for white youth declined.* In fact, "by 1991, a black juvenile was 579 percent more likely to be arrested for a drug offense than a white teenager." The War on Drugs is also a war on Black youth. Policing Black bodies.

And this racialized trend continues today. After the legalization of marijuana in both Washington State and Colorado, *arrests of white youth for possession of marijuana declined, while arrest rates for Black youth remain significantly higher.*

> According to a national study from the ACLU in 2013, black users are 3.73 more likely to be arrested for possession than their white counterparts, even though both groups use pot at the same rate. As a result, black people are disproportionately slapped with mandatory minimum sentences and languish in prison for decades even as more states consider legalization.[13]

Deeply troubling is the fact that while the vast majority of these Black young men and women are being incarcerated for what amount to minor, nonviolent property crimes, in addition to the loss of freedom they experience while incarcerated, they are at tremendous risk for physical and sexual abuse.

PHYSICAL ABUSE IN JUVENILE DETENTION CENTERS

It is much more difficult than one might imagine to find accurate data on the mistreatment of young men and women locked up in juvenile detention centers. The Annie E. Casey Foundation's report *No Place for Kids*, published first in 2011 and updated in 2015, tracks reports of the mistreatment of incarcerated young men and women by combing the only two publicly available sources for abuse reports: lawsuits and news accounts. According to research reported by the Annie E. Casey Foundation, "42 percent [of juveniles in detention or camps] said they were somewhat or very afraid of being physically attacked, while 45 percent reported that staff 'use force when they don't really need to,' and 30 percent said that staff place youth into solitary confinement or lock them up alone as discipline."[14]

One of the most chilling accounts about the abuse of young men incarcerated in a juvenile detention center comes from the Dozier School for Boys in Florida, where young men were systematically abused for decades.

The men remember the same things: blood on the walls, bits of lip or tongue on the pillow, the smell of urine and whiskey, the way the bed springs sang with each blow. The way they cried out for Jesus or mama. The grinding of the old fan that muffled their cries. The one-armed man who swung the strap.

They remember walking into the dark little building on the campus of the Florida School for Boys, in bare feet and white pajamas, afraid they'd never walk out.

For 109 years, this is where Florida has sent bad boys. Boys have been sent here for rape or assault, yes, but also for skipping school or smoking cigarettes or running hard from broken homes. Some were tough, some confused and afraid; all were treading through their formative years in the custody of the state. They were as young as 5, as old as 20, and they needed to be reformed.

It was for their own good.[15]

Kalief Browder[16] was sent to Rikers Island, the infamous New York jail that jets fly over on their way to landing at La Guardia airport, when he was just sixteen years old. Browder had been accused of stealing a backpack. He spent three long years, including more than four hundred days in solitary confinement, at Rikers Island, *never having been convicted of any crime*. During his time at the prison he was repeatedly bullied, beaten—by guards and fellow prisoners—and raped. At age twenty-two, after having been released on bail, still having only been accused but never convicted of stealing a backpack, Browder committed suicide. This kind of tragedy should never occur in the United States. But sadly it does, and far too often.

Regardless of how you might feel about the treatment of people convicted of crimes, it is critically important to remember that the abuses we are detailing here are being experienced by children, most of them Black, the vast majority of whom were incarcerated for nonviolent property crimes. We ask, does any child deserve to have their body policed and abused in such a way, regardless of the crime they have been convicted of? Would you want your son or daughter to be treated this way? Of course not. And these *children* should not be treated this way either. They deserve to be respected and to have the opportunity to be resocialized so that they enter adulthood with an education, with some training, and with at least a chance of becoming contributing members of our society.

RAPE IN JUVENILE DETENTION CENTERS

After decades of activism to bring the phenomenon of prison rape to the attention of lawmakers and the public, in 2003 the Prison Rape Elimination Act (PREA) was passed. PREA required that all facilities that incarcerate people must report on an annual basis the number of rapes that are reported, as well as other information about the assault, like the assailant's gender and rank—inmate or staff. The Bureau of Justice Statistics compiles this data, and it is readily available for anyone to examine. As we note in our 2016 book, *The Social Dynamics of Family Violence*, reported rapes represent only about 10 percent of the actual number of rapes that occur. Scholars estimate the difference between official reports and the actual number of cases by conducting surveys of inmates. Interestingly, the 10 percent report rate is nearly identical to the rates we see on college campuses, in the military, and in adult prisons. There are many reasons why people don't report rape, including shame, embarrassment, fear of retaliation, and, in the case of boys and men, a presumption of being gay. Rape victims often believe, wrongly, that they did something to facilitate or incite the rape. If they are raped by a staff member or guard, they may fear that they will not be believed or that they will face disciplinary action.

Data from the most recent Bureau of Justice Statistics report on juvenile rape reveal that in the previous twelve months, 10 percent of boys and 8 percent of girls reported being raped by either another inmate or a guard.

Because this measure is restricted to rapes that occurred in the previous twelve months, similar to rape in the military or on college campuses, the rate of boys and girls who have been raped *at any time during their incarceration* will be much higher. And, as noted, as a direct result of significant underreporting, these numbers are a gross underrepresentation of the actual percentage of boys and girls who are sexually victimized.[17] By the time they are released, we estimate that as many as 40 to 50 percent of all boys and girls who are detained in juvenile facilities will have been raped by another inmate or a guard.

Overall, boys report significantly higher rates of sexual abuse than girls, which is the opposite of what we find in the "free world," where one in five women report being raped in their lifetimes compared to one in seven boys and one in thirty-three adult men. This pattern of rape in

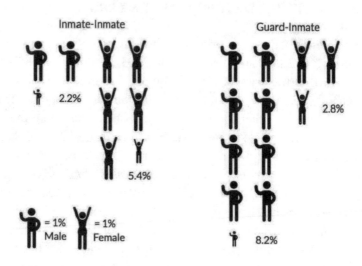

Reported Rapes in Juvenile Detention

juvenile facilities mimics what we see in adult prisons; incarcerated men have a significantly higher rate of rape than incarcerated women. Also similar to adult facilities, girls are more likely to be sexually abused by another inmate, whereas boys are more likely to be raped by a guard.

It is especially important to note that these statistics are only based on children locked up in juvenile facilities. A disturbing number of young men are incarcerated in adult prisons, including those serving life without the possibility of parole, and their experiences are not captured in this data. Based on conversations we have had with staff at Parchman Prison in Mississippi, we can speculate confidently that the rates of rape are significantly higher for boys incarcerated alongside adult men, including convicted child molesters.

Boys report that they are more likely to be sexually abused by a guard than by another inmate. Despite the fact that women make up only 44 percent of the guard staff, an overwhelmingly majority, 89 percent, of boys reported that the person who sexually abused them was a female guard. Even more disturbing, 85 percent of the boys who reported sexual victimization by a guard indicated that they had been victimized more than once in the previous year, and 20 percent reported *more than eleven incidents in the previous twelve months*.

When asked about the process by which the sexual contact was initiated, boys described two themes that are common in other settings, particularly in middle and high schools, where women sexually abuse boys: grooming and "relationship." Among the boys who were incarcerated, they reported that grooming behavior included providing "favors" and gifts in "exchange" for sex. Boys also reported that the female guards who abused them presented the abuse as if it were a "relationship." They wrote the boys letters, sent them pictures, talked inappropriately to them about other aspects of their lives, and even contacted them when they were transferred to other facilities.

A case from Woodland Hills,[18] a juvenile detention center in Tennessee, provides an interesting and unfortunately common illustration:

> A *Tennessean* investigation found suspicious indications of female staff abuse of male students at Woodland Hills, including a female kitchen employee who transmitted chlamydia to a 17-year-old youth through a sexual encounter, and later lived with another male she had a relationship with at the facility.

Among the many negative outcomes of this kind of sexual abuse is that it often leaves the victim believing that he or she was in some way responsible for the abuse because they accepted gifts or because they were made to believe that the abuse was part of a consensual relationship. Sexual molestation of children by adults is a crime. Even if the child is led to believe that he or she "wants" the relationship, sexual contact by adults with children always constitutes abuse precisely because it is based in a power relationship that muddles the ability of the child to give consent freely. In the case of the rape of juveniles by guards, consent is impossible *precisely because of the power the guard has to impact the victim's daily life*, withholding food or restricting access to privileges to recreation time or telephone calls or visits, or even locking them in solitary confinement.

The boys and girls who are confined in juvenile detention centers are there almost exclusively as the result of being convicted of committing nonviolent crimes, and they are subjected at very high rates to sexual abuse while they are confined. Nearly 10 percent of juveniles reported experiencing a sexual assault in the previous twelve months,[19] which means that our young people are at significantly greater risk for rape while in a detention facility than in the "free world." Given all the negative outcomes for rape victims, we can be sure that as they serve their time and are rehabilitated and prepare to reenter society with the hopes of becoming productive adults, unless their experiences with sexual violence are addressed, they will face significant obstacles in reentry and ultimately in living healthy, productive lives—a set of challenges that is great enough for juvenile offenders without the additional burdens of being a rape survivor.

JUVENILE LIFE WITHOUT PAROLE (JLWOP)

Without a doubt, the data and stories that make up this chapter are deeply disturbing. Yet, buried inside the story of the overincarceration of Black youth, visible only to those parents and families it impacts and the few researchers and activists who pay attention to it, is perhaps the most deeply disturbing phenomenon of all: juvenile lifers, those girls and mostly boys who are sentenced to life in prison without the possibility of parole.

> Life in prison without the possibility of parole gives no chance for fulfillment outside prison walls, no chance for reconciliation with society, no hope. Maturity can lead to that considered reflection which is the foundation for remorse, renewal, and rehabilitation. A young person who knows that he or she has no chance to leave prison before life's end has little incentive to become a responsible individual. (*Graham v. Florida*, 2010)[20]

The United States is the only country in the world that allows children under the age of eighteen years old to be sentenced to life in prison without the possibility of parole. Currently there are more than 2,500 people who committed their crimes when they were under the age of eighteen who are serving life sentences without the possibility of parole.

Proponents of life sentences will argue that there are some crimes so heinous and the perpetrators so dangerous that for the good of public safety they must be locked away until their death, never allowed to enter our society again. An interesting perspective when we consider serial killers like Charles Manson, an adult when he was convicted, who was sentenced to life in prison *with the possibility of parole*. Though he has never been paroled, and he probably never will be, he has the *opportunity* every few years to apply. Even Charles Mason can hold on to the hope, if he chooses, that he can adopt behaviors that will impact the possibility that he will once again be free of a life behind prison walls.

Opponents of life sentences without the possibility of parole for individuals convicted as juveniles argue that juveniles are not fully developed cognitively, intellectually, or emotionally—they are not good decision makers—and thus sending them to prison for the rest of their lives is an inappropriately harsh sentence, regardless of the crime they were convicted of. In fact, the concept of juvenile life without the possibility of parole is recent. As far back as 1899, criminal justice reformers were clear that juveniles needed to be treated differently than adults, and many state laws included provisions for handling juvenile crime differently from adult crime. Not until the 1990s did courts begin to transfer some juvenile offenders to adult court. Initially, very few juvenile cases were handled in adult court, but during the crack epidemic and the rise of juvenile homicide (which tripled between 1980 and 1993),[21] the expansion of policies allowing juveniles to be tried in adult court and sentenced as adults began. Despite the fact that juvenile homicides continue to decline today, more and more juveniles are sentenced to life without the possibility of parole, a sentence which amounts to nothing more than a long, drawn out death sentence.

THE CASE OF HENRY MONTGOMERY—INCARCERATED FOR FIFTY-THREE YEARS AND COUNTING

In 1963, seventeen-year-old Henry Montgomery was convicted of killing a sheriff's deputy in Louisiana. Henry was sentenced to life without the possibility of parole. Henry Montgomery has been incarcerated nearly sixty years!

Based on a 2012 ruling by the U.S. Supreme Court that rendered unconstitutional the sentencing of juveniles convicted of murder to *mandatory* sentences of life without the possibility of parole, in 2015, Henry's case for parole, *Montgomery v. Louisiana*, made it to the Supreme Court. The case was ultimately turned back to the State of Louisiana on the grounds that state courts, not the U.S. Supreme Court, should rule on cases of parole. Henry is still waiting to learn if the Louisiana state parole board, which will conduct its hearing inside the state prison where Henry is incarcerated, will give him the chance to argue that he is rehabilitated and no longer a threat to public safety.

We would never argue that growing up in difficult circumstances is an excuse for committing crime. That said, the majority of those juveniles who were sentenced to prison for life without the possibility of parole experienced circumstances that are unthinkable to most of us, the kinds of circumstances that would typically mitigate a sentence—not eliminate it, but perhaps shorten it. For example, juvenile "lifers" experienced high rates of violence in their homes (79 percent witnessed violence regularly) and in their communities (54 percent). Nearly half of all juvenile lifers experienced physical abuse at home; the vast majority of girls (77 percent) and 20 percent of boys experienced sexual abuse at home. Most juvenile lifers are poor, many were not in school in the weeks leading up to the crime, and just less than half were in special education classes, an indicator of some limited or delayed cognitive ability.[22] Many of these *children* engaged in violence as a direct result of the violence and abuse they experienced at home. Some were convicted of killing their abuser or a father or stepfather who was abusing their mother. Others joined gangs in response to a lack of supervision at home and found themselves entangled in circumstances they may not have fully understood. These experiences don't excuse behavior, but they do provide a lens for helping us to understand the circumstances in which children find themselves engaged in behaviors that ultimately land them in adult courtrooms, sentenced to life without the possibility of parole.

As was the case with Kuntrell Jackson, a quarter (25 percent) of juvenile lifers were convicted of "felony murder accomplice liability," which means they may not have even been present at the time of the murder. Similar to the case of Kuntrell Jackson, many juvenile lifers had "priors" that were factored into their sentences, even as their life circumstances were not. Of course we have to ask the question, how many juvenile "lifers" were first exposed to the juvenile justice system as a result of a disciplinary action at school? The ultimate in the school-to-prison pipeline. The ultimate in policing Black bodies.

As with everything else we have explored in this book, the sentencing of juveniles to life in prison without the possibility of parole is deeply structured by race: both their race and the race of the victim. According to the research of the Sentencing Project,

The proportion of African Americans serving life sentences without the possibility of parole for the killing of a white person (43.4%) is nearly twice the rate at which African American juveniles are actually arrested for taking a white person's life (23.2%). Conversely, white juvenile offenders with black victims are only about half as likely (3.6%) to receive a life sentence without the possibility of parole as their proportion of arrests for killing blacks (6.4%).

In other words, the probability that a juvenile will be given a life sentence without the possibility of parole is double if the offender is Black and the victim is white and half as likely if the offender is white and the victim is Black.

Because the majority of juvenile life sentences without the possibility of parole are handed down in just five states—California, Florida, Louisiana, Michigan, and Pennsylvania—that have mandatory sentencing guidelines that do not allow judges to consider mitigating factors when sentencing juveniles, the Sentencing Project and others advocate for changes in sentencing guidelines that allow judges' discretion in sentencing juveniles.

The school-to-prison pipeline is also a mechanism for cordoning off an already segregated population to a place of seemingly no return. Segregation in education is the first step in the cordoning-off process, and incarceration seals the deal. As Michelle Alexander writes in *The New Jim Crow*,

It is fair to say that we have witnessed an evolution in the United States from a racial caste system based entirely on exploitation (slavery), to one based largely on subordination (Jim Crow), to one defined by marginalization (mass incarceration). While marginalization may be far preferable to exploitation, it may prove to be even more dangerous. Extreme marginalization, as we have seen throughout world history, poses the risk of extermination. Tragedies such as the Holocaust in Germany or ethnic cleansing in Bosnia are traceable to the extreme marginalization and stigmatization of racial and ethnic groups. As legal scholar john a. powell once commented, only half in jest, "It's actually better to be exploited than marginalized, in some respects, because if you're exploited presumably you are still needed." Viewed in this light, the frantic accusations of genocide of poor blacks in the early years of the War on Drugs seem less paranoid. The intuition of those residing in ghetto communities that they had suddenly become disposable was rooted in real changes in the economy—changes that have been devastating to poor black communities as factories have closed, low-skill jobs have disappeared, and all those who had the means to flee the ghetto did. The sense among those left behind that society no longer has use for them, and that the government now aims simply to get rid of them, reflects a reality that many of us who claim to care prefer to avoid simply by changing channels.[23]

Before they have even had a chance to grow into adulthood, the school-to-prison pipeline cordons off *future* Black families and Black communities, ensuring unfettered access to the opportunity structure, including educational opportunities, jobs, and homeownership, to *future* white families and white communities. Policing Black bodies by paying it forward for future generations.

The school-to-prison pipeline functions to literally remove Black young men, many of them *children*, far too many of them *permanently*, from society and is nothing short of devastating to Black youth, Black families, and Black communities. For those who do return, far too many return with the wounds not only of the incarceration itself but also of severe physical and sexual abuse. Those who do return, return with a felony record, already one-third of their way to three strikes. Is this how our society values Black bodies relative to the value of a sixty-five-cent carton of milk? Policing Black bodies.

5

THE PRISON-INDUSTRIAL COMPLEX

The New Plantation Economy

FEDERAL PRISON INDUSTRIES—UNICOR OFFICIAL WEBSITE

FPI Inmate Programs

FPI is, first and foremost, a correctional program. The whole impetus behind Federal Prison Industries is not about business, but instead, about inmate release preparation . . . helping offenders acquire the skills necessary to successfully make that transition from prison to law-abiding, contributing members of society. The production of items and provision of services are merely by-products of those efforts.

FPI Program Benefits . . .

- to society—Rigorous research demonstrates that participation in prison industries and vocational training programs has a positive effect on post-release employment and recidivism for up to 12 years following release. Inmates who worked in prison industries or completed vocational apprenticeship programs were 24 percent less likely to recidivate than non-program participants and 14 percent more likely to be gainfully employed. These programs had an even greater positive impact on minority offenders, who are at the greatest risk of recidivism.
- to the courts, crime victims, and inmate families—In FY 2014, inmates who worked in FPI factories contributed almost $1 million

of their earnings toward meeting their financial obligations, e.g., court-ordered fines, child support, and/or restitution. Many inmates also contributed to the support and welfare of their families by sending home a portion of their earnings.

- to thousands of incarcerated men and women in federal prisons— For many inmates, working in Federal Prison Industries represents an opportunity to learn a marketable skill and gain valuable work experience that will substantially enhance their ability to success-fully reintegrate into society following release from prison. The program teaches inmates pro-social values including the value of work, responsibility, and the need to respect and work with others. Many inmates gain a sense of dignity and self-worth that they had lost or never before experienced.
- to private sector businesses—During FY 2014, FPI purchased more than $272 million in raw materials, supplies, equipment, and ser-vices from private sector businesses. More than half of these pur-chases were from small businesses, including women and minority owned and disadvantaged businesses.
- to the Bureau of Prisons—FPI contributes significantly to the safety and security of federal correctional facilities by keeping inmates constructively occupied. Inmates who participate in work programs and vocational training are less likely to engage in institutional misconduct, thereby enhancing the safety of staff and other in-mates.[1]

FPI is an integral component of the Federal Bureau of Prisons (Bureau or BOP), https://www.unicor.gov/About_FPI_Programs.aspx.

Incarceration has become a multibillion-dollar industry[2] that *relies* on incarcerating nearly 2.5 million citizens on any given day in the United States. We spent the entirety of chapter 3 exposing the causes of mass incarceration, and in this chapter we deal with one remaining cause: *the pure profitability of incarceration*. Like so many issues we interrogate in this book, the system of profiting off of incarcerated bodies and exploit-ing their labor is thinly disguised as something positive for those people whose bodies are being locked in a "rental" cage, their labor exploited for profit, as well as something positive for society, as the opening descrip-tion from the Federal Prison Industries website suggests.

The term "prison-industrial complex" (PIC), first coined by Angela Davis and employed by many other scholars and activists, including Eric

Schlosser, refers to two aspects of mass incarceration: the profit that is made simply by incarcerating people and the profits that are made by dozens if not hundreds of private and public corporations by exploiting the labor of incarcerated people. Though both of these sources of profit are intertwined, in order to understand the real power of the prison-industrial complex it is critical to understand the role that each plays separately as well as the ways in which these two strategies reinforce each other and fuel not only profit but mass incarceration. Given the enormous profits associated with incarceration, we have reached a point of no return. Unless some dramatic legislation is passed that would make it unconstitutional to make a profit off of incarcerating human beings and off of the labor of the incarcerated, we see no evidence that the train that is mass incarceration will be slowed down or ever turned around. And of course the costs of mass incarceration are born almost entirely by the Black community and by whites who live in poverty, groups whose interests are not represented in the halls of Congress, bodies whose lives have no value in a capitalist economy built on racist policies and practices.

THE ECONOMICS OF THE PIC: THE CASE OF CORECIVIC

The economic benefits a prison brings to a community, except for the possible increases associated with census discrepancies, are debatable.[3] Though a few jobs are created, prisons are actually very expensive to run. Though in some cases the inmates themselves contribute to the cost of their own incarceration, their contributions, usually based on fines and fees and occasionally on the wages they earn by working in prison industries, are but a small fraction of the cost to lock them up. They don't pay rent, they don't pay for food, and they obviously don't contribute toward upkeep and maintenance. This structure is a physical space that while providing housing for the convicted receives little in return directly from the inhabitants themselves. And as we argued in our discussion of mass incarceration, as our society began to incarcerate more people, the costs to the citizens of the United States who bear the burden of mass incarceration grew exponentially.

Incarceration is extremely expensive. Rough estimates indicate that it costs most states many times more to incarcerate an inmate per year than to educate a citizen in college for that same year. At an average cost of

$31,286 per year to incarcerate a single person, when multiplied by ap-
proximately 2.2 million prisoners nationally, one arrives at the figure of
nearly $70 billion per year for incarceration in the United States. None of
these estimates of course address the costs of supervision, probation, and
parole, where, ironically, previously incarcerated people find that their
once exploitable labor is no longer exploitable. But that's another story.

Hence, there has to be another method to pay for, whether in the
public or private facility, the built environment of the prison. Even the
most basic economic analysis would conclude that the prison loses money when there are empty cells. Thus, just as college campuses must enroll
enough students to fill the dorms, prisons rely on being at "full capacity."
As some others, including Marc Mauer, executive director of the Sentencing Project, and we have suggested, part of the explanation for the
rise in incarceration rates is the fact that building and expanding prisons
means that we must continue to fill them. We must impose harsher and
longer sentences; we must arrest more and more people vis-à-vis dragnet
or stop-and-frisk policies. In short, we must continue to find new and
creative ways to funnel inmates into prisons. And we argue here that this
funnel is not being filled with white-collar offenders such as Bernie Madoff (ponzi scam artist), Ken Lay (Enron CEO), or Martha Stewart, but
rather by vulnerable, unempowered populations, primarily young, poor,
Black men. Policing Black bodies.

When we consider the overall cost of incarceration and supervision
and the costs of police practices like stop and frisk, this war on Black
bodies that Nixon initiated in 1972 is extremely expensive to our society,
the costs being borne almost exclusively by us, the average taxpayer. One
question we have to ask in the cost-benefit analysis is whether the price is
worth it. Are we getting what we are paying for? Part of the answer lies in
our interrogation of the prison-industrial complex: the labor that is extracted from these otherwise unexploitable Black bodies, as we shall see,
generates profits for both public and private corporations, but none of it,
of course, is returned to the citizens whose taxes pay for incarceration.
The prison-industrial complex is the latest version of the plantation economy. White men make profits on the bodies and labor of Black men.

> As early as the early 1990s, then President George H. W. Bush worried
> about paying for the outcome of the War on Drugs, the cost of mass
> incarceration.

[President] Bush looked toward innovative new ways to expand the nation's carceral institutions while cutting the cost of imprisonment. Worried about the severe problem of prison overcrowding, Bush endorsed lease-purchase agreements, whereby private firms built correctional facilities and leased them back to the federal government in the long term. "This approach would enable us to bring new institutions into operation much more quickly and would allow the government involved to spread out its acquisition costs over 20 or 30 years," Bush wrote hopefully in a memorandum. To house new offenders entering correctional institutions without further straining state resources, the Anti-Drug Abuse Act proposed using civil property seized in forfeitures to fund prison construction.[4]

And thus the movement to privatize prisons was born, a collaboration among federal and state governments and private corporations, using forfeiture funds, including those seized during drug raids, to expand the carceral state. As we noted in our discussion of mass incarceration, even if a person is *never convicted* of the crime for which he or she was arrested, the forfeitures seized are not returned; instead they belong to the law enforcement agency that collected them.

CoreCivic, formerly Corrections Corporation of America, which builds and staffs private prisons, built its first prison in 1984 in Texas. According to their financial disclosures, CoreCivic currently operates 88,500 beds (incarcerating approximately 75,000 inmates) in sixty-six facilities—from California to Oklahoma to Montana to the District of Columbia—and has plans to build more. CoreCivic also manages eleven correctional facilities that are owned by state or federal governments. In their annual disclosure, CoreCivic reported a *daily profit* of approximately $24 per bed filled, or *$1.8 million per day in profit, $221 million in profit for calendar year 2015*—all for incarcerating bodies, primarily Black bodies. In addition, CoreCivic and other private prison companies have written "occupancy guarantees" into their contracts, *requiring* states to pay a fee if they cannot provide a certain number of inmates.

This private corporation, founded in 1983, employs approximately fifteen thousand personnel and trades on the New York Stock Exchange (CXW); as of June 6, 2017, CXW stock traded at $29.26 per share. You may have CXW in your mutual fund portfolio.

PROFITING OFF PRISON LABOR: EXPLOITING THE UNEXPLOITABLE

Whereas many prison farms, like Parchman and Angola, are self-sustaining—the inmates grow all their own food and produce all of the textiles, including uniforms and cell mattresses, that are needed within the prison—a new phenomenon is the entrance of prisons into the global economy. Prisons that were once producing goods only for their own consumption are now producing goods for state agencies as well as multinational corporations. In some cases the inmates are paid a pittance and are then charged by the prison for the costs of their incarceration. In other cases, the prisoners are not paid a wage; instead a portion of their "wages" is paid directly to the prison, ostensibly to offset the cost of incarcerating them. Regardless of how the wage is paid, we are unable to find a case in which inmate labor is compensated at fair market value; rather, inmates receive a sub–minimum wage—typically less than $1 per hour[5]—and as a result state agencies and corporations make money and the prisons cut costs by exploiting the labor of bodies, primarily Black bodies.

Another way to think about this is to use the analogy that Michelle Alexander employs in her book *The New Jim Crow*. If mass incarceration functions as the new Jim Crow, a mechanism to segregate and cordon off Black bodies far away from mainstream society, then the prison-industrial complex functions as a new form of sharecropping whereby the labor of Black bodies is extracted at far below its value and the profits accrue to white-owned institutions, much as they continue to accrue to plantation owners even into the twenty-first century.

Let us be clear. We have absolutely no problem with inmates working. We would imagine that it provides them with something meaningful to do, a welcome distraction from the endless days, weeks, months, and years of isolation from mainstream culture. In many prisons, a job offers an inmate an opportunity to get out of the cage for a few hours a day; on prison farms, inmates get a chance to be outside eight hours a day, even though it may be hot and humid, as it often is in the Mississippi Delta. At least they are outside. In some cases the work that inmates do helps them to build skills that they can take with them after they are released—which might range from assembly work to leather and sewing work to high-tech factory work—which, in theory at least, would qualify them for a job, that is, as long as they don't have to "check the box." As we argued extensively in our interrogation of mass incarceration, many incarcerated people enter prison with fines and fees as well as other debts, such as child support, that continue to accrue during their period of incarceration, and we wholeheartedly support the opportunity that work provides an inmate to earn a wage that can be applied toward that debt, including contributing back, directly in some cases, to the cost of their incarceration. That said, the meager wages that inmates are paid would require them to work for long hours every week, for years, in order to pay off the debts they owe. An inmate with a debt of $1,500 who is paid fifty cents an hour would have to work forty hours a week for seventy-five weeks (nearly a year and a half) in order to pay the debt. We recently corresponded with a man incarcerated in the New York state prison system, the same person we were trying to send the book from Amazon, who told us that he earns thirty-two cents an hour sewing sweatshirts. Because the water in the prison is too dirty to drink, all of the inmates purchase bottled water. At ninety cents a bottle. It takes this man three hours of work to earn enough to buy a bottle of water. That's the equivalent of someone making minimum wage (approximately $8 an hour) paying $25 for a bottle of water. When put this way, this experience is nothing short of absurd! Policing Black bodies, be they in Flint, Michigan, or Attica.

Of grave concern is the role of the prison-industrial complex in the hyperexploitation of Black bodies for the sheer purpose of generating profit for state agencies and multinational corporations. It is especially problematic when the inmate doing the work is paid such a pittance that they are not able to make any dent in their debts. An inmate may labor for years, generating profit for state agencies or corporations, while the debt associated with their incarceration decreases minimally, ultimately delaying their release or following them back into the "free world." Coincidence? We don't think so.

So, perhaps you are saying to yourself, OK, but McDonald's and Starbucks employ millions of people around the globe. How much does the exploitation of prison labor contribute to their corporate coffers? How big a problem is this anyway? On the one hand, we believe that the hyperexploitation of one human body is too much. On the other hand, this is a reasonable question, and though there are no estimates on the percentage of profits that are derived from the hyperexploitation of Black, incarcerated bodies, what we do know is that most of us touch *dozens of products every single day* that are produced by prison labor. And if you are working or living on a public university campus, just like the one where we work, you are likely sitting in a chair, typing at a desk, and sleeping in a bed that was produced by incarcerated bodies. The cleaning supplies used to keep the bathroom on your hall clean were manufactured in a prison. And even if you believe that the person responsible for purchasing your chair and desk, your filing cabinet, and the bed in your dorm room is of high moral conscience and would never be in the business of exploiting someone's labor, what you need to know is that they probably did not purchase these items knowingly, and most likely they did not have a choice.

In the Commonwealth of Virginia, all public institutions, including the campus where we are employed, must purchase all furniture and cleaning supplies from a company called Virginia Correctional Enterprises. As we can attest from our personal experience, all new employees who will be making purchases for their units must attend a series of purchasing trainings, detailing how to use the purchase card, what *cannot* be purchased using state funds (strippers, Kleenex), and so forth. An entire training is dedicated to teaching new employees the "ropes" when it comes to purchasing things like office supplies, pizza, and furniture, all of which must be done using online procurement systems that are owned and operated by the commonwealth. When we run low on paper for the copy machine or ink for the printer, we cannot simply run over to Staples or Office Depot and buy supplies over the counter. All of these types of purchases must be made from preapproved vendors via the online procurement system. In Virginia this system is called eVA. Part of the purchasing training includes directions for purchasing furniture from "VCE." Unless an employee reads the fine print or, as luck would have it, someone like us who knows something about prison industries is being trained, it is unlikely that anyone sitting in the training would notice or realize that "VCE" stands for Virginia Correctional Enterprises. The furniture and cleaning supplies being purchased through the required procurement system were produced by inmates as part of the prison-industrial complex. The shiny online catalog looks so similar to what you would find on any mainstream website that the actual source is difficult to detect.

We wrote the first draft of this chapter while sitting in chairs and working at a table in one of the libraries on the campus where we are employed. Surrounding us is a set of really nice-looking lounge chairs in which students are studying, relaxing, or taking a nap. Comparing the lounge chairs to the Virginia Correctional Enterprises online catalog, we have determined that these are the "Old Dominion" lounge chairs that retail to our university for $600 per chair. According to investigative research, inmates who work for Virginia Correctional Enterprises in the furniture factory earn *fifty-five to eighty cents per hour*. In contrast, according to the Bureau of Labor Statistics, the figures for June 2016 reveal that the average American worker engaged in the production and manufacture of furniture earned $20.36 per hour, or a wage more than twenty times greater than made by those "employed" by Virginia Correctional Enterprises. Perhaps this wouldn't be so troubling if our units could buy the chair for one-twentieth of the price given that the laborer earned only one-twentieth of the wage! This is, however, not the case. In fact, one state agency, Virginia Correctional Enterprises, is allowed to generate significatn profits by hyperexploiting the labor of incarcerated laborers and not selling the commodity at a reduced cost, even to other state agencies! It is estimated that in 2013 Virginia Correctional Enterprises earned nearly $55 million in profit.[6] Its seems clear to us that taxpayers are being gouged twice, first for the cost of incarcerating millions of people who are not paid enough for their labor to cover the costs of their own incarceration, and second by charging above fair market prices for commodities that state agencies are forced to purchase with their state funding from another state agency that keeps the profits. You can buy a similar chair at IKEA, which happens to be less than twenty miles from our campus, for significantly less, perhaps $300, or even order the same chair, shipped for free, at Wayfair.com and have it delivered right to our office. As a taxpayer, how would you want us to spend state funds?

This frustration is not limited to state agencies. In many states, local, small, and even large businesses also argue that they are harmed by prison industries that compete with them in the local market, all while paying significantly reduced labor costs. For example, Kurt Wilson,[7] CEO of American Apparel, a company familiar to most people, complained to Congress as recently as 2013 that his company, which in addition to making inexpensive T-shirts, pants, and shorts manufactures military uniforms, is unable to sell its merchandise to the U.S. military as a direct result of the extensive and well-funded lobbying efforts of UNICOR. Because of a government contract, awarded to UNICOR *without soliciting other bids*, the U.S. military is required to purchase all its military uniforms from UNICOR. Kurt Wilson argued that his company is being unfairly denied the opportunity to compete for a huge government contract that he believes his company can fulfill. To make matters worse, Wilson notes that UNICOR pays its "employees," inmates in federal prisons, between 23 cents and $1.15 an hour, whereas American Apparel must pay its employees at least minimum wage, or approximately $7.50 an hour at the time of his complaint to Congress. Additionally, it's not rocket science to conclude that American Apparel, were they to be awarded a government contract for military uniforms, would make significantly less profit because they are required to pay a minimum wage that UNICOR is not required to pay. The "Made in America" label takes on a whole new meaning when we consider practices like those of UNICOR. American Apparel must compete not only with textiles made in Singapore, but with those made by inmates in the United States.

The hyperexploitation of the labor of incarcerated people is by no means limited to the types of prison industries that we have exposed so far. In fact, it seems that when it comes to harnessing labor at very low cost, there is almost no limit to the ingenuity of the person or business or department of corrections in identifying and creating more and more ways to extract labor from inmates at a fraction of the cost that is required by minimum wage laws.

For example, the practice of partnering with the state and local Department of Transportation (DOT) has been popular for many years. As you drive along interstate highway systems, you may see inmates digging ditches, picking up trash, mowing, and doing other sorts of highway labor. As with "factory labor," this form of inmate labor is expanding. Inmates now use heavy construction equipment, such as jackhammers, in various projects, including the construction of tunnels in Pennsylvania. (These same inmates managed to smuggle the jackhammers "home" and used them to tunnel out of their home, the Western Pennsylvania Penitentiary in Pittsburgh!)

And yes, inmates still do make license plates.

This form of inmate labor has been popular for decades. Because the work is often backbreaking, it is difficult to find laborers willing to do the work, and if unionized, this labor would be very expensive. It is also reminiscent of, and most likely inspired by, the chain gangs popular in the nineteenth and twentieth centuries, especially in the South. Many municipalities, counties, and states post significant savings to taxpayers by relying on inmate labor for these sorts of projects. This use of prison labor is not, however, without controversy.

In communities that have recently suffered significant declines in manufacturing jobs, local residents are becoming more vocal in their critique of these practices. In a rural Iowa community, for example, critics of this practice note that inmates have "taken" the jobs of countless citizens. In a community that has seen a decline in agricultural manufacturing, specifically meatpacking, this loss of jobs is serious, and local citizens, many of whom are now unemployed or underemployed, resent the fact that jobs they could take are now being filled by prison inmates.

> In the case of the State liquor warehouse, 12 workers just lost good-paying jobs to prisoners who are paid *37 cents an hour*. Currently, 500 state government jobs and 190 private sector positions are being filled by prisoners.[8]

The data are relatively clear that in most communities that vote to have a prison located and built there, the majority of the well-paying jobs, especially jobs as corrections officers or guards, do not in fact accrue to local folks. Though prisons *may* bring some jobs into a community, especially jobs as corrections officers, this gain is offset by the fact that the inmates may themselves be competing with local citizens for jobs both in the free market and in the prison itself, doing maintenance, mowing, and a variety of facilities work.

For much of the last century, prisons were engaged in industries that provided goods for local markets. Prison farms like Parchman in the Mississippi Delta and Angola in Louisiana have for decades targeted a portion of their prison-grown agricultural produce, mostly vegetables and more recently goods like catfish and cotton, to local merchants for sale and consumption in local communities.

After loosening the laws that prohibited direct competition between prisons and free enterprise, prison enterprises have expanded to include goods that are produced in factory settings. At the Eastern Oregon Correctional Institution, a medium-security state prison located in Pendleton, Oregon, that incarcerates about 1,500 people, inmates are engaged in textile factory work making the denim uniforms for all the inmates in the entire Oregon state prison system, a practice that is seen in nearly every state in the union. What is unique about the work clothes produced at the Eastern Oregon Correctional Institution is their popularity. Under the tagline "Clothing Made on the Inside to be Worn on the Outside," clothes and hats sewn in the Prison Blues Garment Factory, appropriately named "Prison Blues," are marketed for purchase over the Internet![9]

At first glance this form of inmate labor seems nothing but positive. As extolled on the Prison Blues website, inmates learn a marketable trade that they can take with them when they reenter the "free world." Also, they keep busy during the day, and they earn some money, which is used to pay for their expenses in prison as well as toward their financial obligations that they have with the state, including child support.

However, industries like this, be they agricultural or manufacturing or service, by definition, as with public works, take job opportunities away from local citizens. For example, the economy is quite depressed in the agricultural regions of the Mississippi Delta, and in the case of catfish farming in Mississippi, local free-world farmers face competition not only from imported product from Vietnam but locally as well. That the Mississippi Department of Corrections has a strong hold in the farm-raised catfish market means that local farmers have less of an opportunity to make a living with this agricultural commodity.[10] In competitive markets, as opposed to restricted markets like the state procurement system in Virginia, where companies compete to sell their products, by paying wages that are significantly below market value, products produced by inmates can be sold at lower prices and for a higher profit margin, often running "free world" business that pay even a minimum wage, forget about a living wage, out of the market. Thus, the exploitation of inmate labor can contribute to unemployment and lower wages in local communities.

Perhaps the most recent change in incarcerated labor, and the one that seems to be the most controversial and disturbing, is the use of inmate labor for a variety of service sector work that is subcontracted through "middleman companies" for some of the nation's leading manufacturers, including IBM, Boeing, Motorola, Microsoft, AT&T, Texas Instruments, Dell, Compaq, Honeywell, Hewlett-Packard, Nortel, Lucent Technologies, Intel, TWA, Nordstrom's, Revlon, Macy's, Pierre Cardin, Target Stores, Victoria's Secret, Toys"R"Us, Starbucks, and the Parke-Davis and Upjohn pharmaceutical companies, which have all engaged with prisons in order to exploit inmate labor in order to produce commodities or in some cases to staff call centers.[11] Eat a burger at McDonald's or Wendy's lately, and it is highly likely that the uniform worn by the fast-food worker was sewn in a prison. Work on a computer lately, and it's quite possible that the circuit board was manufactured in a prison. Even the Victoria's Secret panties you gave or received as a Valentine's or anniversary gift may have been sewn by inmates.

The next time you call customer service, you may be speaking with an inmate who is staffing a call center located directly inside the prison walls. "When New York residents call the Department of Motor Vehicles, for example, they might get an inmate at Greene Correctional Institution in Coxsackie, near Albany, or at Bedford Hills Correctional Facility for Women near White Plains, on the border with Connecticut."[12]

One can easily come to the conclusion that this is a positive movement in the evolution of the carceral state because prison industries, both public and private, provide work, offer opportunities to learn job skills that are transferrable, and allow inmates to earn some money while they are on the inside, otherwise locked in a cage. However, critics, including many inmates at the Twin Rivers Corrections Unit, are skeptical of the underlying reasons for this evolution in prison industries. They do not necessarily believe it is indicative of a *rehabilitative movement* in prisons but rather is driven entirely by companies seeking another way to maximize their profits.

> Others suspect that DOC's motives are more pecuniary than pure-hearted, noting that by shaving nearly 50 percent off the top of an inmate's paycheck, the department slashes its own expenses while subsidizing the companies in the program, which aren't required to pay for inmates' health insurance or retirement. "They figure that if somebody's sitting around, doing their time and doing nothing, they don't make any money off them," Strauss says. . . . Richard Stephens, a Bellevue property-rights attorney, is suing DOC on the grounds that the program is unconstitutional, allows businesses that use prison labor to undercut their competitors' prices, and unfairly subsidizes some private businesses at the expense of others. . . . *Private businesses are "paying prison workers less than they're paying on the outside, but they aren't reducing the markup to the consumer" they're pocketing the profits.* Another key difference, Wright notes, is that prisoners can just be sent back to their cells whenever business goes through a lull; "on the outside, they have to lay off workers. It's much more difficult," Wright says.[13]

And despite the wages they may be earning, there is no prison industries work program that allows an inmate to earn enough to pay off the fines and fees that are attached to their incarceration. Thus, if one were to believe that allowing inmates to work is a means to working off the kind of debt we described in our discussion of mass incarceration, they would be flat-out duped.

The use of inmate labor allows middle-level companies to underbid their competitors by cutting their labor costs. And prisons benefit as well because by engaging their inmates in this sort of economic production and then charging inmates for their own incarceration, they are able to keep the costs of running the prison down. Paul Wright, an inmate at Twin Rivers, sums it up:

> "They need to know that they are buying these products from a company that is basically getting rich off prisoners." Wright, sent to Twin Rivers for first-degree murder in 1987, *believes parents would be disturbed to know that their child's GameCube was packaged by a murderer, rapist, or pedophile.* These companies spend a lot of money on their public image," Wright says, "but then they're quick to make money any way they can."[14]

IS IT LEGAL TO EXPLOIT INMATE LABOR?

Yes, in fact it is legal to pay inmates less than minimum wage, to exploit their labor. In fact, it is perfectly legal to require incarcerated individuals to work for free, which is often the case on prison farms like Parchman where the inmates hoeing okra or tending hogs may get a chance to consume some of the fruits of their labor in the mess hall, but they will not be paid a wage, no matter how small, for their work.

Men incarcerated at Parchman were required to build the table on which lethal injections are performed. Imagine building the contraption that would eventually kill you.

How is this possible? Inmates laboring for slave wages can thank an obscure clause in the Thirteenth Amendment to the United States Constitution. According to the documents housed at the Library of Congress and available online, the Thirteenth Amendment to the Constitution declared that

> Neither slavery nor involuntary servitude, *except as a punishment for crime whereof the party shall have been duly convicted,* shall exist within the United States, or any place subject to their jurisdiction.

Formally abolishing slavery in the United States, the Thirteenth Amendment was passed by Congress on January 31, 1865, and ratified by the states on December 6, 1865. Emphasis ours.

According to legal scholar Kamal Ghali,[15] "The punishment clause appears to be aimed at an important concern. The drafters sought to free the slaves, but took pains to ensure that they did not inadvertently curtail the power of state governments to punish criminals." And to this we add that the drafters left the door wide open for prisons to *legally enslave incarcerated bodies.*

Black Codes were enacted to allow prison farms like Parchman and Angola to incarcerate Black bodies to do the intensive agricultural labor that previously enslaved bodies had performed. The convict leasing system allowed prisons to contract the bodies they incarcerated out to local businesses in exchange for a fee. Mass incarceration puts 2.5 million people in prison; all of their bodies are legally available to be enslaved for labor, by the prisons themselves as well as by multinational corporations like McDonald's and Victoria's Secret. A magical transformation occurs: the very bodies that are deemed unexploitable outside prison walls suddenly become hyperexploitable once they are incarcerated. The same young Black man who can't get a job in the local McDonald's finds himself in a prison factory sewing uniforms for the very McDonald's worker he will never become. Policing Black bodies.

The more prisons that are built for profit rather than rehabilitation, the more people who must be incarcerated. Prisons only make money when the cells are occupied. Policing Black bodies.

As Angela Davis so aptly put it, once prisons got into the business of incarceration in a capitalist economy, there was no other option but to grow: "Corporations that appear to be far removed from the business of punishment are intimately involved in the expansion of the prison industrial complex."[16]

The more prisons provide labor for corporations, the more prisons will be built. Don't believe us? Read the financial disclosure forms of Core-Civic in which they brag about the almost limitless opportunities for expansion. In his exposé after a four-month stint working as a correction-

6

POLICING BLACK WOMEN'S BODIES

You are in the last days of your pregnancy and you realize that you are going into labor. Soon you will be bringing a new life into the world. Now imagine your wrists are bound by handcuffs that attach to a chain wrapped around your waist and leg irons that are chained together, limiting your ability to walk. This is a practice known as shackling.

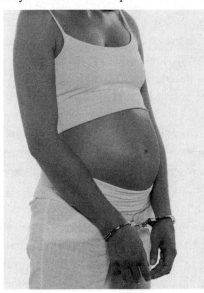

Across the United States, prison policy dictates that people be shackled whenever they are transported outside the prison. Many states make no exceptions for women in labor, childbirth or postpartum recovery. And, even in states like New York that have banned the shack-

the school-to-prison pipeline is largely replaced by the sexual-abuse-to-prison pipeline. Though women and men are both incarcerated for drugs and financial crimes, digging more deeply we see that even these pathways to prison are different. An overwhelming number of women are incarcerated for drug use, not drug dealing. Similarly, when women are incarcerated for "financial" crimes they are usually crimes like passing bad checks, not manipulating financial instruments like Bernie Madoff did. Women do commit murder, but the majority of women incarcerated for homicide murdered their abusive partners, often after having endured decades of abuse and a dozen failed attempts to leave. And the vast majority of women who are incarcerated have children under the age of eighteen with whom they were living and for whom they were providing the majority of support immediately prior to their incarceration.

Women's bodies are *sexual bodies*, which means that they can be abused but also that their sexuality, and reproductive capabilities in particular, can be policed, and this is particularly true for Black women's bodies.

SO, HOW MANY WOMEN ARE IN PRISON?

Though women make up only 10 percent of the incarcerated population in the United States, they are the fastest-growing demographic group that is entering prison. Since 1980 the number of women in prison has risen by 700 percent. At the start of the twenty-first century, the incarceration rate for white men has grown by 4 percent, and for Black men it has increased by 21 percent; but for women, both white and Black, the incarceration rate has grown at a rate of 50 percent.

In 2015, more than 1.25 million women in the United States were under the control of the criminal justice system; the majority, just over one million, are on probation or parole, while slightly more than two hundred thousand are incarcerated in jail (109,100) and prison (106,232), which amounts to half of the incarcerated population in the European Union, an entity with a population of twice as many people! The United States leads the world in every category of incarceration, including women. And, as with everything we deal with in this book, race matters; Black women's bodies are incarcerated or otherwise under the control of the criminal justice system at twice the rate of white women.

WHY ARE MORE WOMEN GOING TO PRISON?

As is the case for men, a major contributor to the incarceration of women has been the often uneven application of drug laws; from 1984 to the present, the percentage of women incarcerated for drugs doubled from 12 to 24 percent. Compared to men, more than half of whom are incarcerated for a violent crime, more than half of women are incarcerated for either drugs (24 percent) or property crimes (28 percent).

Though people commit all kinds of crimes for all kinds of reasons, the majority of women who are incarcerated have a personal history that is inextricably linked to their criminal behavior. The vast majority of girls and women who are incarcerated have been victims of sexual and/or intimate partner violence. More than three-quarters of incarcerated women reported that they were victims of intimate partner violence prior to their incarceration. In other research we've conducted, we've documented a high correlation between incarceration and intimate partner violence for women. In some cases, women are incarcerated for murdering their abusive partners. In others, their illegal behavior is related to the abuse, for example, using drugs or alcohol or committing property crimes like check fraud. In other words, the majority of women who are incarcerated for drug possession offenses are, among other things, self-medicating to relieve the pain associated with sexual and intimate partner violence. Many of those incarcerated for property crimes are, among other things, engaged in criminal behavior in order to amass the resources necessary to leave abusive relationships, be it incest or intimate partner violence.

Not surprisingly, women come to prison with mental health issues, which are likely exacerbated by the policing they experience while incarcerated. Based on a survey of one hundred thousand incarcerated people, the Bureau of Justice Statistics found that nearly two-thirds of women in prison have suffered from mental health ailments, nearly double the percentage of their male counterparts. When women exhibit mental health symptoms in prison, they rarely receive the services they need. Citing a 2015 study on the mental health services in New York City's jail, Cohen pointed out that at Rikers, "older white men were directed towards mental health services, while younger black and Hispanic men and women were directed to solitary confinement, and self harm. I don't think that fact reflects different rates of mental illness, I think it demonstrates racial bias."[1]

THE SEXUAL-ABUSE-TO-PRISON PIPELINE

The relationship between abuse and being pulled into the criminal justice system is strong for boys, but it's dramatically more powerful for girls.

A 2015 study conducted collaboratively by the Human Rights Project for Girls, the Georgetown University Law Center on Poverty and Inequality, and the Ms. Foundation for Women identifies a "sexual-abuse-to-prison pipeline for girls." Though the data vary from state to state, between 80 and 95 percent of girls in juvenile detention were sexually assaulted or raped before they arrived there, and more than half had experienced physical abuse or dating violence as well. Much like adult women who self-medicate with drugs or pass bad checks in order to generate the resources necessary to leave an abusive relationship—putting down a security deposit on an apartment, perhaps purchasing transportation—girls who are victims of incest and partner violence engage in similar strategies. The primary difference for girls is that they are subjected to even more surveillance. For example, if they are self-medicating with alcohol they can be arrested for underage drinking, and they can be arrested for status offenses like truancy and vagrancy or for hanging out in a park or on the streets when they are supposed to be at school. It is not uncommon at all for girls who are experiencing incest by their fathers or mothers' boyfriends to run away simply to get away from the abuse.

As part of our research on intimate partner violence, we interviewed women who were escaping violent relationships, and among them were several who had been victims of incest and two who had been forced into child prostitution. Most if not all of them engaged in these same strategies for self-medicating the pain and seeking escape from the violence.

Evie is one of the women we interviewed.[2] The particulars of her life may be unique, but the general patterns of a lifetime of abuse are quite typical for low-income Black women. Evie grew up in a liquor house where her father prostituted her. Liquor houses are a sort of unregulated social club. Usually they are apartments in public housing projects. In a typical liquor house, a man allows a woman, and often her children, to live rent free upstairs in exchange for her, and her children, running the liquor house on the main level of the home. And, not surprisingly, this arrangement usually involves an exchange for sex with the woman whenever he desires it.

Typically, liquor houses are open nearly twenty-four hours a day. Evie and other women we interviewed told us that they were horrible places to grow up because customers, mostly men, come in at all times of the day and night to get a drink and a plate of food, play cards, and buy cigars or cigarettes. A typical liquor house not only stocks liquor, wine, and beer but often also serves cold sandwiches during the afternoon and fish, pork chops, and french fries in the evening. Evie talked almost with pride about how she could make the sandwiches and even pour a shot of whiskey by the time she was ten. But her face turned dark and tears filled her eyes as she talked about the men she encountered there and what they made her do—employing the euphemism that she had to "sit on their laps."

When we inquired about the men who frequented the liquor houses, Evie, who was in her fifties when we interviewed her, told us that of course there were the locals, men who lived in the projects, but the primary customers were white male executives from R. J. Reynolds Tobacco Company who lived in the more affluent parts of town. These men would come during their lunch hour and at happy hour, usually after four in the afternoon, to consume alcohol and cigarettes and have sex before returning to their quiet, white middle-class neighborhoods.

> Some of the Reynolds men got paid on Wednesday. They'll come in, maybe, and buy . . . give me a five, and maybe they done bought four drinks and I would have the change. Sometimes they would sell fish in there. And a lot of times, some of the guys would get the cigarettes and change cigarettes for drinks. And it was just like, I wonder that the people that lived out by a car [in the suburbs]. There was nice section. But they would come in our neighborhood and drink and buy women and stuff like that.

Evie was initially lured into this work and ultimately into a childhood of forced prostitution by her father, who told her she could earn a little money making sandwiches and pouring drinks. Evie recalls that by age twelve she was frying fish and managing the food side of the operation. In addition, she admitted that her father required her to work regularly as a child prostitute; in her words, she was required to "perform favors" for the men in the liquor house.

> You can't imagine what it's like to have to sit on the laps of men when you are a ten-year-old. I hadn't even learned to ride a bike yet.

Tragically, we found that though child sexual abuse and incest were quite common among adult women who later found themselves living in violent intimate partner relationships, each of the twenty-five Black women we interviewed had been sexually abused as children—every single one of them. Black girls' sexual bodies are policed by the adult men in their lives—most often fathers and stepfathers—and then, when they self-medicated or ran away, their bodies were policed by the criminal justice system.

> And in a perverse twist of justice, many girls who experience sexual abuse are routed into the juvenile justice system *because of* their victimization. Indeed, sexual abuse is one of the primary predictors of girls' entry into the juvenile justice system. A particularly glaring example is when girls who are victims of sex trafficking are arrested on prostitution charges—punished as perpetrators rather than served and supported as victims and survivors. Once inside, girls encounter a system that is often ill-equipped to identify and treat the violence and trauma that lie at the root of victimized girls' arrests. More harmful still is the significant risk that the punitive environment will re-trigger girls' trauma and even subject them to new incidents of sexual victimization, which can exponentially compound the profound harms inflicted by the original abuse.
>
> This is the girls' sexual abuse to prison pipeline.[3]

So, how come so many Black girls and women are in prison or on parole or probation? Because they are sexually abused as children and rendered invisible and ignored by the very services that we should be marshaling to help them, because girls and women make difficult choices to save their lives that often result in them being ensnared in a criminal justice system that continues to abuse them. Policing Black girls' and women's bodies.

CRIMINALIZATION OF PREGNANCY

Girls and women have been subjected to the sexual policing of their bodies since the beginning of time, and there is no evidence, in the United States or globally, that this will end anytime soon. Consistently, across the twenty-five or thirty years in which statistical data have been collected on crimes of sexual and intimate partner violence, about half of all women living in the United States have been or will be a victim of some sort of sexual or intimate partner violence in her lifetime. And, not surprisingly, the rates are higher for Black women, as our own interviews confirmed.

One of the more recent strategies for policing Black women's bodies is what we term the criminalization of pregnancy. The criminalization of pregnancy is a movement in state legislatures and the criminal justice system more widely whereby women who engage in behaviors that "harm" the fetus they are carrying are increasingly being charged with crimes. The most common scenario involves women who use drugs or abuse alcohol while they are pregnant and who are charged with child endangerment or, worse yet, if the fetus is born dead, with fetal homicide.

In her influential 1997 book, *Killing the Black Body*, Dorothy Roberts devotes an entire chapter to interrogating the criminalization of pregnancy in which she details not only the cases but, more important, the laws that are used to prosecute and ultimately to imprison women for their behavior while pregnant. According to Roberts, the first cases of prosecuting women for endangering their babies through their behavior while pregnant took place in the early 1990s. At that time the primary focus of the prosecutions was on poor Black women who gave birth to crack babies. Roberts argues persuasively that this movement began as an attempt to deal with what many in the public perceived as an "explosion of crack babies." Dorothy Roberts recounts the case of twenty-eight-year-old Cornelia Whitner who in February 1992 gave birth to a healthy baby. Upon conducting a urine test on the baby, traces of crack were discovered. The baby was healthy, and in her court hearing Whitner begged to be sentenced to a residential treatment program in order to address her addiction and become a good parent. The judge responded, "I think I'll just let her to go to jail." He sentenced her to a startling eight-year sentence.[4]

These laws, called "fetal harm laws," are controversial but also compelling for those who believe that criminalizing women's behavior is a solution to drug problems. Instead, what Roberts and others note is that these laws end up forcing women to make difficult choices about their reproductive lives. Women can choose to continue with their pregnancies and risk going to prison—often for very long sentences—or they can "choose" to have an abortion, which will limit their prosecution to drug possession, allowing them to escape the more rigorous charge of child endangerment. We wonder what kind of a choice this is.

Additionally, the criminalization of pregnancy, because of its focus on drug laws, was justified as part of the larger War on Drugs, a justification that allowed for the otherwise repulsive policing of pregnant bodies. As Dorothy Roberts explains, the "crack epidemic" was critical to the ushering in of an era of criminalizing behaviors during pregnancy. We agree that crack is a highly problematic drug: it is highly addictive, because it is smoked it produces an instantaneous high, and because it is cheap it was confined primarily to inner-city Black communities that were already highly policed and resource poor. Dorothy Roberts argues persuasively that crack became an easy target for the War on Drugs, and low-income Black women became the "poster child" providing a powerful and visual rationale for this war. And chief among their major offenses was delivering babies addicted to crack. "Crack babies" quickly became of primary concern to policy makers, not necessarily because they were addicted to crack per se, but because of the *perceived, but not necessarily substantiated, claim of the burden they would place on society*, a burden that could have been avoided had the mothers simply behaved responsibly, at least according to the instigators of the War on Drugs, including Presidents Nixon and Reagan. Dorothy Roberts explains,

> Always pictured trembling and shrieking in an overcrowded hospital ward, the crack baby suffered from multiple ailments that often killed him. But these images that induced pity for the helpless victim were eclipsed by predictions of the tremendous burden that crack babies were destined to impose on law-abiding taxpayers. Permanently damaged and abandoned *by their mothers*, they would require costly hospital care, inundate the foster care system, overwhelm the public schools with special needs, and ultimately prey on the rest of society as criminals and welfare dependents. It was estimated that Americans were already spending an additional $200 million a year "to keep up with

the crack onslaught" leading to the startling prediction that crack babies "will cost this nation in remedial medical and developmental costs
over the next decade." . . . This frightening portrait of damaged crack
babies may have caused as much harm as the mothers' crack use
itself.[5]

Thus, the solution to the crack epidemic was clear: prevent poor Black
women from becoming pregnant. And one strategy for achieving this
goal, in addition to forced contraception, a subject that Roberts takes on
in great detail in her book, was the criminalization of drug use during
pregnancy, a strategy fueled by the hope that these policies would provide
a deterrent effect. The criminalization of pregnancy and the control of
women's sexuality is nothing short of policing Black women's bodies.

As the research on deviance in general and drug use in particular
points out, *perceptions* about who uses drugs and *beliefs*—founded or
not—about the relative dangers associated with using different drugs can
shape which offenses are reported to agents of the criminal justice system, which offenders officers choose to arrest, who prosecutors choose to
prosecute, and the types of sentences judges and juries impose. You need
not look any further for confirmation of this than the case of "affluenza
teen" Ethan Couch, who killed four people while he was driving drunk
and was sentenced only to probation and no jail time, or the Stanford
swimmer Brock Turner, who was convicted of rape and sentenced to only
six months in jail. Both men, we note, are white and affluent.

One deliberate outgrowth of the War on Drugs, or as Ehrlichman
termed it the "War on Black people," was the development of a stereotype or belief that Blacks used crack, as Dorothy Roberts notes, a drug
that was defined not only as extremely dangerous but substantially more
dangerous than drugs that white people were supposedly using, including
cocaine. Belief in this stereotype led to treating pregnant mothers who
were suspected of using drugs differently depending not so much on the
actual drugs they were using but on their racial identity. For example,
studies of differential treatment of pregnant women find that regardless of
similar or equal levels of illicit drug use during pregnancy, Black women
are ten times more likely than white women to be reported to child welfare agencies for prenatal drug use.[6] This racial disparity can only be
explained by the power of hegemonic ideologies in shaping perceptions.
Simply put, when a pregnant Black woman is discovered using drugs, this
confirms our stereotype of Black women as crackheads, and therefore she

and her unborn child are referred to child welfare agencies or agents of the criminal justice system. In contrast, when a pregnant white woman is discovered using drugs, this appears to be an isolated event. It doesn't match the stereotype, and thus she is not referred to child welfare agencies or agents of the criminal justice system; rather, she is offered placement in a drug treatment program. The Black mother is believed to be deliberately endangering her children, and the white mother is simply engaging in an individual behavior that needs an intervention. The white mother is an addict; the Black mother is a potential murderer. Disparities in the treatment of Black and white mothers who are discovered using drugs during pregnancy shine a bright light on the racialized design of the criminal justice system, a system whose purpose and intent is to police Black bodies. The case of pregnant women is not so different from the kinds of cases we described in our discussion of the school-to-prison pipeline—which child is arrested and handcuffed and charged with a crime for "stealing" a carton of milk in the middle school lunch room? Black bodies are policed differently than white bodies.

The relatively steep rise over the last thirty years in the incarceration of women has created additional challenges for those charged with incarcerating the bodies of girls and women, primarily because women have distinct needs, including pregnancy, childbirth, and parenting.

MOTHERING FROM BEHIND BARS

Obviously both men and women who go to prison may be parents—men leave approximately five million children behind—yet there are significant and unique challenges that shape mothers' incarceration experiences differently than fathers'. For starters, 75 to 80 percent of incarcerated women are mothers of *minor children*; the average incarcerated woman leaves two children under the age of eighteen behind when she goes to prison. This translates into at least one million children in the United States, on any given day, whose mothers are incarcerated. To make matters even more complicated, the majority of incarcerated mothers (64 percent) *lived with their minor children* immediately prior to their incarceration as compared to fewer than half (44 percent) of incarcerated fathers.

Providing care and custody for her minor children is a main concern for most mothers who are incarcerated. The majority of children of incarcerated mothers live with a grandparent (52.9 percent), 28 percent live with their fathers, and 25.7 percent live with another relative. The remaining 20 percent are placed in foster care or with "a friend." In contrast, when fathers are incarcerated, in nearly all cases (89 percent), the children live with their mother, and fewer than 2 percent are placed in foster care. The stresses and challenges that mothers who are incarcerated face are far more complex than those faced by fathers, including challenges to child custody, which can be a major stressor not only for women but also for their children.

The overincarceration of Black bodies results in 7 percent of Black children having a parent in prison, *a rate that is nine times greater than that of white children* and more than double the rate of Hispanic children. Because of a confluence of factors, including the overincarceration of Black bodies, higher rates of poverty in the Black community, and the under- and unemployment of Black people, Black children are more likely to be placed in foster care than either white or Hispanic children, who are more likely to remain living with a relative during the term of their mother's confinement. Black children are more likely than children of other racial and ethnic identities whose mothers are incarcerated to languish in foster care, which puts them at significantly greater risk for sexual and physical abuse, neglect, and ultimately being ensnared in the criminal justice system themselves. This is nothing short of the *intergenerational policing of Black bodies*.

On the "up" side, incarcerated mothers report significantly more contact with their children during their periods of incarceration than fathers do. More than half (60 percent) of mothers report weekly contact with their children as compared to only 40 percent of fathers. As with nearly everything in the criminal justice system, weekly contact, though, has downsides as well, especially in-person contact.

We talked with women who had been incarcerated about their experiences when family members visit. And though they craved visits, especially with their children, many decided at the end of the day that the "price" they and their families paid for a visit wasn't worth it. In most prisons, in order to have in-person contact visits, the inmate must submit to a strip search, and the visitors are also searched more vigorously than for visits that separate the parties by Plexiglas. The women we talked to not only resented the strip searches and the fact that these searches left them even more vulnerable to sexual harassment and abuse, but many also worried that their children, especially their teenage daughters, would also be subjected to inappropriate touching in the search process. Many decided that the price for a hug simply wasn't worth the requisite policing of their bodies. And for mothers of teenage girls, this was one of the very few ways they could control or have any power over the policing of their daughters' bodies by corrections officers: by refusing contact visits.

Women not only leave minor children behind, but 6 percent enter prison while pregnant. Incarcerating pregnant bodies, managing labor and delivery, and facilitating mothering from behind bars are all challenges faced by a criminal justice system that incarcerates nearly a quarter of a million women. And at the rate of growth we are witnessing today, with women, both Black and white, being incarcerated at rates never before seen, we can only expect these challenges to require increasingly nuanced and costly solutions.

PREGNANT BEHIND BARS

Approximately twelve thousand women (6 percent) entering state prison each year are pregnant at the time of their admission to a correctional facility. The majority of these pregnant women are sentenced to longer terms than the remainder of their pregnancy, and thus the correctional institution must have a policy and set of practices for handling prenatal care, labor and delivery, and postnatal care. As with many other policies and practices inside correctional institutions, there are few federal regulations, and as a result there is wide variation in protocols and experiences across states and even within institutions under the same department of corrections. However, the majority of research, journalistic reports, and our own interviews confirm that the policies and practices are based on a "sameness" ideology that puts both mothers and their children at risk. The sameness ideology results in a set of standards that are applied equally to all incarcerated bodies, regardless of their needs as individuals or, in this case, as a class: pregnant women.

SAMENESS/DIFFERENCE DEBATE

One of the most important questions facing researchers and policy makers concerns *sameness and difference* among male and female inmates. The sameness/difference debate is a long-standing one in feminism. At the crux of the argument—a point that pits proponents of liberal feminism against those who embrace radical feminism—is the question of whether men and women have significant enough differences to be treated differently or whether men and women are just different versions of each other and thus treatment ought to be the same. Let us start with an example unrelated to incarceration. As we all know, both men and women participate in market labor; they are employed. One of the critical issues facing employees and employers is the issue of family leave and child care. Liberal feminists argue that because, until now at least, only women experience pregnancy and childbearing, accommodations should be made to insurance policies and workplace practices that allow for women who are pregnant, are nursing, or have just given birth to complete these "life tasks" without incurring penalties as employees. Thus organizations should, though of course not all do, create maternity leave policies and provide lactation spaces and a minimal level of child-care support. Because the federal government *refuses* to require a reasonable standard for accommodations by employers, the availability of these policies and accommodations varies greatly from employer to the employer. Those of us who have ever used these policies and accommodations know full well that they are nearly always woefully inadequate, unless, for example, you are lucky enough to work at Google or Netflix. The *only* federally mandated policy, the Family and Medical Leave Act or FMLA, requires only that employers provide twelve weeks of *unpaid leave* and the assurance that an employee who takes such a leave to care for a family member who is ill or to welcome a new family member via birth or adoption will be able to return to his or her job after the twelve weeks. Additionally, the FMLA is only mandated for employers with fifty or more employees; the majority of women of childbearing age work for companies with fewer than fifty employees, and thus there is no guarantee that they will be covered even by this practically useless national policy. For the record, the United States is the *only* industrialized economy, and only one of three countries on the planet, that does not have some sort of paid maternity or family leave policy. Now that's embarrassing.

Radical feminists reject the idea of modifying the workplace to accommodate female employees and instead advocate an entire transformation of workplace structures and family life such that neither is incompatible with the other and both men and women will have the opportunity to participate in both spheres as they choose. Though far from complete, the family leave policies in Scandinavian countries approximate this perspective more closely; both men and women are offered identical parental leave, and in fact maternity leave improves—both the amount of time and the percent of pay—when fathers take a leave as well. Scandinavians argue that these policies and practices create more equity at work *and* at home and that both institutions—workplaces and families—are strengthened as a result.

In terms of incarceration, policy makers clearly recognize that there are some differences between male and female inmates, the key differences being related to women's reproductive capacities. Yet these "differences" rarely result in differential protocols. Instead, inside of jails and prisons, all inmates, regardless of their gender or their gender-specific needs, are treated the same. As viewed through the lens of feminism, a minimum set of policies are developed to accommodate the specific needs of women's bodies (a liberal feminist approach) rather than changing the structure of the prison itself to address the unique challenges women's bodies present (a radical feminist approach), and as a result of insisting on treating male and female inmates the "same," some unique and troubling practices have developed.

As part of another research project we conducted that focused on citizens reentering after periods of incarceration for felony convictions, we interviewed Kezia, a thirty-something Black woman, about a year after she had been released from prison after serving a five-year sentence for possession of crack cocaine. She was pregnant with her youngest child at the time she was first incarcerated in state prison, and she finished her pregnancy and delivered her child while incarcerated. Her experience, sadly, is typical of pregnant incarcerated bodies.

Kezia grew up in the housing projects in Winston-Salem, North Carolina, and like so many poor, young Black women, when she was a young teenager she started hanging around on the corner with older guys. She became sexually involved with these older men because she was bored, because it made her feel like an adult, and because these men, who were dealing drugs, had money. By the time she was sixteen years old she was a mother, and by the time she entered prison in her mid-twenties she had four children and was pregnant with her fifth. The father of her children is a drug dealer who has been in and out of prison during all of the years Kezia has been involved with him. Essentially they live together when he is "free," she gets pregnant, and he is arrested for dealing drugs and is sent back for another stint in the penitentiary. Like so many other women living in this environment filled with drugs, dealing, and the repeated cycle of incarceration, Kezia took "the rap" for the father of her children. In an attempt to save the father of her children from the life sentence he faced under the three-strikes habitual felon law, during a raid on their apartment Kezia lied and told the officers that the drugs they found belonged to her, not to the father of her children.

When Kezia was arrested and sent to prison, she was about six months pregnant. As is the case for all women entering the North Carolina Department of Corrections, Kezia was sent to a women's prison in Raleigh, North Carolina, where the majority of women inmates in North Carolina are housed. Because she was sent to the largest women's prison in North Carolina and there were many other pregnant women there, she was housed in a unit specifically for pregnant women and women who had just delivered babies, a maternity ward of sorts behind bars. There were at least two positive consequences to this. First, it facilitated the delivery of pre- and postnatal care, and thus Kezia probably received better pre- and postnatal care than if she had been housed in the general population or in a prison or jail without such a unit. Second, when she went into labor, there were other women who could help her. She recalls that when she was in the early stages of labor, not quite sure that it had officially begun, women who had recently given birth and those who had been incarcerated in the unit longer than she had directed her to immediately notify the guards so that she could be transported to the hospital for the remainder of her labor and delivery. Had they not given her this advice, she suggested that she would have labored in her cell much longer without assistance or medical supervision.

As is standard practice in any transport of an inmate, laboring or not, Kezia was shackled for her trip to the hospital. Specifically, she was put in handcuffs that were attached to a "belly chain," and her feet were put into leg irons that were then shackled together, the "inmate shuffle" her only way to move. Thankfully she was still in the early stages of labor, when contractions are milder; nevertheless, any woman who has experienced labor would likely protest this action as one that would be not only uncomfortable but would constitute inhumane treatment that would violate human rights treaties.

After being transported to the labor and delivery unit of the local hospital, as is standard practice with all inmates receiving treatment in a "free world" hospital, once in the bed, Kezia's hands and ankles were shackled to the bedrails. One of the authors can confirm this practice based on personal experience. Hattery recalls working in a hospital during summers in college and witnessing male inmates being shackled just this way as they waited for, completed, and recovered from angiograms. The only "support" Kezia was allowed in her room during labor and delivery were the guards, stationed with pump shotguns to be sure she didn't attempt to escape. No one held her hand or helped her with breathing or even offered her a supportive smile.

The logic behind this practice of shackling is that any foray by inmates into the "free world" presents an opportunity for the inmate to escape. And many inmates who attempt escape take their chances during this type of transport. As a result, inmates are always shackled and guarded during any and all transport and during their entire stay in the "free world." You might recall seeing inmates transported this way in airports, on buses, or in hospitals or courtrooms. Inmates are even shackled if they are lucky enough to be granted permission to attend the funeral of a parent or other immediate family member.

Advocates of shackling do have cases to point to when the failure to do so resulted in a tragedy. For example, while we were writing this chapter in June 2016, Larry Gordon, an inmate in custody in Berrien County, Michigan, who was *not* handcuffed, managed to wrestle a gun away from a guard, wounding several people and killing two bailiffs before he was shot and killed. These kinds of stories contribute to the legitimate concern for public safety when inmates are transported in the "free world."

We understand the logic behind this practice, for at stake is the public safety of our society. An inmate's comfort must always be weighed against the likelihood that they pose an escape risk and the probability that if they were to escape this would threaten public safety. We wonder, though, about the practice of shackling pregnant women as they labor and deliver their babies. We are certain that any specialist in obstetrics and gynecology would argue that this practice, especially the practice of shackling through the delivery, puts both the mother and the infant at risk for medical complications. And any woman who has had a baby and perhaps any man who has witnessed it would conclude that this practice constitutes cruel and unusual punishment and violates even those few basic human rights retained by incarcerated bodies. We wonder, has the need to adhere to the principle of "sameness" been taken to an unnecessary extreme in cases like Kezia's and others like hers that occur every single day in this country? Similar to the criminalization of pregnancy, we argue that shackling during childbirth is a direct response to women's sexuality, it violates their basic human rights, and it is nothing short of policing women's bodies.

Once a mother, shackled in leg irons, delivers her infant into the world and the medical staff have certified that mother and baby are "doing well," the baby is taken to the nursery, and as soon as she is stable, often less than twenty-four hours after giving birth, the incarcerated mother is returned to the same corrections facility she left just hours before. Postnatal care, whatever that entails, is now in the hands of the prison medical staff. The baby is placed in temporary custody of the state, and the mother has but twenty-four hours to make arrangements for a designated relative to take custody of the child from the neonatal unit.

Before we interviewed Kezia, we had read the literature and journalistic accounts, and thus we were not surprised when she recounted that she barely saw her child and that her child was taken away from her almost immediately and turned over to the custody of a relative, in this case Kezia's mother. What we were not prepared for was the process that Kezia described.

Kezia talked about how she was back in the women's prison just hours after she had given birth. Thankfully for Kezia, because this was not her first birthing experience, she knew what to expect in terms of postpartum bleeding and care. But we wondered about the first-time mother who is forced to return to a prison cell with little access to supplies and perhaps less access to advice about how to ease the first few days after giving birth. Would she know about "Tucks" and the other remedies women rely on to ease the pain of an episiotomy? Would she know how much postpartum bleeding was normal and when she should be concerned? Would she be prepared for her breasts to swell and become engorged, even though she had been given medication to halt her body's natural production of breast milk?

We learned something even more troubling from Kezia as she re-counted that day. We learned that the process for arranging for care for the infant is unnecessarily burdensome and in all likelihood results in more children being taken into foster care than is necessary.

Kezia was not allowed to contact her family members about the birth of her baby until *after* she was returned to her cell deep inside the North Carolina Correctional Facility for Women. Once she was safely back in prison, Kezia was allowed a fifteen-minute phone call to arrange for her mother to pick up her baby and take temporary custody. And the clock started on the twenty-four-hour time limit for the baby to be "claimed" when the child was born, not when Kezia made the phone call to her family. Kezia recalls having barely enough time to reach her mother, give her mother the necessary information about which hospital the baby had been born at, and for her mother to drive several hours to the hospital to take custody of the baby. Kezia had forgotten to tell her mother in this most important fifteen-minute phone call that the baby was born with red hair. This would be an especially important fact because Kezia and the father of her children are both Black. So when her mother arrived at the hospital looking for Kezia's daughter, she initially dismissed the child that the hospital claimed was Kezia's because the baby had red hair. By some miracle, Kezia's mother was able to place a phone call to the cor-rections facility and get confirmation that this was in fact Kezia's baby. Had any more unexpected events arisen or any more time passed, Kezia's daughter would have been placed in the foster care system as an "aban-doned child."

Why couldn't the mother call the designated family member *before* she left the correctional facility to labor and deliver the baby, thus giving the family member more time to make arrangements? Or why couldn't the mother—or even the hospital—contact the designated relative imme-diately after the baby was born? What would happen to babies whose mothers were incarcerated half a day's drive from their extended family, as is very often the case in states like North Carolina or New York, where incarcerated women are typically housed in facilities far away in distant counties? We understand that there are public safety concerns. Maybe there is some logic behind not allowing the inmate multiple phone calls or for preventing family members from arriving at the hospital while the incarcerated mother is still there. Perhaps these are simply "safety" meas-ures designed to limit or even prevent contact between the incarcerated mother and her family. But weighing the welfare of the child and the costs—financial and otherwise—associated with foster care against the requirements for "sameness" and public safety, it is not at all clear that the policies and procedures are the most appropriate for all parties concerned. The costs of treating women as if they are the same, at least in this case, are too high and contribute significantly to the many negative consequences that children whose mothers are incarcerated experience. Policing Black bodies, even those of a newborn baby.

WHAT HAPPENS TO THE CHILDREN?

Kezia's case illustrates the special circumstance when an inmate is pregnant while incarcerated. And her case is critically important because it highlights some of the problems in policy and procedure that result from the "sameness" approach as well as some of the contributing factors to the negative consequences experienced by children whose mother is incarcerated. Yet these cases occur only 6 percent of the time. Far more common and equally problematic are the policies and procedures that are designed to address the more common situation when mothers are incarcerated and they leave their minor children behind.

As is the case with labor and delivery, there are no federal or even state laws that govern the policies and procedures that apply when mothers are arrested or sent to prison. The implementation of policies and practices are often left to the discretion of arresting officers or individual corrections institutions, and this increases the variation dramatically. Both the lack of any universally applied principles and the specific implementation of policies and practices are troubling. For example, depending on the nature of the situation and the arresting officer's disposition, when mothers are arrested, they are not always given, nor are they entitled to, any time to make arrangements for their minor children, even those who are living with them, which is the case more than 60 percent of the time. If a mother is not given any time to make arrangements, her minor children may be taken into custody alongside her—there are even some reported cases in which toddlers and elementary school children have been handcuffed and transported either to the police station or to child protective services. We can only imagine the emotional and psychological impact on a child who witnesses such an event. The impact is compounded by the fact that the child may not have any idea where they are headed, who will be designated as their caregiver, where they will sleep that night and for many nights after that, or when they will be able to see their mother again. We as a society pronounce that we are troubled by the intergenerational cycle of incarceration, yet our policies and procedures work against our expressed goal to break the cycle. The lack of a standard and humane policy for dealing with minor children whose mother is being arrested is a case in point.

Or perhaps the expressed goal is not the actual goal. As Michelle Alexander argues in *The New Jim Crow*, as Robert Ehrlichman declared, the United States is engaged in a war on Black bodies, and what is more efficient than implementing policies and procedures (or the lack thereof) that increase the likelihood of perpetuating the intergenerational cycle of incarceration? Policing Black bodies.

As noted previously, the majority of children whose mother is incarcerated are cared for by their grandmothers, but too many are also relegated to foster care. Either way, one of the primary hurdles many incarcerated mothers face is the struggle to retain legal custody of their minor children.

The relationship between incarcerated mothers and their minor children is also a critical humanitarian concern. Because fewer maximum-security prisons are available for women, they are often incarcerated far from their homes; over 60 percent of mothers in prison are incarcerated more than one hundred miles from their children, making visits financially prohibitive and often impossible. This phenomenon is exacerbated in states that are the most segregated by geography.

For example, in New York State, the majority of incarcerated women come from the boroughs of New York City, and yet more than half are incarcerated in correctional facilities that are located in the western region of the state, like Albion, a medium-security facility that houses more than 1,200 female inmates. It is located near Brockport, New York, a more than eight-hour drive by car from New York City. Imagine, as is the case for many families, that the only transportation to the prison is by bus, a ride that is likely to take twice as long. Building prisons and housing inmates so far from their families not only makes maintaining relationships difficult, but it can add to the likelihood that mothers will lose custody of their children. Legal policies that were put into place as part of the welfare reform acts of the mid-1990s, signed into law by President

Bill Clinton, included such a policy that may result in the permanent loss of custody for incarcerated mothers. As Nancy Sokoloff writes in her 2003 essay,

> Reunification laws became more punitive in 1997 under the Adoption and Safe Families Act (ASFA), which states that if a mother does not have contact with a child for six months, she can be charged with "abandonment" and lose rights to her child. Likewise, if a child has been in foster care for fifteen of the prior twenty-two months, the state may begin proceedings to terminate parental rights. However, women are often transferred from one facility to another, thus missing important deadlines and court dates that can result in termination of their parental rights. . . . The threat of losing their children is quite real. [7]

And this burden is carried disproportionately by Black women and their children. Policing Black bodies.

Though some mothers have their parental rights terminated by the state while they are incarcerated, most seek to regain or reestablish custody upon release. In order to do so, they must prove themselves fit and appropriate caregivers, including establishing a residence and a source of income, both of which are impeded by the bans on social welfare that we described in our discussion of mass incarceration. Mothers reentering the "free world," especially if they have a drug felony conviction as Kezia did, will likely find that they are banned for life from receiving any of the benefits provided by Temporary Assistance for Needy Families (TANF), including cash assistance, food stamps, access to public housing, and even student loans. As we discussed earlier, we understand the intention of the ban, which was designed ostensibly to ensure that people with drug felony convictions can't use welfare or student loans to pay for drugs, but at the end of the day, the people hurt most by these policies are the children, who through no fault of their own and with nowhere else to go find themselves in unstable housing situations and without adequate food, clothing, and other basic necessities. And, as Beth Richie notes, many find themselves without a mother as well:

> The woman will need an apartment to regain custody of her children, she will need a job to get an apartment, she will need to get treatment for her addiction to be able to work, and initial contact with her children may only be possible during business hours if they are in custody of the state. The demands multiply and compound each other, and

services are typically offered by agencies in different locations. Competing needs without any social support to meet them may seriously limit a woman's chances for success in the challenging process of reintegration.[8]

And of regaining custody of her children. Policing Black women's bodies.

Conducting the research for this book has provided us with many opportunities to ask the question why, to wonder about policies that may make sense in the halls and recesses of Congress and that may even seem appropriate to the average person. And yet, when we think about incarcerated mothers and policies like those we described here that significantly increase the possibility that these mothers will lose permanent custody of their children while they serve a two- to five-year sentence for drug possession or passing bad checks, we really have to wonder, do we hate incarcerated women so much that we would punish their children in this way? Over a missed phone call that costs $15 a minute and can often be limited to one try per week, or an in-person visit that may involve a long day of driving or an even longer trip on a bus that a child's caregiver simply cannot make? As parents, we find this deeply disturbing. And add on top of this that most of the women who are losing their parental rights wound up in prison as a direct or indirect result of sexual and intimate partner violence. Most of the women who are losing their parental rights are poor; their children are already leading a life that is stacked against them. We can't imagine the pain that these policies create and the additional, unnecessary hardship that it places on mothers and their children. Policing Black women's bodies. Policing Black children's bodies. Policing Black families. Both inside the prison and outside the prison walls.

Black women's bodies are policed, sometimes in the same way and sometimes in different ways than Black men. Black women's bodies are policed precisely because of their sexuality and reproductive capacity. Black women who are incarcerated have their bodies policed twice: first by the men who rape and physically abuse them and second by a criminal justice system that criminalizes their pregnancies and shackles their pregnant, laboring bodies. The policing of Black women's bodies, like the school-to-prison pipeline, polices future bodies by creating an intergenerational prison cycle, ensuring an almost endless supply of Black bodies to police.

7

POLICING TRANS BODIES

Ms. Diamond, 36, had lived openly and outspokenly as a transgender woman since adolescence, much of that time defying the norms in this conservative Southern city.

But on the day she arrived at a Georgia prison intake center in 2012, the deliberate *defeminizing* of Ms. Diamond began. Ordered to strip alongside male inmates, she froze but ultimately removed her long hair and the Hannah Montana pajamas in which she had been taken into custody, she said. She hugged her rounded breasts protectively.

Looking back, she said, it seemed an apt rite of initiation into what became three years of degrading and abusive treatment, starting with the state's denial of the hormones she says she had taken for 17 years.

"During intake, I kept saying: 'Hello? I'm trans? I'm a woman?'" Ms. Diamond recounted in a phone conversation from prison. . . . "But to them I was gay. I was what they called a 'sissy.' So finally I was like: 'OK, I'm a sissy. Do you have a place where sissies can go and be OK?'"

They did not provide one, she said. A first-time inmate at 33 whose major offense was burglary, Ms. Diamond was sent to a series of high-security lockups for violent male prisoners. She has been raped at least seven times by inmates, her lawsuit asserts, with a detailed accounting of each. She has been mocked by prison officials as a "he-she thing" and thrown into solitary confinement for "pretending to be a woman." She has undergone drastic physical changes without hormones. And, in desperation, she has tried to castrate and to kill herself several times.[1]

Laverne Cox, aka Sophia Burset, is the most well-known, perhaps the *only*, image we have of a transgender inmate. Laverne Cox's character, prominently featured in the Netflix hit series *Orange Is the New Black*, is also the most unrealistic example of what trans inmates face in prison. Unlike the typical trans inmate, Cox's character is housed according to her gender identity; she is allowed to dress as she chooses, within the confines of a uniform of course; and she is clearly allowed to continue on her hormone regimen. And though we applaud any representation of a positive trans figure in mainstream media, we are concerned that this (mis)representation may minimize and render invisible the reality of life in prison for incarcerated trans people. Indeed, Ashley Diamond's experience is far more typical, and it is precisely this policing of trans bodies that we unpack in this chapter.

Before we dig down into the experiences of trans inmates, we want to ensure that everyone is on the "same page" with regard to language. Gender identity refers to how individuals identify in terms of their gender. Transgender is the identity of individuals whose sex assigned at birth—"It's a boy!" or "It's a girl!"—is different from the gender they believe themselves to be. Transgender individuals may choose a variety of ways in which to achieve congruence or gender affirmation: some choose to adopt the traditional dress and mannerisms of the gender with which they identify, some have body modification procedures (for example, breast augmentation or mastectomy), and some have gender congruence surgery, including procedures to reconfigure their genitals. The term "cisgender" refers to individuals whose sex assigned at birth is congruent with their gender identity. Finally, terms like "queer," "gender queer," "gender nonconforming," and "gender fluid" refer to individuals who don't identify with either identity in the binary—male or female—but rather view their gender identity as more fluid. Individuals who identify as gender queer or gender fluid may prefer pronouns like *they*, *their*, and *them* as opposed to *he* or *she* or *him or her*.

TRANS PEOPLE AND POLICING

Trans people's bodies are policed in many different ways. In the spring of 2016, North Carolina passed legislation that was signed into law by Governor Pat McCrory that requires trans people to "use the bathroom that corresponds to the gender on their birth certificate." Though there has been public outcry at the so-called bathroom bill as well as a series of legal maneuverings—a lawsuit was filed by the Department of Justice based on the argument that the law violates the Civil Rights Act, and a mandate from the Department of Education was sent to all public schools, including universities, detailing the ways in which this law violates Title IX (gender equity)—this is but one example of the ways in which trans bodies are policed. This law, in particular, and those who support it have argued, erroneously, that trans people pose a threat to the rest of us when we use public bathrooms. Proponents of these kinds of policing policies use fear tactics—they argue that adult men will dress up as women in order to enter women's restrooms and sexually abuse children and rape girls and women—in order to generate support for this type of discriminatory law. In fact, there are no documented cases of this scenario actually occurring. What does happen is that trans people and people whose bodies don't conveniently fit into the stereotypes we have of gendered bodies are often harassed when they attempt to use the appropriate bathroom.

One of our colleagues, Betsy Lucal, wrote a piece all the way back in 1999 in which she describes how her own body is policed:

> Each day, I negotiate the boundaries of gender. Each day, I face the possibility that someone will attribute the "wrong" gender to me based on my physical appearance. I am six feet tall and large-boned. I have had short hair for most of my life. For the past several years, I have worn a crew cut or flat top. I do not shave or otherwise remove hair from my body (e.g., no eyebrow plucking). I do not wear dresses, skirts, high heels, or makeup. My only jewelry is a class ring, a "men's" watch (my wrists are too large for a "women's" watch), two small earrings (gold hoops, both in my left ear), and (occasionally) a necklace. I wear jeans or shorts, T-shirts, sweaters, polo/golf shirts, button-down collar shirts, and tennis shoes or boots. The jeans are "women's" (I do have hips) but do not look particularly "feminine." The rest of the outer garments are from men's departments. I prefer baggy clothes, so the fact that I have "womanly" breasts often is not obvious (I do not wear a bra). Sometimes, I wear a baseball cap or some other type of hat. I also am white and relatively young (30 years old). My gender display—what others interpret as my presented identity—regularly leads to the misattribution of my gender. An incongruity exists between my gender self-identity and the gender that others

perceive. In my encounters with people I do not know, I sometimes conclude, based on our interactions, that they think I am a man. This does not mean that other people do not think I am a man, just that I have no way of knowing what they think without interacting with them. . . . My identity as a woman also is called into question when I try to use women-only spaces. Encounters in public rest rooms are an adventure. I have been told countless times that "This is the ladies' room." Other women say nothing to me, but their stares and conversations with others let me know what they think. I will hear them say, for example, "There was a man in there." I also get stares when I enter a locker room. However, it seems that women are less concerned about my presence there, perhaps because, given that it is a space for changing clothes, showering, and so forth, they will be able to make sure that I am really a woman. Dressing rooms in department stores also are problematic spaces. I remember shopping with my sister once and being offered a chair outside the room when I began to accompany her into the dressing room. . . . Women who believe that I am a man do not want me in women-only spaces. For example, one woman would not enter the rest room until I came out, and others have told me that I am in the wrong place. They also might not want to encounter me while they are alone. For example, seeing me walking at night when they are alone might be scary.[2]

As uncomfortable as Betsy's experiences are, thankfully she has not, to our knowledge, been assaulted or arrested. This is, of course, not the case for nearly half of all people whose bodies challenge our notions of gender, especially trans bodies.

Trans bodies are at particularly high risk for being policed by the use of physical and sexual violence. Among people who identified as trans or gender nonconforming in kindergarten through high school, 35 percent reported physical assault and 12 percent reported experiencing sexual violence.[3] Nearly every week an incident of the beating, sexual assault, and/or murder of a trans woman makes the news. Trans women are particularly vulnerable to physical and sexual violence by men—both in the "free world" and while incarcerated—for a variety of reasons, including the belief on the part of perpetrators that they were "tricked," believing initially that the trans person was biologically female. This is particularly common among trans women who are engaged in sex work. Many trans women sex workers report that they were solicited precisely because they are trans and that their identity was no surprise to the john who later assaults her and claims he was "duped." This was the claim former NFL player Eric Green made when he was sued in 2010 by Angelina Mavilia, a transgender woman, whom he met at a casino in January 2009 in Scottsdale, Arizona—at that time Green was playing for the Arizona Cardinals. Mavilia agreed to go back to Green's condo and have sex with him. She alleged that when Green had trouble penetrating her, he forcibly sodomized her. Green claimed that he didn't know that Mavilia is a transgender woman and "freaked out" when he realized her actual identity. Mavilia claims that Green knew of her identity, and that is exactly why he solicited her for sex.

Fundamentally, as is the case with all sexual violence, trans individuals are raped and sexually assaulted in an attempt to police their bodies, which do not conform, in very specific ways, to societal and cultural expectations. As we have argued in our work on violence against women, sexual violence is the preferred tool for policing bodies that transgress gender and/or sexual identity because the violence itself targets the site of the transgression. Rape is a tool that reminds a sexual minority or trans or gender queer person that their very existence outside of socially accepted norms is unacceptable. And what more powerful mechanism to reinforce this unacceptability than by an act that specifically targets the unacceptable body parts. Sexual violence is a tool for policing how people identify and how they present themselves—in short, who they are allowed to be. Sexual violence is a powerful tool that ensures that dominant cultural norms remain dominant and that opportunities accrue to those who mind the body police.

TRANS BODIES AT RISK FOR POLICING

According to the national report *A Blueprint for Equality: A Federal Agenda for Transgender People*, published in 2015 by the National Center for Transgender Equality,[4] 16 percent of transgender people and 21 percent of trans women have been incarcerated in their lifetimes. Among Black transgender people, nearly half (47 percent) have been incarcerated, a rate that is ten to fifteen percentage points higher than the rate for all Black folk. The overincarceration of Black trans people is the result of two forces that will be familiar because they are factors in the overincar-

ceration of other marginalized populations: poverty and its related consequences and status offenses.

For the most part, every disadvantage that accrues to transgender people is worse for trans people of color, particularly Black trans people.
According to the report *Injustice at Every Turn: A Report of the National
Transgender Discrimination Survey* published in 2011,[5] 15 percent of
transgender people live on less than $10,000 a year, a rate of poverty that
is *four times* the national average. Many factors contribute to poverty
among trans people, including job discrimination, which is legal in most
states. Transgender people also experience high rates of unemployment,
nearly double the national unemployment rate, and nearly 50 percent
report being fired from a job. As a result of class factors such as poverty
and unemployment, as well as the fact that housing discrimination is
legal, 20 percent of trans people report that they were homeless at least
once. Sadly, many trans people had family or friends who had the capacity to provide them a place to live but refused to do so. As we know from
our examination of mass incarceration, as a direct result of structural
factors, including where one lives, the job one has, and the inability to
pay fines or bail, the poor are significantly more likely to be arrested and
incarcerated than people with more money, and this pattern applies to
trans people as well and to Black trans people in particular.

As a direct result of poverty, homelessness, and job discrimination,
many trans people are arrested and incarcerated for status offenses. More
than half of all trans people report being harassed by the police in public
places like parks and bus stations, and they are often arrested. Sixteen
percent of trans people report that their only way to get the money they
needed to pay rent and buy food is to pursue ways of making money in
the illegitimate economy, especially by engaging in sex work and selling
drugs. Quite obviously, both of these "occupations" put trans people at
significantly greater risk for being incarcerated. Unable to pay fines or
post bail, the majority find that they will be locked up, at least pending a
hearing, in the local jail. In these ways, the experiences of trans people
are not that different from other marginalized groups, only more severe.
Just like juveniles who find themselves locked up for status and drug
offenses, and just like the majority of Black people who are incarcerated
for nonviolent offenses like drug possession, many of whom are unable to
pay fines or post bail, trans people, and Black trans people in particular,
have extremely high rates of incarceration.

TRANS ISSUES IN PRISON

There have been trans inmates incarcerated since at least the early parts of the twentieth century. In our many visits to Parchman Farm—the Mississippi State Penitentiary—visitors can see the booking photographs of an inmate that was incarcerated first as a man and many years later, on an unrelated conviction, as a woman. That said, the significant increase in the sheer number of individuals who identify as trans has created many challenges for prisons, and as a result of the mistreatment of trans inmates by prison staff, many if not most trans inmates report that they experience physical and sexual abuse during their periods of incarceration.

And though all trans bodies experience the risk for violence inside prison walls, we focus our attention on trans women because they are far more likely to be incarcerated and, once incarcerated, are far more likely to report being physically and sexually abused while detained than are trans men.

The risks for trans women begin when they are taken into custody and assigned to a cell. Although there are many different factors taken into consideration when an inmate is assigned to a cell, because of the complete sex-segregated nature of jails and prisons, the most important and first factor that is considered is the inmate's gender. And assignment by gender is quite simply "gender assigned at birth," or, put more plainly, the genital test. If an inmate has a penis, that inmate, regardless of how they identify in terms of their gender, regardless of whether the inmate also has breasts, regardless of any other qualities, will be assigned to and incarcerated in a men's housing block or prison.

And, as noted above, trans individuals transition in many different ways. Perhaps not surprising, the least common transition undertaken by trans people is genital surgery; only 33 percent of trans individuals have any surgery at all, and 14 percent of trans women and 21 percent of trans men[6] report that they are not at all interested in genital surgery. And even for those who are, there are many barriers to obtaining genital surgery, not the least of which is the cost, which can run from $7,000 to $20,000 for transitioning from male to female and upward of $50,000 for transitioning from female to male. Of course there are other surgeries as well, including breast augmentation, mastectomy, facial feminization surgery, and procedures like electrolysis. One of our colleagues who transitioned from male to female indicated that the total cost was nearly $100,000, and very few health insurance policies cover any of these costs. Furthermore, there are other "costs" associated with surgery, including taking time off of work, which most people in the United States, even those with relatively good jobs, cannot afford to do. Thus, as a result, even among trans individuals who would like to have surgery, very few can afford it. We note that this has been a point of criticism in Caitlyn Jenner's "coming out" on the cover of *Vogue*. Many in the trans community, including Laverne Cox and Janet Mock, made it clear that Jenner's experience was highly shaped by social class and that Jenner's experience does not represent the typical trans experience.

There is no question that incarcerating trans women in male prisons and cell blocks is dangerous and highly problematic for a variety of reasons. According to one of the leading researchers on the rape of trans people in prison, 59 percent of trans women incarcerated in male prisons report being raped.[7] This is an extraordinarily high rate of rape, more than ten times greater than the rate for cisgender inmates in men's prisons.

Prison officials argue that there are very few options for incarcerating trans inmates safely in a sex-segregated prison system. Though there is absolutely no evidence of this, opponents of incarcerating inmates by their self-identified gender identity argue that doing so puts cisgender women in danger of being sexually assaulted by trans women with penises. This is not a new concern as this is the same fear expressed in debates about bathroom use or housing trans students in residence halls on college campuses. And just as is the case with bathroom bills and housing on college campuses, there is absolutely no evidence that incarcerating trans women in women's prisons puts cisgender women at risk. If anything, all people incarcerated in women's prisons are at risk for sexual violence by guards and other cisgender inmates.

In some of the largest prison systems—New York and California—some jails and prisons have addressed this dilemma by designating LGBTQ blocks where any inmate who identifies in the LGBTQ community and who feels unsafe in sex-segregated units may apply to be housed. This may be, for now, the safest and most appropriate solution to the issue. That said, there are very few jails and prisons with the space to set up these kinds of blocks, and thus they are extremely uncommon. Furthermore, this approach assumes that all members of the LGBTQ community are respectful of each other or even share the same needs.

Another strategy that prison officials utilize to ensure the safety of trans inmates, and trans women incarcerated in men's prisons in particular, is administrative segregation, more commonly known as solitary confinement. There are, of course, many problems with solitary confinement as well, including the fact that long-term solitary confinement has been identified by the United Nations as "cruel and unusual punishment." Solitary confinement is deemed cruel and unusual primarily because it significantly restricts an inmate's human contact and because it imposes additional burdens on those in solitary confinement. At the core of solitary confinement is the concept "solitary," and thus inmates are allowed only minimal, if any, contact with other inmates. Solitary confinement also limits the contact between an inmate and the guard. Food is passed through a basket or "wicket" on the cell door. When inmates are transferred from their cells to the shower, where they are locked in alone, or to the yard, the guards rarely talk to the inmate except to yell at them.

Inmates we interviewed at a rural prison in Pennsylvania told us over and over again that solitary confinement was not to protect them; it was the ultimate form of punishment. They complained that the total segregation from human contact "messes with your mind" and causes serious mental health problems. They told us of the ways in which solitary confinement also allowed the guards to restrict access to their other guaranteed civil rights, including three meals per day. For example, one inmate reported that he was taking medication that made him tired, and when he didn't jump up quickly enough and run to the wicket when the guard came by with his breakfast, the guard reported that he had "refused food" and he did not receive his breakfast. "All human privileges are gone; they treat you like a dog. They bring you food, they throw it to you, you shower in a cage, you exercise in a cage. Just because I'm wearing orange [the color of the jumpsuit for inmates confined in solitary] doesn't mean I'm not human."

At the Mississippi State Penitentiary at Parchman, inmates in solitary confinement are taken outside for their "exercise time" and put in cages that look like large dog kennels. Occasionally there may be more than one inmate in a set of these "kennels" at a time and they can holler back and forth to each other, but that is the upper limit of their contact with other inmates. Furthermore, because solitary confinement requires a one-to-one ratio of inmates to guards and typically a one-to-two ratio anytime an inmate is moved, for example, to the shower or to the exercise cages, understaffing can result in inmates incarcerated in solitary confinement having fewer opportunities than inmates in the general population to take showers and get exercise time. Though all incarcerated people, including those in solitary confinement, are supposed to get at least one hour per day to shower or exercise, we heard reports at Parchman that inmates in solitary confinement were often realistically getting time in the dog kennels only once or twice a week as a result of understaffing, bad weather, and a variety of other factors that restricted their movement. Finally, solitary confinement does not ensure that an inmate will not be harassed or raped: 37 percent of trans women *housed in solitary confinement* in men's prisons reported that they were sexually harassed or assaulted by guards.[8]

In addition to their safety, trans inmates face additional challenges during periods of incarceration; for example, only nineteen state prison systems have any policy on transgender health care.[9] And though there is some variation by state and institution, in the majority of jails and prisons, the most common approach to providing ongoing health care for trans inmates is the "freeze-frame" approach. The freeze-frame approach dictates that the inmate is provided the exact same medical care that they were receiving before being incarcerated. For example, if a trans woman had been receiving a certain amount of estrogen and androgen blockers before being incarcerated, she would continue to receive that same amount during the period of incarceration. There are several problems associated with the freeze-frame approach. For example, for an inmate who desires to transition but has not been receiving hormone therapy under "official" medical care prior to being incarcerated, there will be no treatment available under the freeze-frame approach. And because the freeze-frame approach is predicated on existing medical records, this can present an additional problem for low-income trans inmates. Because hormone therapy is very expensive, many low-income trans people obtain hormones on the black market and therefore do not have prescriptions and are not officially "under medical care." Thus, when they are admitted to prison, they will not receive any hormone therapy. This will have disastrous effects in that it will put the trans inmate into an immediate reversal of their transition; trans women who have been growing breasts will see their breasts shrink, and trans men who have been growing facial hair will experience this reversing.

Additionally the freeze-frame approach assumes that a constant level of hormone therapy is medically appropriate. Transitioning, like many other hormone-related medical treatments such as thyroid replacement or medication to control diabetes, typically varies based on a variety of factors, including the time between diagnosis and the onset of treatment, age, stress, and diet. Similarly, the amount of hormone necessary to maintain a trans person's physical changes may vary, and thus the freeze-frame approach is not necessarily what would be medically indicated. Lastly, the freeze-frame approach does not allow for the transition to continue; instead it prescribes delivering the same hormone treatment that the inmate was receiving prior to incarceration, which in effect stalls the transition and does not allow it to progress according to the inmate's wishes. According to the World Transgender Health Standards of Care, transitioning at the desired and medically supervised pace is not only the most appropriate treatment protocol, but to slow or stop the transition when this is not medically recommended or when this contradicts the desire of the trans individual can cause emotional and psychological stress, as was the case with Ashley Diamond whose narrative opens this chapter.

As part of a project focused on solitary confinement that we participated in during the spring of 2017, we interviewed Aretha, a trans woman incarcerated in a rural Pennsylvania prison. In contrast to so many cases of trans women in solitary confinement, we were pleased to learn from Aretha that she was incarcerated in solitary confinement because of a disciplinary action for which she was found responsible, not as a strategy for housing trans inmates. Despite not receiving formal medical treatment for her transition—prior to being incarcerated, Aretha was ordering hormones over the Internet—she was receiving hormone treatment under Pennsylvania's freeze-frame approach. Though Aretha desired to continue her transition and pressed the medical staff to provide increased hormone therapy, compared to many incarcerated trans bodies her experiences were significantly better.

Though the freeze-frame approach may currently be the "best-case scenario," unfortunately the vast majority of jails and prisons have no trans health policy. Absent any health policy, most jails and prisons simply discontinue hormone therapy upon the trans inmate's admission. This practice is in clear violation of the World Transgender Health Standards of Care. But even without the standards of care protocols laid out by knowledgeable medical professionals, it is only common sense that immediate withdrawal—going cold turkey—from hormone therapy has significant negative physical and psychological outcomes. For a trans woman, an immediate withdrawal from hormones is exactly like medically induced menopause, the type that occurs when a woman has a hysterectomy, and results in many more symptoms—for example, night sweats, hot flashes, and depression—than the slower transition that occurs during a naturally occurring menopausal process.

Along with sexual and physical abuse, denying incarcerated trans people appropriate medical care is nothing short of policing their bodies. And just as sexual and physical violence are used to police trans bodies by targeting the very body that stands in opposition to gender norms, the physical impact of denying incarcerated trans people appropriate medical care polices their bodies by literally stopping or even reversing the transition of their bodies. It forces them to live in bodies they believe are incongruent with their gender identity. These policies are the ultimate form of policing. Policing Black bodies. Policing Black trans bodies.

CeCe McDonald is in many ways a very typical trans woman. CeCe knew from a very early age that she was different from the other boys. She had disdain for her boy's body, boyish clothes, and even her name. At the same time, she remembers at age nine being enthralled by her mother's clothes and perfume. She adopted very feminine qualities, and as a result she was bullied at school and at home, which is not uncommon: 44 percent of trans youth report being bullied. [10] During a fight with her uncle over a note she had written to a boy, he threw her to the ground, choking her. She left home at fourteen and never returned.

Like the 40 percent of trans youth who report having been homeless, [11] CeCe could not live at home and had to learn to make a life on the streets. CeCe began selling drugs and by age fifteen was involved in prostitution. Not surprisingly she experienced harassment, violence, and rape.

CeCe started hanging out at a youth drop-in center for LGBTQ teens and caught the attention of a case worker who helped CeCe complete her GED and enroll in community college. She was also able to begin seeing a psychiatrist who diagnosed CeCe with gender dysphoria, and with that diagnosis she was able to begin appropriate hormone treatment therapy. As one can imagine, as her body began to change to match her internal gender identity, and as she found a community and was attending school, CeCe was finally feeling good and doing well. She even went through the often unnecessarily burdensome bureaucratic process to have her name legally changed. She had her first apartment and was using her community college training to prepare for a career in the fashion industry.

All of this fell apart on the night of June 5, 2011. CeCe and her roommates were going grocery shopping, something they preferred to do at night, where under the cover of darkness they were less likely to be subjected to stares, catcalls, and harassment.

> Gathered outside the dive bar were a handful of cigarette-smoking white people, looking like an aging biker gang in their T-shirts, jeans and bandannas, motorcycles parked nearby. Hurling the insults were 47-year-old Dean Schmitz, in a white button-down and thick silver chain, and his 40-year-old ex-girlfriend Molly Flaherty, clad in black, drink in hand. "Look at that boy dressed as a girl, tucking his dick in!" hooted Schmitz, clutching two beer bottles freshly fetched from his Blazer, as CeCe and her friends slowed to a stop. "You niggers need to go back to Africa!"[12]

According to CeCe, she and her friends asked to be left alone and tried to move along the sidewalk past the bar. Molly Flaherty hurled more insults and threw a glass tumbler that hit CeCe in the face. A fight broke out between CeCe and Molly, which left both bleeding. Once CeCe realized she was OK, she ran and didn't realize that Schmitz was behind her. Terribly afraid, CeCe put her hand into her purse and wrapped her hand around a pair of fabric scissors that she carried regularly because she used them in her fashion classes. Schmitz lunged at CeCe, and she instinctively pulled out the scissors. Accounts differ whether CeCe stabbed Schmitz or whether Schmitz lunged at her. Either way, Schmitz had the scissors three and a half inches in his chest, and he was bleeding profusely. What CeCe did not know about Schmitz was that he was a self-declared racist, even having a swastika tattooed on his stomach. Much of Schmitz's racist behavior, including the tattoo, was inadmissible in court, and CeCe was convicted by an *all-white jury* and sentenced to forty-one months in prison. The Minnesota prison system does not have an LGBTQ block, and CeCe served her entire sentence—she was released after nineteen months for good behavior and with credit for nearly a year's time served between her arrest and her conviction—in solitary confinement.

It is quite clear when it comes to trans bodies that changes in law and policy must be enacted as soon as possible in order to ensure the safety of all bodies. Bathroom policies must be repealed, corrections systems must design appropriate protocols not only for assigning trans inmates to housing but also for addressing their health-care needs as medically recommended, and laws at the state and federal level must be passed that protect trans bodies in all aspects of life, in employment, housing, education, and, yes, bathrooms. As Valerie Jenness and Sarah Fenstermaker argue, corrections departments must seriously address the "facts about the rape of transgender women in carceral environments built for men and only men."[13] Trans people are citizens of the United States, and trans bodies deserve to be free from all forms of policing.

8

POLICE KILLINGS OF UNARMED BLACK MEN

We—we know—we know the risk you are taking, and we say thank you to every police officer and law enforcement agent who is out tonight protecting us—black, white, Latino, of every race, every color, every creed, every sexual orientation. When they come to save your life, they don't ask, if you are black or white. They just come to save you!

We also—we also reach out. We reach out our arms with understanding and compassion to those who have lost loved ones because of police shootings—some justified, some unjustified. Those that are unjustified must be punished. Those that are justified, we must apologize to. It's time to make America safe again. It's time to make America one again. One America!

What happened—what happened to—what happened to, there's no black America, there's no white America, there is just America?! What happened to it? Where did it go? How did it float away?

—Rudy Giuliani, former New York City mayor, remarks to the Republican National Convention, Cleveland, Ohio, July 2016

One of our primary aims in writing this book was to provide a conceptual framework for interpreting police killings of unarmed Black men as only one form of policing Black bodies that must be understood in the wider context of different forms of policing of Black bodies, including mass incarceration, the school-to-prison pipeline, and the prison-industrial complex. Though the vast majority of Black men who are murdered are

killed by other Black men, Black men who are killed by the police constitute a different phenomenon; they are not murdered by their peers but in
acts of state-sanctioned violence. As we will demonstrate, many unarmed
Black men who are killed by the police were caught in the same dragnet
that pulls Black men into the criminal justice system in record numbers.
Those who argue that the most promising strategies for reducing police
killings of unarmed Black men include teaching anger management or
breathing techniques miss the point. Police killings are not simply a matter of policing gone wrong. Rather, police killings of unarmed Black men
are simply another outgrowth, tragic but not necessarily unintended, of
building a society squarely on racist practices that define Black bodies as
"less than," which wages a war on Black people because it is the only
legal means to remove them from mainstream society in a century in
which it is no longer ethical to move oppressed people onto reservations
or engage in eugenics or genocide.

Chris Hayes, in his book *A Colony in a Nation*, argues that police
shootings of unarmed Black men are a predictable if undesirable consequence of a system of racial domination that includes both regular contact
between the citizens of the state (white people) and the members of the
colony (Black and Brown people) and a requirement to police the bodies
of the colony, Black bodies. In comparing the racial caste system in the
United States, where citizens of the nation and members of the colony
live in geographic proximity, to the typical European colony, in which the
citizens of the nation live in one geography (England, France) and the
members of the colony live in another (Congo, Kenya), he writes,

> The borders must be enforced without the benefit of actual walls and
> checkpoints. This requires an ungodly number of interactions between
> the sentries of the state and those the state views as the disorderly
> class. The math of large numbers means that with enough of these
> interactions *and enough fear and suspicion on the part of the officer*
> who wields the gun, hundreds of those who've been marked for moni-
> toring will die.[1]

Policing Black bodies. Deliberately.

The U.S. Department of Justice review of Ferguson's police department after the shooting of Mike Brown revealed that, like many other
municipalities, the Ferguson Police Department was militarizing by purchasing implements from the U.S. military, including tanks, tactical gear,

flak jackets, and weapons.[2] And when the tools of war are unleashed on the Black community, innocent, unarmed people will be murdered by the police.

> At the close of the last century, the New York City Police Department switched from full-metal-jacket bullets to hollow points. It was a move meant to spare lives—in theory, anyway: The old bullets had a tendency to pass through their targets and endanger bystanders, while hollow points expand after impact, inflicting greater damage to internal organs but also increasing the likelihood that the bullet will slow to a halt inside the body. And so, on February 2, 2012, when Officer Richard Haste shot 18-year-old Ramarley Graham—who was unarmed, standing in his own bathroom—the hollow-point bullet did just that. Less than a millisecond after being fired, the Speer Gold Dot 9-mm. round struck Graham's chest and blossomed as it bore a jagged tunnel through his aorta, trachea, and right lung. Seconds later, Graham was all but dead, facedown on the tile floor.
>
> There was no video. The NYPD offered a tidy and by-now-familiar explanation: A police officer thought a young, unarmed black man had a gun and, fearing for his life, made a fatal miscalculation.[3]

In his book *Rise of the Warrior Cop: The Militarization of America's Police Forces*, Radley Balko makes clear the connection between the militarization of the police and policing Black bodies.

> Today's armored-up policemen are a far cry from the constables of early America. The unrest of the 1960s brought about the invention of the SWAT unit which in turn led to the debut of military tactics in the ranks of police officers. Nixon's War on Drugs, Reagan's War on Poverty, Clinton's COPS program, the post-9/11 security state under Bush and Obama: by degrees, each of these innovations expanded and empowered police forces, always at the expense of civil liberties. And these are just four among a slew of reckless programs.[4]

But the militarization movement in law enforcement is not limited to arming police officers with the tools of war; it is also arming police officers with a way of thinking that Dave Grossman, otherwise known as "Professor Carnage," refers to as "killology." In his report titled "Professor Carnage," Steve Featherstone details the curriculum that Dave Grossman has delivered to tens of thousands of police officers over the last two decades and that he details in his book *On Killing*, which has sold more than half a million copies.

> Dave Grossman has transported his approach to soldiering, an ideology he refers to as "Killology," seamless to the world of law enforcement. Grossman trains tens of thousands of police and other law enforcement agents to think of themselves as warriors. The police are soldiers in the war to protect American public safety. And, that war is ultimately a war on Black bodies, a war on Black men. Every state of war requires a state enemy and police officers are taught that Black men are that enemy of the state and sometimes they must be killed.[5]

Extending Grossman's argument, when police officers kill a Black man, they haven't committed a crime, any more than when an American soldier kills a member of the Taliban. They have done their job. They have eliminated the enemy, the threat to the American way of life, the threat to public safety. Policing Black bodies. When we analyze the (lack of) accountability for police officers who kill unarmed Black men—they almost never go to prison—through this lens, we expose the logic of state-sanctioned violence, of the warrior police. Police officers who kill unarmed Black men (or any American citizen) don't go to prison because they haven't committed an individual act of violence, they've engaged in state-sanctioned practices to control the enemy. They are fighting the war on Black people.

When we read and hear testimony of police who have killed an unarmed Black man, one of the most common defenses they invoke is that they feared for their life, that the Black man seemed wild, out of control, huge, like a monster. And this misperception is confirmed by experimental research. A 2017 study published in the American Psychological Association's *Journal of Personality and Social Psychology* showed that white people perceived Black men as more muscular, heavier, taller, stronger, and more dangerous than white men the same size and weight.[6]

On September 16, 2016, Tulsa, Oklahoma, female police officer Betty Shelby shot and killed forty-year-old Black man Terence Crutcher while he stood by his disabled vehicle. She killed Crutcher because, as she put it, she feared for her life. Although Crutcher was unarmed, Officer Shelby said she believed he was about to reach for a weapon. In her widely viewed *60 Minutes* interview that took place on April 2, 2017, when asked why she shot Crutcher, she responded, "Because it was an odd behavior. Zombie-like, I—I—it's the best I can . . . . Zombie-like."[7] Officer Shelby was acquitted just a few weeks later on May 17, 2017.

Like so many other police officers, Officer Shelby saw Crutcher as a big scary Black man. Often police officers report perceiving the unarmed Black men they kill as significantly bigger than they really are, as monsters. Darren Wilson, the police officer who shot and killed unarmed Black teen Michael Brown, described Brown as huge, like a monster. Wilson and Brown are about the same size and weight. Wilson was never indicted.

According to Featherstone, "Jeronimo Yanez, the police officer who shot and killed Philando Castile in front of his girlfriend and her four-year-old daughter during a routine traffic stop in a Minneapolis suburb last July [2016], had attended a seminar on warrior policing co-taught by Grossman. Yanez shot Castile seven times, at point-blank range, because he mistakenly believed that Castile was reaching for the gun in his pocket instead of his wallet." Despite substantial forensic evidence, Yanez was acquitted of all charges on June 16, 2017.

Police killings of unarmed Black men must be understood as nothing short of state-sanctioned violence. Policing Black bodies.

One of the most common critiques of this argument is that police also kill unarmed white men. Black police officers kill unarmed Black men. These facts do not contradict our argument that police killings of unarmed Black men are a form of state-sanctioned violence. Rather, these facts reinforce our argument. As Chris Hayes argues in his book *A Colony in a Nation*,

> The Colony is overwhelmingly black and brown, but in the wake of financial catastrophe, deindustrialization, and sustained wage stagnation, the tendencies and systems of control developed in the Colony have been deployed over wider and wider swaths of working-class white America. . . . Maintaining the division between the Colony and the Nation is treacherous precisely because the constant threat that the tools honed in the Colony will be wielded in the Nation; that tyranny and violence tolerated at the periphery will ultimately infiltrate the core. American police shoot an alarmingly high number of black people. But they also shoot a shockingly large number of white people.[8]

Police violence waged on Black bodies is highly controversial and highly emotionally charged. Peruse any Facebook or Twitter feed after the next police killing of an unarmed Black man or the failure to indict or convict the next officer who has killed an unarmed Black man, and you will witness the vitriol, more often than not fueled by emotions not facts.

Though writing this chapter is emotionally painful for us, our argument is not driven by emotion but fact. We are empiricists, and the data for this chapter comes from a variety of official sources.[9] But first a caveat: when it comes to police shootings, getting accurate data can be quite challenging, in part because police departments censor critical information about police shootings or don't make reports of them at all.

> The FBI's Supplementary Homicide Report, or the CDC's National Vital Statistics System, these records are often censored of critical information (such as the names of the officers involved), lack independent evaluation of the justification for the shooting, and are selectively published. The FBI data, for instance, are not only incomplete, but may be structurally biased by the reporting behaviors of police, as the majority of the 17,000+ police departments in the United States do not file fatal police shooting reports, or do so only selectively. According to Gabrielson et al., Florida departments have failed to file reports since 1997.[10]

Thus, we owe a tremendous debt to those scholars who have addressed these issues before us.

The official U.S. Department of Justice reports on Ferguson, Missouri; Chicago, Illinois; and Baltimore, Maryland, though mostly ineffective in achieving any real change, help to guide us in this inquiry by providing facts. We also owe a debt of gratitude to the journalists who, in some cases, risked their lives in places like Ferguson and Baltimore to bring us the voices and images of the people living there, often while they protested not only the killing of a member of their community but also the treatment they have been subjected to, often for decades, at the hands of the police.

This lack of transparency and accurate reporting by police departments when it comes to police shootings was illuminated in response to the mass shootings of five Dallas police officers by ex-army private Micah Johnson on July 7, 2016. In the immediate aftermath of the deadly rampage, Dallas police chief David Brown announced that the department would *finally* put up an official department web page that offered transparency into the use of deadly force in Dallas County. Implied here is that prior to these tragedies, such data had not been publicly available.

In the summer of 2016, the governor of North Carolina signed a law that allowed police departments to select the police body camera videos they would make available to the public. Isn't the whole point of police body camera videos that they be available so that citizens can see with their own eyes the interactions between police and the community? Perhaps the answer lies in the ideology of "killology." The state feels no more burden to release statistics and images from police shootings of unarmed Black men than they do from the missions of American soldiers in Iraq and Afghanistan. State-sanctioned violence is protected whether it takes place in Fallujah or Ferguson. Policing Black bodies.

We are interested not only in providing witness, through description, of the unarmed Black men who are killed by the police but in understanding the processes by which these killings occur—we are interested in exploring answers to the "why" question. In fact, police utilize a variety of racist practices, including those developed as part of the War on Drugs and others that we outlined in our discussion of mass incarceration and the school-to-prison pipeline, to pursue Black men as part of the war on Black bodies.

When it comes to understanding the context in which violence escalates and tragically ends in yet another police shooting of yet another unarmed Black man, the research of Charles R. Epp, Steven Maynard-Moody, and Donald P. Haider-Markel, reported in their 2014 book *Pulled Over: How Police Stops Define Race and Citizenship*, provides a lens into understanding this context. Based on their research, Epp, Maynard-Moody, and Haider-Markel unpack the ways that "routine" traffic stops lead to the types of escalating violence that result in police shootings of unarmed Black men like Philando Castile and the tasing and beating deaths of Black women like Sandra Bland.[11]

Based on more than a thousand interviews, their careful research reveals that police stops fall into two categories: legitimate stops and "fishing expeditions." Legitimate stops involve behaviors like speeding ten to twenty miles over the speed limit, erratic driving patterns that might signal distracted driving, running stop signs and stoplights, and the like. Their research revealed that there were very few racial differences and no racial disparities in legitimate stops in terms of either the likelihood of being stopped or in the way drivers experienced the stop. Both Blacks and whites who reported on these kinds of stops indicated that they were over quickly; usually the officer simply wrote a ticket, and the driver was allowed to go on their way.

In sharp contrast, fishing expeditions were highly racialized in terms of both the likelihood of being stopped and the driver's experience of the stop. When President Obama proclaimed after the death of Philando Castile that Blacks are 30 percent more likely to be pulled over, he was referencing these fishing expeditions. And in fact this is exactly what Epp, Maynard-Moody, and Haider-Markel argue took place in the case of Philando Castile. Fishing expeditions involve officers pulling over people they suspect might be engaged in criminal activity, the "might be" being a very loose term. As Epp, Maynard-Moody, and Haider-Markel argue, because the officer has no legitimate reason to stop the motorist, the driver often becomes suspicious and agitated. The "warrior police officer," engaging their "killology," approaches the driver, who is already suspicious of the police officer's motive, and the violence escalates rapidly, too often resulting tragically in the officer taking the life of the motorist.

One might say, well, this is good if police officers are preemptively stopping people who might be engaged in criminal activity. But, as Epp, Maynard-Moody, and Haider-Markel's data reveal, in fact rarely is the person stopped engaged in any criminal activity. In fact, though white motorists are pulled over less often than Black drivers, and they are less likely to be subjected to having their vehicle searched, white drivers are 20 percent more likely to be discovered with evidence of criminal activity, such as drugs or stolen goods. In other words, police officers "get it right" 20 percent more often when they pull over white drivers, but because they pull over white drivers 30 percent less often, the question remains, how many white people engaged in criminal activity are missed in these racially motivated fishing expeditions? And how many Black bodies are policed and even murdered over fishing expeditions that had no basis in reality and ended in unnecessary tragedy?

No wonder Black people often report feeling harassed by the police. Blacks interviewed by Epp, Maynard-Moody, and Haider-Markel reported that when they saw the blue police lights flashing in their rearview mirrors, they hoped it was for a legitimate stop, even though that meant a fine, instead of a fishing expedition, which could result in them being beaten, tased, or even killed.

And by the way, isn't it illegal to pull someone over because you think they might commit a crime? Or because they have a broad nose, or because they look like a suspect in the area who has recently committed a crime, as was the case with Mike Brown? At a minimum, these police practices violate the Constitution. At the tragic end, they result in the loss of a life, too young, sometimes in front of children, as was the case with Philando Castile and Fritz Severe, a homeless, unarmed Black man who was shot by Miami police officer Antonio Torres, who rolled up and fired five shots into Severe's body, killing him in front of more than fifty horrified kids. Deaths that are like pouring gasoline on an already burning blaze that characterizes the relationship between police and the Black communities they are charged to protect. Deaths that punctuate the state-sanctioned war on Black bodies.

The killing of Black men by the police is nothing new. It has been taking place for the entire history of the United States. Though our focus is on unarmed Black men killed by police officers, there are many high-profile cases that involve what we consider to be police surrogates—vigilantes—who take it upon themselves to police Black bodies that they perceive to be transgressing expectations for behavior. George Zimmerman was not officially a police officer, but he was a neighborhood watch captain whose defense in the shooting death of Trayvon Martin was that he was protecting his community from a young Black man he perceived to match the description of some young men who had recently burglarized homes in his community, never mind that Trayvon Martin *lived* in the community and was simply walking through the neighborhood on his way home armed with only a bag of Skittles and an iced tea.

In 1955 in the southern community of Money, Mississippi, fourteen-year-old Emmett Till from Chicago was killed by two white men—Roy Bryant and his half-brother J. W. Milam—after he had allegedly flirted with a white woman, Bryant's wife, at the Bryants' convenience store. Emmett Till's murderers were tried and acquitted by an all-white jury who spent only thirty minutes or so deliberating the case. A few weeks after the trial, Bryant and Milam confessed to the crime.

On January 24, 1956, *Look* magazine publishes the confessions of J. W. Milam and Roy Bryant, two white men from Mississippi who were acquitted in the 1955 kidnapping and murder of Emmett Louis Till, an African-American teenager from Chicago. In the *Look* article, titled "The Shocking Story of Approved Killing in Mississippi," the men detailed how they beat Till with a gun, shot him and threw his body in the Tallahatchie River with a heavy cotton-gin fan attached with barbed wire to his neck to weigh him down. The two killers were paid a reported $4,000 for their participation in the article.[12]

We deliberately chose to focus our analysis on police killings of unarmed Black men for the same reasons that most of the issues we dissect in this book focus on Black men's bodies, with Black women's bodies being the focus of an entire chapter devoted to their unique experience. Though no death is more or less tragic than another, Black men are far more likely to be killed by the police, just like they are ten times more likely to be incarcerated and significantly more likely to be trapped in the school-to-prison pipeline. And though homicides of Black men rarely make the news, in places like Chicago where they are considered "routine business," police shootings of unarmed Black men often garner significant attention, including public protests, and as a result, we have an abundance of data to inform our analysis.

All of that being said, we are highly critical of the lack of attention that the murder of Black women's bodies has generated, and thus we pause here to acknowledge their lives lost. As is the case with the murder of Black men, though most Black women who are murdered are murdered by Black men—most often their intimate or ex-intimate partners—and not by the police, their lives are no less valuable, and the importance of their stories, and especially honest discussions of intimate partner violence, is no less important. We have taken up this mantel and written four books in which we highlight and interrogate intimate partner violence in the Black community: *African American Families, Intimate Partner Violence, African American Families Today: Myths and Realities*, and our most recent book, *The Social Dynamics of Family Violence*.

Of course there are Black women who are killed by police, either by being shot while in their custody or, as was the case in one of the most high-profile cases, that of Sandra Bland, they die later in police custody. Ms. Bland was stopped on a stretch of road leading to Prairie View College in Prairie View, Texas. The violence escalated quickly, and she was restrained, arrested, and placed in a jail cell. She was found dead on July 13, 2015, three days after being jailed. The coroner in Waller County, Texas, ruled the death a suicide, though her family and many others are disputing that claim. Extending the analysis of Epp, Maynard-Moody, and Haider-Markel, we can speculate that Sandra Bland was the victim of a fishing expedition, or what otherwise might be termed "driving while Black," in a neighborhood where she was not expected to be, but otherwise she was doing nothing wrong. The violence in this case escalated rapidly, and Sandra Bland died as a result. Policing Black bodies.

Once again, in our home county of Fairfax, Virginia, Natasha McKenna died in February 2015 while in police custody in the Fairfax County jail. She was handcuffed and was allegedly resisting being put into a restraint chair when she was tased four times, which delivered a shock of fifty thousand volts each time. She died with her hands cuffed behind her back, her legs shackled, and her face covered with a mask. She was diagnosed with schizophrenia and by all accounts needed mental health services more than she posed any real threat to police.

Malissa Williams's death is one of those that involved a police shooting. Williams was killed in an automobile along with Timothy Ray Russell. They were shot 137 times by thirteen Cleveland police officers. Malissa Williams was doing nothing except sitting in a car. Officer Michael Brelo, who fired forty-nine of the shots, was tried and found *not guilty of all charges*. The judge in the case ruled that because he could not determine which bullet or bullets killed Malissa, he could not hold anyone accountable for her murder. [13]

As little attention as the lives of Black women murdered receive, even less attention is paid to the deaths of trans and queer people, especially those who are Black or Latinx, an issue that was brought to the nation's attention when on June 12, 2016, Omar Mateen went on a shooting rampage, killing forty-nine people and injuring another fifty-three at the Pulse nightclub in Orlando. All of the news reports at the time indicated that Mateen's choices that night were deliberate: targeting a gay club on Latin night. What could be clearer than his determination to police Black and Brown queer bodies? Yet another of the violent tragedies that took place while we were writing this book. Too many lives taken too soon, all because these bodies transgressed norms for behavior held by Mateen and, sadly, by millions of Americans, including some police officers.

As is the case with Black women, white men are also murdered by the police. And their lives are of no less value. We can hear the same pain in a mother's voice, regardless of her race or the race of her child, a life always taken too soon, as was that of Dylan Noble, a nineteen-year-old white male who was killed by two police officers in Fresno, California. He was unarmed and was shot while he was lying on the ground.

But, as is the case with mass incarceration, the school-to-prison pipeline, and exonerations, just to name a few issues, the bodies of Black men are significantly more likely to be policed; their unarmed bodies are shot and killed by police 2.5 times more often than are the bodies of white men. And, compared to police killings of unarmed white men, more often than not the police killings of unarmed Black men are both a symptom of and generate a response to the decades-long tension between the police and the Black community.

The overall lack of transparency and high levels of tension between police officers and Black communities across the United States result in hundreds of unnecessary deaths each year. State-sanctioned violence in the war on Black bodies permits police officers to decide whom to target and whom to kill, with virtually no threat of criminal sanction or institutional civil liability. Police who kill are in fact almost never held responsible for their actions. The data paint a very clear story: of the 102 cases in 2015 in which an unarmed Black person was killed by police, only 10 cases resulted in officers being charged with a crime. And to date, nine of the ten officers who were charged with killing an unarmed Black man have seen the charges dropped or have been acquitted. The war on Black bodies is a war fueled by "killology." State-sanctioned violence is justified to remove, by any means necessary, into prisons or even death, Black bodies that act as if they are full citizens of the nation rather than marginalized members of the colony, to use Chris Hayes's framework.

SAY THEIR NAMES

As with most things, some of the police killings of unarmed Black men have received more attention in the news than others, perhaps because they were more egregious; perhaps because they were captured on cell phone video and the videos went viral, shared for all the world to see; or perhaps because the Black community where they were killed was already more organized and could quickly respond with civil disobedience or erupt into a protest. We all know the names and the stories of Black men including Trayvon Martin, Michael Brown, Philando Castile, and twelve-year-old Tamir Rice. The book's appendix contains a list of some

Revolutionary Gaze by **Suzanne Scott Constantine**

of the high-profile police killings of Black men and the outcomes for the police. It's an incomplete list, but it illustrates all of the troubling patterns we examine in this chapter, including police killings of unarmed Black men and the lack of accountability for the police who engage in a state-sanctioned war on Black bodies. Say their names. Remember their names.

Another example of this is the killing of Prince Carmen Jones, who was shot eight times on September 1, 2000, by a Prince George's County, Maryland, police officer. Prince George's County is home to the highest concentration of wealthy Black Americans living in the United States. Prince was doing nothing illegal at the time. He was a student at the esteemed historically Black university (HBCU) Howard University in Washington, D.C., and a close friend of Ta-Nehisi Coates, who was then a fellow student and who is now a national correspondent for the *Atlantic*, where he writes about cultural, social, and political issues as these apply to Black Americans. The 2000 murder of Prince Jones comes (back) onto the radar screen of the reading public in large part because Coates writes about it in his 2015 best-selling National Book Award winner, *Between the World and Me*.

Strikingly similar in its pattern, Coates writes that police followed Jones from Prince George's County, Maryland, to Fairfax County, Virginia, where we currently live, because they suspected he might be a drug dealer they were looking for. According to Coates, Corporal Carlton B. Jones, who is Black, was sitting in an unmarked SUV when he saw Prince Jones and then fired sixteen shots at the Howard University student who was sitting in his Jeep. Eight of the shots hit Jones, and he died as a result—as is always the case, too early, his potential never fully developed, the world deprived of another Black man whose contributions to society will never be realized.

Ironically, the police officer in the case testified that he was looking for a man about five feet four inches tall and weighing 250 pounds. Prince Jones's body, as confirmed by the coroner, was six feet three inches tall and weighed only 211 pounds. Though Coates did not have the benefit of the work of Epp, Maynard-Moody, and Haider-Markel as he attempted to understand the shooting death of his friend, we imagine he would also characterize Jones's murder as a fishing expedition gone terribly wrong.

As in almost all the other police shootings of unarmed Black men we have researched, the officer was never held accountable. The county did, however, make an award to Prince Jones's family.

> The jury awarded $2.5 million in damages to Prince Jones's daughter, Nina, who is 6; $1 million to his mother, Mabel Jones; and $200,000 to his father. The jury award is one of the highest for a police misconduct lawsuit in county history.[14]

The monetary award does not erase the grief that a family has for their son, or the father they will never know any more than in any other police killing of an unarmed Black man.

As Coates so eloquently writes, "This officer, given maximum power, bore minimum responsibility. He was charged with nothing. He was punished by no one. He was returned to his work."[15] State-sanctioned policing of Black bodies.

The week of July 4 through July 7, 2016, was one marked by intense violence between police and the Black community. We were writing this book at the time, and it seemed as if the violence would never stop rolling across our TV and social media accounts. Each day brought more violence and, sadly, more death. On July 4 (early morning of July 5), two Baton Rouge, Louisiana, police officers, in an execution-style shooting, killed thirty-seven-year-old father of five Alton B. Sterling. Less than forty-eight hours later, on July 6, 2016, thirty-two-year-old Philando Castile was shot and killed by Minneapolis police as he sat in his car with his girlfriend and her four-year-old daughter. The police let him die in front of his girlfriend and her daughter. His girlfriend, Diamond Reynolds, captured the entire police stop—as we have noted, yet another fishing expedition that escalated into violence—on her cell phone. Live-streaming his murder on Facebook, and replayed over and over on cable news outlets and on personal cell phones and computers, the world was able to witness not only the police shooting of an unarmed Black man but the events that led up to it. Like so many others who watched the video, we were horrified for Reynolds's four-year-old daughter, who not only witnessed the murder but at one point verbally comforted her mother. We are astounded by the courage and calm Reynolds displayed while her boyfriend lay next to her dying and the police officer continued to keep his pistol trained on Castile. And we could not believe our eyes when none of the first responders attempted to give Castile mouth-to-mouth or CPR; none of them even bothered to call the EMTs. "Killology" at work. State-sanctioned policing of Black bodies.

Just a day later, acting out of anger and possibly symptoms of PTSD, in downtown Dallas, Texas, late on Friday, July 7, and into the early morning hours of July 8, 2016, a sniper, twenty-five-year-old Micah Johnson, unleashed a barrage of bullets from a high-powered automatic long rifle, killing five police officers and wounding eleven more. One civilian, a woman, was hit in the leg by stray bullets. According to reports, Johnson was very upset with what was happening with regard to police killing Black men, and he was also upset with the Black Lives Matter movement.

On July 8, 2016, thirty-seven-year-old Lakeem Keon Scott killed one person and injured three others, including a police officer, when he opened fire outside a Days Inn in Bristol, Tennessee. Like the sniper in Dallas, Scott expressed distress over the police killings of Black men. It is important to note that police officers are killed every year by civilians, including sixty-three in 2016. Most police officers who are killed by civilians are not killed in retaliation, though each year a few are, but rather they are killed while responding to a crime or while engaging and/ or chasing suspects.

All told, these shootings across the July Fourth holiday left eight people dead and fourteen others wounded. Six of the eight deceased were white, and five were police officers.

Just when we thought that was it, again, in Baton Rouge, on July 17, 2016, just a week after the shootings in Dallas and Tennessee, three Baton Rouge police officers were killed and five others were injured when a sniper, Gavin Long, of Kansas City, Missouri, open fired on them in what was described as an ambush. We were not alone in wondering when the violence would stop. And of course it won't, at least not until we address the causes of the violence: the policing of Black bodies and the "killology" culture of police departments that are engaged in a state-sanctioned war on Black people.

THE THIN BLUE LINE . . . ARE BLACK MEN INCLUDED?

Black men who are police officers themselves, though they sometimes are the shooter, as was the case in the murder of Prince Jones, are also not immune to becoming the victims of this kind of violence. There are a surprising number of cases in which white police kill Black officers, perhaps because they see them as Black men first and police officers second.

Though police-on-police shootings are not all that common, they are seriously racialized. Black officers make up only 10 to 12 percent of all local police officers, yet in 90 percent of police-on-police shootings the victims are Black and the police shooter is white. Black officers are nine times more likely to be shot by fellow officers than their representation on police forces.

On May 28, 2009, in New York City, white police officer Andrew P. Dunton shot and killed twenty-three-year-old police officer Omar Edwards, who is Black.[16] Dunton has since been promoted to sergeant in the New York Police Department.[17] In Chicago, police officer Howard Morgan, who is Black, was shot twenty-eight times by four white police officers. On June 23, 2017, an off-duty police officer, who is Black, was shot by an on-duty officer who is white. "The officer, who lives near the site of the incident, first approached the North Pointe-area scene and was told to get on the ground. After complying with the on-duty cops' orders, *the off-duty officer was recognized and informed he could stand up. Once standing, the off-duty officer was shot.* . . . The off-duty cop, Tate added, identified himself upon arrival and complied with all commands. The white officer who shot him has argued that he 'feared for his safety.'"[18]

Policing Black bodies is "blind" in these cases, at least in the sense that it doesn't discriminate based on the status of the Black man who was killed. As was the case in nearly every police killing of an unarmed Black man, the officers who murdered other officers were never convicted for the crimes they committed.

As many Department of Justice reports have demonstrated, from Ferguson, Missouri, to Missoula, Montana, the culture of a police department is perhaps the most powerful force in shaping the specific ways that Black bodies are policed as well as the overall relationship between the police and the Black community.

In response to the police killing of Freddie Gray in Baltimore in April 2015, city leaders, Baltimore residents, and even the police department called for an investigation by the U.S. Department of Justice. The report, released in August 2016, coincidentally as we were writing this chapter, was scathing. Not only did the U.S. Department of Justice find racial bias, but they found gender bias as well, including evidence that the police department's response to sexual assault was termed "grossly inadequate." With regard to racial bias, the U.S. Department of Justice report identifies all of the same patterns that we see in other communities and in other research. Specifically, the research reported that Black residents were three times more likely to be stopped and frisked, that the vast majority of the time police officers stopped and frisked Black bodies without any suspicion or probable cause—they were fishing expeditions—and that police officers used excessive force, often after a suspect was detained and under the control of the arresting officer, which tended to escalate the violence and result in unnecessary injury and even death. One Black man was subjected to stop and frisk thirty times in four years!

One might say, well, this is good, police officers are proactively policing the city of Baltimore. In fact, as the report reveals, there is ample evidence that rather than getting people off the streets of Baltimore who are actually engaged in crime and making the city safer, the vast majority of the time the fishing expeditions yielded nothing. In the case of stop and frisk, conducted without suspicion or probable cause, only 3.7 percent of the police interventions resulted in identifying someone who had an out-standing warrant or was engaged in any criminal behavior. Confirming the research conducted by Epp, Maynard-Moody, and Haider-Markel, when conducting vehicle stops, despite stopping Black motorists many times more often than white motorists, white drivers who were stopped were 50 percent more likely to have illegal drugs than Black motorists. Though Blacks and whites use drugs at rates that are very similar, in Baltimore, police officers arrested Black bodies five times more often than whites for drug possession. Policing Black bodies.

> Racial disparities in BPD's [Baltimore Police Department's] arrests are most pronounced for highly discretionary offenses: African Americans accounted for 91 percent of the 1,800 people charged solely with "failure to obey" or "trespassing"; 89 percent of the 1,350 charges for making a false statement to an officer; and 84 percent of the 6,500 people arrested for "disorderly conduct." Moreover, booking officials and prosecutors decline charges brought against African Americans at significantly higher rates than charges against people of other races, indicating that officers' standards for making arrests differ by the race of the person arrested. [19]

These findings are not only incredibly troubling, but they reinforce what others have argued. Chris Hayes, as we detail in our discussion of mass incarceration, found the exact same patterns in Ferguson. And these findings provide the context for analyzing police shootings of unarmed Black men.

Perhaps Freddie Gray had reason to resist as police officers dragged him, fully handcuffed, into the paddy wagon where he would sustain lethal injuries. Perhaps he was being unfairly targeted, without suspicion or probable cause. Perhaps he had done nothing wrong. Perhaps he had experienced or witnessed fishing expeditions or police brutality. Is it any wonder that the streets of Baltimore erupted into violent riots after Fred-die Gray's death? It's not too far-fetched to speculate that many of those rioting in the streets had been subjected to fishing expeditions or been stopped and frisked for no good reason or been victims of excessive police force or been arrested for loitering. All of this is, in many ways, reminiscent of the Black Codes of the Jim Crow era. As if all of this isn't bad enough, one interpretation of the findings in the U.S. Department of Justice report is that the Baltimore Police Department is wasting resources by unnecessarily policing Black bodies, all the while claiming that the city does not have the money to pay the proposed $15 minimum wage. Perhaps the city could pay a living wage to Black and Brown laborers if they didn't waste so much money policing their bodies!

Redditt Hudson, in his insightful article, "I'm a Black Ex-Cop, and This Is the Real Truth about Race and Policing,"[20] published in the middle of that violent week in July 2016, provided an insider perspective on the culture of police departments and how a culture can shape the likelihood that police will engage in brutality against and even murder the Black bodies they police. Redditt argues that 15 percent of police officers will do the right thing all the time, 15 percent will abuse their authority every time they have the opportunity, and 70 percent could "go either way." Without any accountability for the abuse of authority by the 15 percent of officers who engage in brutality and violence, the lesson for the 70 percent who could "go either way" is that there are no consequences for engaging in brutality, violence, or even murder. Redditt goes on further to argue that in police departments that refuse to hold officers who abuse their authority accountable, a culture develops that is shaped primarily by the abusive 15 percent. As the poisonous culture becomes more deeply rooted in the department more and more of the 70 percent who could "go either way" engage in abuses of their own authority, they "become part of the problem." He describes one of the deepest cultures of abuse, the Chicago Police Department.

> About that 15 percent of officers who regularly abuse their power: a major problem is they exert an outsize influence on department culture and find support for their actions from ranking officers and police unions. Chicago is a prime example of this: the city has created a reparations fund for the hundreds of victims who were tortured by former Chicago Police Commander Jon Burge and officers under his command from the 1970s to the early '90s.
>
> The victims were electrically shocked, suffocated, and beaten into false confessions that resulted in many of them being convicted and serving time for crimes they didn't commit. One man, Darrell Cannon, spent 24 years in prison for a crime he confessed to but didn't commit. He confessed when officers repeatedly appeared to load a shotgun and after doing so each time put it in his mouth and pulled the trigger. Other men received electric shocks until they confessed.

The torture was systematic, and the culture that allowed for it is systemic. I call your attention to the words "and officers under his command." Police departments are generally a functioning closed community where people know who is doing what. How many officers "under the command" of Commander Burge do you think didn't know what was being done to these men? How many do you think were uncomfortable with the knowledge? Ultimately, though, they were okay with it. And Burge got four years in prison, and now receives his full taxpayer-funded pension.

Not only does the culture of the police department influence the ways that officers treat those they are stopping and frisking or those they catch in a fishing expedition, but as Redditt's blog points out, the culture of the police department can also include policies and protocols that encourage coercion and even torture in order to extract confessions, often from innocent people. In our next chapter we examine the ways in which these false confessions lead to innocent men going to prison, often for decades, for crimes they did not commit. It's quite interesting to note here that two of the counties that lead the United States for false confessions and wrongful convictions are Cook County, Illinois, where Chicago is located, and Dallas County, Texas.

The purpose of writing this book was to gather data to demonstrate our hunch that in communities where tensions between police and Black communities are high, we see *all of the policing practices* that we explore in this book: from riots to mass incarceration to a burgeoning school-to-prison pipeline to a disproportionate rate of wrongful convictions to, as we explore here, the shootings of unarmed Black men by the police. It should come as no surprise that Black Lives Matter "protestors took to the streets of Chicago in June 2017 after video of the 2014 shooting of Laquan McDonald was released. The video appears to show a police officer shooting McDonald, but the officer was indicted the week before the video was released." Not only was McDonald's murder—he was shot sixteen times in thirteen seconds as he ran away from the police—horrible to watch, but his murder was the straw that broke the back of Chicago's Black community, a Black community that has watched too many young Black men murdered, too many Black men locked up, and nearly one hundred Black men to date released after serving decades for crimes they did not commit, based largely on convictions that relied on confessions that were likely beaten out of them by Chicago police officers. The Black community in Chicago was ready, for good reason, to explode, and Laquan McDonald's murder was like setting a match to a tanker truck full of gasoline.

The belief that we are all equally policed renders invisible the facts and prevents us from addressing the causes of these tragedies. Policing Black bodies through the lens of "killology" results in lives lost, always prematurely, and often when the victims are still very young men. Tamir Rice was twelve. Trayvon Martin had just turned seventeen. While we wring our hands and scream about tighter gun control laws, which we endorse by the way; the lack of a clear analysis; the perpetuation of the belief that police murders of unarmed Black boys and men are simply the result of a few "bad apples"; and the refusal to name the factors that lead to these tragedies—racism, unconscious bias, racial profiling, and torturing out false confessions—means nothing less than the policing of Black bodies will continue, and more and more families will have to bury their sons, fathers, and partners.

One thing we found interesting and perplexing in writing this painful chapter was the regularity with which mayors, police chiefs, and officers themselves, in press conferences and at memorials and funerals, invoked a "we are one America" theme. We are not one America. As Chris Hayes argues, we are a colony in a nation, a colony ruled by a nation that endorses the state-sanctioned policing of Black bodies, removing them, by whatever means necessary, out of the mainstream so that white Americans can continue to live in a nation filled with exclusive access to the opportunity structure, all while believing the lie of the American Dream.

9

THE ULTIMATE FAILURE: EXONERATION

Imagine that you are eighteen or nineteen years old, or even twenty, and you have your whole life ahead of you; possibly you have a passion that you think you can translate into a paycheck or even a career. Maybe you already have your eye on a potential person you think you could settle down with and call yourselves a family, or maybe you are simply enjoying the freedom that so many of us enjoy in these short years between adolescence and adulthood. Imagine that in the blink of an eye all of your dreams and hopes come crashing down on top of you. Imagine that your worst nightmare has come true. Imagine that you are not only arrested but convicted of a crime you didn't commit. Imagine that you sit before a jury being called the most filthy and vile names—rapist, murderer—because the crime of which you are accused is so heinous. Imagine that you believed what you were taught, that the laws that give rights to defendants are there to prevent what is happening before your very eyes. Imagine that you stand before a judge who sentences you to spend the rest of your life in prison or, worse, to stand in line to be executed. If you are one of the nearly 1,500 men and women who have been exonerated at the time of this writing, you don't have to imagine. This is what happened to you.

The case of Darryl Hunt is, in the words of his attorney Mark Rabil, the quintessential southern crime: Darryl Hunt was a Black man who was accused of the rape and murder of a white woman, Mrs. Deborah Sykes. The case tore at the racial dividing line that is part of the history of Winston-Salem, North Carolina, just as it is in so many southern communities. The aftereffects of the case still reverberate in

Winston-Salem, and there is still much reconciliation and repair that needs to be done. But let's get to the story.

On August 11, 1984, a copy editor for the *Winston-Salem Sentinel*, an afternoon newspaper, twenty-six-year-old Deborah Brotherton Sykes was found brutally raped and murdered behind an apartment complex in downtown Winston-Salem. She had been raped and murdered on her way to work in the early morning hours. In September of 1984, Darryl Hunt, a nineteen-year-old Black man, was arrested and charged with the rape and murder. In June of 1985, Darryl Hunt was tried and convicted of rape and first-degree murder. He was sentenced to life in prison.

From the moment Mr. Hunt was arrested, a handful of local residents who were convinced from the very beginning of his innocence banded together to advocate for Mr. Hunt. Finally, after Mr. Hunt had spent nearly twenty years in prison, an investigative journalist at the local newspaper, the *Winston-Salem Journal*, began what turned out to be a nearly yearlong investigation that culminated in an eight-part series that ran in December 2005.[1] Based on her work and some other breaks that had come in the case—including Mr. Hunt's attorney, Mark Rabil, who was able to secure a DNA test not only of Mr. Hunt but also of another man who they suspected was the real perpetrator— nearly two decades after his conviction, on Christmas Eve 2005, Mr. Hunt was released from prison, and in February 2006 he was exonerated, making him the 150th person to be exonerated. Sadly, fewer than ten years after regaining his freedom and working to rebuild his life, Mr. Hunt took his own life. In the words of his attorney, Mr. Hunt's death sentence was finally executed.

The main reason that we know so little about false convictions is that, by definition, they are hidden from view.[2]

As we were analyzing the data for this chapter in the summer of 2016, we were reminded that one of the hot spots for police brutality is the city of Chicago in Cook County, Illinois.[3] Cook County is also the home to more exonerations—produced by wrongful convictions—*than any other county in the United States*. To put this into perspective, Cook County has three times the number of exonerations (ninety-six) compared to New York City (thirty-two), which has a population of twenty million, or nearly ten times that of Cook County. In this chapter we extend our interrogation to yet another form of policing Black bodies, locking up Black men for decades for crimes they didn't commit, depriving them of not just their freedom but their opportunity to do the things that people do in their early twenties: start a career, start a family, build a life. These men will never get these opportunities back. And though there are specific causes of wrongful convictions that we will explore here, the overall context in which wrongful convictions take place is no different than the brew that produces riots, the shooting of unarmed Black men, mass incarceration, and other mechanisms for policing Black bodies. Therefore, it should not be at all surprising that cities like Chicago, Los Angeles, and New York, which lead the country in locking up Black men and shooting unarmed Black men, cities that have weathered the destruction of riots, also lead the nation in wrongful convictions. Thankfully, for a variety of reasons, they also lead the nation in exonerating those whose bodies they locked up wrongfully for decades.

WHAT IS AN EXONERATION, ANYWAY?

An exoneration is a unique status in the criminal justice system; quite simply it refers to a case in which a person who has been convicted of a crime is later proved to be innocent of that crime. Exoneration is reserved for those people who were "factually innocent" but who despite their actual innocence were wrongly convicted of a crime and served time in prison. In other words, as our friend and exoneree Darryl Hunt was fond of saying, an exoneration "is not a technicality: I was convicted of strong armed robbery but I actually only committed armed robbery. An exoneration means I wasn't anywhere near the crime. I had nothing to do with the crime. I'm completely, factually, innocent."

After all the years we have been studying incarceration and the criminal justice system, we should not be at all surprised that exonerations are controversial, but we are. If we believe that the criminal justice system we have set up in our representative democracy is designed to seek the truth, then any hint that we have gotten it wrong should result in a full deployment of all the resources necessary in order to make it right. And yet, in nearly every exoneration we are aware of, and we've read hundreds of cases, wrongfully convicted and incarcerated people face a steep uphill climb just to get the chance to prove their innocence. Prosecutors fight the admission of new evidence, even when *they withheld exculpatory evidence that could have proved the defendant's innocence.* U.S. Supreme Court justices have even inserted themselves into the debate. The U.S. Supreme Court ruled that those convicted of a crime do not have a constitutional right to have their DNA tested, one of the most common routes to proving one's innocence, even in death penalty cases. Justices Thomas and Scalia have argued, for example, that if one has been duly convicted, and especially if there have been appeals, as is always the case in death penalty cases, one has been provided all of the opportunities to prove one's innocence, and if despite being able to access all of these tools for proving one's innocence a judge and/or jury ruled to convict, then the conviction should stand and the convicted person has *no constitutional right to have a DNA test done* if and when new evidence becomes available. Before we execute someone, wouldn't we want to be absolutely sure we got it right?! A 2014 study by the National Academy of Sciences[4] predicts that one in twenty-five people on death row are innocent. In other words, for every one hundred people we execute, four were innocent. Is that a statistic we can live with, especially in light of the Supreme Court ruling?

The DNA ruling is also important because in many of the cases in which men (almost all exonerees are men) are seeking to prove their innocence, the crime took place before the development of the sophisticated DNA analysis that is available today. Darryl Hunt's case is an example of this. When Deborah Sykes was murdered and forensic evidence was collected, the most sophisticated analysis that could be conducted was blood type analysis. After DNA analysis became available, many exonerees, including Darryl, sought court orders to have the forensic evidence tested. DNA is one of the strongest tools that prosecutors and defendants have in identifying the actual perpetrator of the crime. Thus, the U.S. Supreme Court ruling that denies postconviction DNA testing is a clear statement by the highest court in the land that it is not concerned about ensuring a criminal justice system that works for all. The bodies of the incarcerated do not matter. Policing Black bodies.

As of the time of this writing, in the summer of 2016, more than two thousand individuals have been exonerated in the United States. This is a number that is constantly in a state of flux as more and more individuals are granted the tools and the opportunity to gain their freedom. Thus, for the interested reader, we recommend monitoring the website of the Innocence Project[5] for the most up-to-date count of exonerations.

Scientifically speaking, we don't know how many people there are sitting in our jails and prisons who are factually innocent, primarily because there is no systematic way of gaining an exoneration; they are, in the words of some scholars, accidental. But typically exonerations result from the dedicated work of attorneys like Mark Rabil, Darryl Hunt's attorney, who believe their client is innocent; investigative journalists who pay attention to serious inconsistencies in the evidence, as was also the case with Darryl Hunt's exoneration; and often the inmate's own efforts, like Ronald Cotton, who do their own detective and legal work in order to prove their innocence. Many but not all of these cases finally catch the attention of the Innocence Project, whose mission is to find and free wrongly convicted, innocent people who rot for decades in America's prisons. Innocence Project lawyers and law students commit thousands of hours each year, pro bono, to help free the wrongfully convicted.

Because the cases are handled on an individual basis, it is hard to estimate, but some experts suggest that as many as 6 percent of our incarcerated population is actually innocent. If that statistic is accurate, of the 2.2 million people who are currently incarcerated, as many as 140,000 may be factually innocent, serving decades in prison for crimes they did not commit.

EXONERATION: THE ROLE OF DNA IN SHAPING EXONERATIONS

We cannot underestimate the impact of the role that the science of DNA has played in the more than two thousand exonerations that have been granted. One the exonerees we work closely with, Kirk Bloodsworth, was the first person exonerated from death row as a result of DNA evidence. Darryl Hunt's exoneration, whose case opens this chapter, involved many factors, but DNA was the evidence that finally led to his freedom. Kirk Bloodsworth talks about watching the *Phil Donahue Show* in the early 1990s from his jail cell in the Maryland prison system where he was on death row, having been convicted of the rape and murder of nine-year-old Dawn Hamilton. He recalls that he was not the only inmate watching the *Phil Donahue Show* that day to make the connection between this new scientific protocol that could map the unique DNA of every individual with only a small sample of blood, hair, or semen and the possibility of proving one's innocence.

For all of the power that DNA holds for many innocent people seeking to prove their innocence, either as a defendant or as one of the thousands of innocent people who are already locked up, rotting away in prison, DNA is only one important tool that innocent people can utilize in order to prove their innocence and be granted an exoneration. In fact, DNA data tip the scale for the innocent in only 10 percent of all exoneration cases.

Exonerations are a fascinating case study for sociologists because they involve all of the elements that sociologists study—race, gender, social class—and the criminal justice system. More specifically, as we shall see, the intersectional nature of the phenomenon makes exonerations a nearly perfect test of intersectional theory. Exonerations require discussions of power and relationality, not to mention social justice. The typical person who is wrongly convicted of a crime has very little power in a system that is stacked against them. Police, prosecutors, and even judges often collude, more interested in locking up another Black man than in seeking justice. Ironically, many sociologists claim that they use intersectional theory, that their work focuses on "race, class, and gender," but they shy away from analyzing exonerations, perhaps because of the invisibility of prisons and of exonerations in particular, or perhaps because they wrongly assume that the system of justice works. What is clear is that Patricia Hill Collins's call to social action throws the door wide open for researchers whose work could be harnessed to assist the thousands of people wrongly convicted and sentenced to spend arguably the best years of their lives locked so far away from public view that they are, by and large, totally forgotten.

We published our first piece of research on exoneration in 2010, and we continue to be amazed by the fact that sociologists give almost no attention to this fascinating and tragic social problem. The vast majority of research on exonerations is conducted by law professors and published in law reviews. And, as useful as their research is, and we certainly owe a debt to our law colleagues, they ask different kinds of questions than we do. They are interested primarily in the causes of exoneration, which we will address here as well, but not so much in the patterns of exoneration—who is exonerated, what types of crimes lead to wrongful convictions, and who are the victims. In order to answer these questions, we built a unique data set using a variety of sources, including data provided by the Innocence Project (New York City), data from University of Virginia professor Brandon L. Garrett,[6] data from the Centurion Ministries, and finally data from the National Registry of Exonerations at the University of Michigan Law School.

Additionally, we scoured the profiles of exonerees and searched the local newspapers where the crimes had originally occurred for any additional data, particularly data on the race of the victim, which was often not reported in the case summary published by the Innocence Project or contained in other data sources. Because exonerations continued to occur throughout the time we've been writing this book and will continue long after it is published, we hope, we made the decision to "close" the data collection at the end of 2014, which gave us time to construct the database and perform analysis. Our database contains 1,358 cases.

WHO IS EXONERATED?

Part of what is interesting and perplexing about exonerations is the fact that the population of exonerees is distinctly different from the population of prisoners.

For example, though women make up 10 percent of the prison population, there are only a handful of women among the exonerees. This makes sense because the vast majority of exonerations are for murder, rape, and sexual assault, crimes *rarely* committed by women.

Despite being overrepresented in the prison population, Black men are *even more overrepresented in the population of those exonerated.* Six hundred twenty-nine, or 46 percent, of the exonerees in our database are Black men, 40 percent are white, and the remainder are Hispanic men (11 percent). Policing Black bodies.

When it comes to death row exonerations, the numbers are staggering. Of the 159 men exonerated from death row, eighty-four (52 percent) are Black. It is terrifying to think that 159 *innocent men we know of* were on a time line for execution. And, not surprising, Black men's bodies are disproportionately represented among those sentenced to die. Policing Black bodies.

WHO IS THE VICTIM?

Exonerations are interesting not only because of the racial patterns of who is wrongfully convicted and ultimately exonerated, but also in who the victim is. Whereas Black men are more likely to have their bodies wrongly policed, sending innocent Black men to prison, often for decades, for crimes they did not commit, Black bodies are also *less valuable* when it comes to seeking justice. Despite the fact that Black people are vastly overrepresented among the victims of homicide, for example, they are underrepresented among the victims in cases of wrongful conviction and exoneration. Blacks are 43 percent of murder victims, but they are the victims in only 30 percent of exoneration cases. In the majority of cases, 57 percent, the victims in exoneration cases are white.

THE CRIME

Perhaps what is most interesting about exonerations is that they cluster in cases that are otherwise extremely uncommon. Unfortunately, when we built our data set we were not always able to confirm the race of both the victim of the crime and the person exonerated. We speculate that there are at least two reasons for this. First, if most of the research is conducted by legal scholars who are less interested in racial patterns than the facts of the case, they may not report the race of the victim in the case summaries and databases that they develop. Second, in cases of rape where the victim is not murdered, rape shield laws protect the identity of the victim, including her name and her race. Thus, in many cases where we had the race of the exoneree, we often had difficulty identifying the race of the victim. As a result, when we examined the clustering of exonerations that focused on the interaction between the race of the victim and the race of the exoneree, we have a smaller number of cases, 504, to analyze, which is a statistically meaningful sample size, especially for such a relatively rare phenomenon, a total of only 1,358 total cases with which to work.

Though most crimes are intraracial, especially violent crimes like murder and rape, the vast majority of exonerations occur in cases of interracial crime. Even more troubling is that there is one particular interracial configuration that is disproportionately represented among exonerations: despite the fact that Black men murdering white victims account for only 7 percent of all homicides, they account for 56 percent of all exonerations. Drilling down even further, exonerations follow a pattern that is *exactly the opposite* of the pattern of actual crimes that are committed. Black men commit only 16 percent of the rapes perpetrated against white women's bodies, yet the rape and/or murder of a white woman by a Black man is the *most common* crime for which there are wrongful convictions and subsequent exonerations. A crime that rarely occurs accounts for the majority (87 percent) of the exonerations we examined. In other words, *Black men are four times more likely to be exonerated for raping white women compared to the number of times they actually commit this crime.* Policing Black bodies.

This clustering of exonerations confirms the research of other scholars, which reveals that when death penalty cases are analyzed, the most common case in which a death sentence is handed down is the murder of a white person by a Black man. Black bodies are policed both as victims and as offenders. Black bodies *are always valued less*. When Black people perpetrate crimes, it is comparatively easier to send them to the death chamber, and when Black bodies are the victim of violent crime, the perpetrator is held "less" accountable, as if to say a violent crime perpetrated on a Black body is somehow less serious than a violent crime perpetrated against a white body. When Black people kill other Black people, there is often no investigation at all, the assumption often being that the homicide is gang related or that the Black person's life is not important enough to investigate or that the Black person won't even be missed.

WHAT FACTORS CAUSE THE KINDS OF WRONGFUL CONVICTIONS THAT END IN EXONERATION?

In the United States, Lady Justice wears racialized glasses in which the bodies of Black people and white people are policed differently, whether in stop-and-frisk practices, sentencing those found guilty of crime, or, as in the case we are interrogating here, adjudicating some of the most heinous crimes that occur in our society: rape and murder. The policing of Black bodies by devaluing them.

Wrongful convictions are not the result of random mistakes. In fact, they are created by deliberate actions by prosecutors and police officers as well as by "mistakes" by witnesses that are deeply rooted in the kinds of stereotypes white people have about Black bodies, the same kinds of stereotypes we uncovered and illuminated in our interrogation of police shootings of unarmed Black men. In short, if Black men are stereotyped as violent criminals just waiting to commit crimes, then in some ways, from the perspective of many who inhabit white America, both individually and collectively, it doesn't really matter which Black man is locked up when a brutal crime is committed; identifying a Black man to hold accountable seems to be more important than being sure that we are holding the *right* Black man responsible. Wrongfully policing Black bodies.

How do we know this? We were living in Winston-Salem, North Carolina, at the time of Darryl Hunt's release and exoneration. We got to know him, we became friends, and we worked together to identify and advocate for the wrongly convicted as well as to develop a reentry program, the Darryl Hunt Project for Freedom and Justice, that provided support for citizens reentering after a felony conviction as they attempted to get their lives back on track after periods of incarceration. We followed Darryl Hunt's case closely and in real time. One of the most troubling public responses to his initial release from prison was the number of Winston-Salem residents who had been polled by the local newspaper, the *Winston-Salem Journal*, who indicated that he should not be released from prison despite evidence that clearly exonerated him because "he must have done something." In other words, perhaps he did not brutally rape and murder Deborah Sykes, but he must have done something, despite never having been arrested or convicted of another crime, and therefore he not only deserved to but should remain in prison. What?! This echoes the sentiment when police shoot or otherwise murder unarmed Black men: Well, it's too bad that Michael Brown or Trayvon Martin or Freddie Gray or Eric Garner is dead, but they must have done something wrong to have been treated this way by the police. Their death is defined as of less concern. The policing of Black bodies by devaluing them.

But here's the other problem when we get it wrong. When we get it wrong, not only do we send the wrong person to prison, often for decades, but we leave the real perpetrator on the street. And when we leave the real perpetrator on the street, he typically goes on to commit more crimes, as did the real person who brutally raped and murdered Deborah Sykes in 1984, Willard Brown. In fact, when the investigative reporter at the *Winston-Salem Journal* began to dig into the Darryl Hunt case, one of the first things that struck her was that at least two other rapes were perpetrated not long after Deborah Sykes was murdered, and the motive appeared to be the same. The only difference was that the other women Willard Brown raped were spared their lives. But Brown left his DNA, and that was the first indicator that perhaps Darryl Hunt was innocent.

One of the interesting things about exonerations is that they almost always involve a heinous crime—rape or murder—of a white body, and so they tend to receive extensive police work. So, how do the wrong people actually get convicted when the police are doing their jobs? Based on analyzing 1,358 exonerations, we have identified three main causes of wrongful convictions that lead to exonerations: (1) eyewitness accounts that are faulty, (2) prosecutors who engage in misconduct in order to secure a conviction, and (3) false confessions that are often coerced from defendants.

THE FALLIBILITY OF EYEWITNESS TESTIMONY

As the research of others has documented, in 70 percent of the exonerations cataloged by the Innocence Project, the conviction hinged on eyewitness testimony that was later documented to be faulty. What's particularly interesting about eyewitness testimony is that it is commonly believed that such testimony is among the *most reliable* of all evidence. If I saw it with my own eyes, it must be true. It is also commonly believed that our memory of details is heightened rather than diminished during a stressful situation, like witnessing or being the victim of a crime. We hear crime victims all the time report that they deliberately focused on the details, what the suspect looked like and what he wore, committing his license plate number to memory, and so on so that they could provide testimony to the police. And yet, as it turns out, the *research* on eyewitness testimony tells a different story.

Psychologists have demonstrated using experimental designs[7] that even in low-stress situations with relatively long exposures to the "target," eyewitness accounts are ridiculously unreliable. Additionally, psychologists have performed experiments in which they document that cross-race identifications are *significantly* harder to make than same-race identifications.[8] This holds even when researchers' experiments include photos of high-profile individuals, including actors and professional athletes. All of this research is important precisely because the vast majority of exoneration cases involve a white victim who *misidentifies* a Black man. But rarely are these experimental data or experts on the reliability of eyewitness testimony allowed into the defense case. Perhaps judges and courts should be more open-minded about the reliability of scientific evidence.

Added to the difficulty we all have in forming accurate eyewitness memories when we are witnesses or victims in criminal cases, there are also a host of specific problems that apply primarily in the criminal justice setting—namely, the power that police and prosecutors have to influence memory.

The memoir, *Picking Cotton* cowritten by exoneree Ronald Cotton and the victim in the case, Jennifer Cannino-Thompson, details the factors that resulted in Caninno-Thompson wrongly identifying Cotton and testifying against him in court. Ronald Cotton spent more than ten years in prison before he was ultimately exonerated. Though this case may seem bizarre, in fact, the elements are incredibly common.

Ironically, the same summer that Deborah Sykes was brutally raped and murdered in Winston-Salem, North Carolina, and Darryl Hunt found himself ensnared in the racist criminal justice system, Jennifer Caninno was brutally raped just up the road in Burlington, North Carolina. And like that, as with Hunt, Ronald Cotton's journey toward hell was set in motion. In sum, when detectives in the case showed Jennifer Caninno-Thompson a picture of Ronald Cotton as part of a photo lineup, Caninno-Thompson initially identified Cotton's picture. The detective in the case who was administering the lineup reinforced her selection by saying, "We thought so. We thought this was him." Based on this initial identification, Caninno-Thompson was presented with a physical lineup that included Cotton. She identified him again as her rapist, and based on these identifications and her testimony in court, Cotton was sentenced to fifty years to life in prison; ultimately he served ten years before securing his exoneration.

In direct response to the cases of both Ronald Cotton and Darryl Hunt, the photo lineup process used at that time was determined to be so deeply flawed that, in fact, it is now illegal and has been replaced by a significantly revised protocol. Quite simply, detectives must show witnesses one photo at a time rather than a composite sheet that includes pictures of several suspects that the victim views at the same time. Based on flaws in the Darryl Hunt case, in which the eyewitnesses were shown a series of pictures, all mug shots, except Darryl's photograph, which was a color photo, all of the photos must be the same, all in color or all black and white, all close-ups or all "whole body" photos. And investigators are prohibited from giving the witness any feedback like "That's what we thought."

Psychologists who study memory note that when a memory is reinforced with both an image such as a picture and verbal confirmation, an individual will begin to replace the original images in their memory with the image in the photo. As a result of the confirmation that the detective provided to the victim, Jennifer Caninno-Thompson, the image she held of the man who raped her became the image in the photo, and this revision to her memory clearly influenced the identification she made in the in-person lineup. When we've had the chance to meet and talk with Jennifer, she not only confirms this process of memory manipulation, but she goes one step further. Today, three decades after she participated in and contributed to Ronald Cotton's exoneration, and despite the fact that she knows the name and the face of the man who really raped her that summer day in 1984, Bobby Poole, when she has nightmares of that terrible night, she says that she still sees Ronald Cotton's face.

PROSECUTORIAL MISCONDUCT

One of the most common causes of wrongful conviction, and perhaps one of the most insidious and troubling, falls under the umbrella term "prosecutorial misconduct." Some of the specific actions that fall under this umbrella term have been identified by the Innocence Project of New York City, including withholding exculpatory evidence from the defense; deliberately mishandling, mistreating, or destroying evidence; allowing witnesses they know or should know are not truthful to testify; pressuring defense witnesses not to testify; relying on fraudulent forensic experts; and making misleading arguments that overstate the probative value of testimony. The most common type of prosecutorial misconduct identified by the Innocence Project was improper argument, or knowingly eliciting evidence from witnesses on the stand that is actually inadmissible, mis-stating the law, vouching for or otherwise misrepresenting the testimony of experts, intimidating witnesses, and even presenting false evidence.

Though it's possible that instances of prosecutorial misconduct are accidental, we agree with scholars and activists who argue that in the vast majority of cases, prosecutorial misconduct is deliberate and intentional. Research by the Innocence Project found that many prosecutors' offices had multiple cases of prosecutorial misconduct, often perpetrated by the *same prosecutors*. This finding led us to examine the geographic clustering of exonerations, a point to which we will return later.

In cases of prosecutorial misconduct, the prosecutor may, for example, advance a theory of the crime that is absolutely unreasonable or call on experts to testify about evidence that science has proven unreliable. Television shows like *Forensic Files* routinely depict instances of prosecutorial misconduct. It is hard to know how many people are incarcerated based on forensics like hair and teeth identification, which experts now totally discredit, or, as was common in the 1980s and early 1990s, how many prosecutors, including the prosecutor in Darryl Hunt's case, have argued something that seems unbelievable now. During Darryl's second trial in 1994 when DNA analysis first became available and the tests came back and excluded Darryl Hunt as a possible rapist and murderer of Deborah Sykes, the prosecutor argued to the jury that DNA was "junk science." Without an educated jury or a vigorous counterargument by the defense attorney, prosecutors' misconduct can put people in prison for crimes they did not commit.

We certainly don't want anyone to believe that misconduct is limited to prosecutors. Legal scholars and prison reform advocates don't focus much on defense attorney misconduct because it doesn't lead to wrongful convictions, but we should be concerned about it, both because it results in guilty people not being held accountable—they are free to commit more crime—and because it signifies the terrible flaws in a criminal justice system that we are all led to believe is fair and is designed to seek justice above all.

Jon Krakauer, as reported in his 2015 book *Missoula: Rape and the Justice System in a College Town*, conducted a thorough and in-depth examination of rape cases in Missoula, Montana, in an attempt to understand what appeared to be a systematic pattern of inconsistent and often preferential treatment of suspects, especially Missoula football players, accused of rape. His analysis provides us with a framework for better understanding the ways in which wrongful convictions and the exonerations that arise from them can be traced to systematic misapplications of justice. Indeed, the entire criminal justice system is designed in ways that disadvantage both prosecutors and defense attorneys, albeit differently, but nevertheless in ways that rarely produce justice or even seek the truth.

As we demonstrate in the cases we have selected for this chapter, one of the many reasons we see so many exonerations is a result of the "simple" fact that for decades (and even today) in most jurisdictions, prosecutors' major concern is not so much seeking justice, getting it "right," but rather getting a conviction, which allows them to look "tough on crime" and reassure community members that they are safe, which will cast prosecutors in a favorable light when they seek reelection or reappointment. Prosecutors who were "tough on crime" in the 1980s, perhaps partially in response to the War on Drugs and the perception that crime rates were rising, focused more on getting a conviction than on getting it right. Decades later, after DNA analysis became common and investigative journalists have the time to do extensive research, a backlog of wrongful convictions are winding their way through exoneration hearings, and as a result, exonerations have grown exponentially, quadrupling since 2007 when we began studying them.

And of course the same tactics are employed by defense attorneys who fill their coffers by developing reputations for getting defendants off. Need we point to the "dream team" O. J. Simpson assembled or the gifted defense attorney Mark O'Mara who many believe was the key to George Zimmerman's acquittal of the murder of Trayvon Martin? As Krakauer discovered in his research, defense attorneys in rape cases routinely referred to victims' sexual practices, which is not admissible, but once heard by the jurors, even if objected to, can never be unheard. If exonerations teach us anything it's that our criminal justice system is deeply flawed, and in most cases, those with the most resources win: defendants who can afford the most expensive defense team or prosecutors' offices who try poor, uneducated people, dependent upon the defense of public defenders. Justice is rarely served.

THE FALSE CONFESSION

While it's hard for most of us to understand why someone would agree that they committed a crime they did not commit, according to the Innocence Project, upward of 25 percent of those exonerated had originally presented a false confession or confessed to a crime they did not commit.[9] Much like the commonsense belief about eyewitness testimony, jurors generally put a great deal of stock into a confession. If someone confesses to a crime, then they must have done it. Otherwise why would they confess? It's not hard to imagine, then, that police, detectives, and prosecutors will go to great, even illegal lengths to obtain a confession.

False confessions fall into three categories: confessions that are given voluntarily; confessions that are coerced, typically during the police interrogation; and confessions that are given when the person starts to actually believe they committed the crime. How do these three types of false confessions occur? False confessions are the result of two different sets of factors, individual factors and police techniques.

In a fair number of cases, false confessions were obtained from individuals who were unable to fully understand the police interrogation. For example, false confessions have been obtained from juveniles who lacked the intellectual development to distinguish between the hypothetical and the actual as well as adults with diminished capacity or mental impairment, who, like the juveniles, cannot distinguish a story a police officer is painting from the truth. In many of the cases we researched, the scenario unfolds this way. The police officer or detective who is interrogating the suspect asks, "If you were to commit this crime, how would you do it?" The suspect then describes a scenario. The officer then reads the scenario back to the suspect and suggests that, in fact, this is exactly what happened, that it's not hypothetical but actually reflects the facts, including the suspect's true behavior.

Confused by the difference between the hypothetical scenario and reality, juveniles and those with diminished capacity will then agree to the details of the scenario, and the officer will claim that this was a "confession" he or she took from the suspect. A similar variant of this involves telling the suspect all of the details of the crime, offering to write them down, coaching the suspect in what might have happened, and then coercing the subject to "confess" to what the police officer or detective, not the suspect, transcribed.

The second class of false confessions involves people who are not of diminished capacity but who are convinced by *legal* interrogation tactics that it is in their best interests to confess. There are so many variants of these that we illustrate with just a few examples. One common scenario is to interrogate a suspect, usually one who is young or who has never been involved in the criminal justice system before, for hours, denying them an opportunity to rest, go to the bathroom, or have anything to eat or drink. After hours of being detained, the suspect is then told that if he or she will simply tell the officer what happened, he or she will be allowed to go home, call a lawyer, or call their parents. Suspects interrogated in this way report that sleep deprivation and hunger will lead them to admit to anything just so they can go home, especially when the officer has convinced them that by confessing the court will go easy on them.

Another common scenario involves feeding the individual false information, such as telling a suspect that they have found their DNA at the scene of the crime, forcing them to believe they have actually committed the crime. Exonerees who are "tricked" this way relieve the dissonance between what they think they know, or more likely don't know, and the "evidence" presented by the police officer by constructing rational explanations such as a blackout or memory loss. These cases are especially difficult for exonerees because for a period of time they actually convince themselves they have committed some horrible crime, including one exoneree who was falsely led to believe he had killed his parents.

We were surprised to learn that many of the tactics we see on shows like *Special Victims Unit* (*SVU*) are in fact legal. For example, it is perfectly legal and not uncommon for detectives and prosecutors to confront defendants with evidence they know is false in order to get a confession. Exonerees we have talked with told us that detectives confronted them in interrogation rooms and told them that they had evidence, including DNA evidence, that put them at the scene of a crime. Though it might seem unusual that someone could be convinced that their DNA was at a crime scene where they had never been, it's not all that uncommon for people being interrogated under intense, stressful circumstances to admit to things that they know they didn't do or to agree to things that are not true simply so they can get some food or go home. This is especially common when defendants are young, uneducated, or even intellectually challenged. Does it come as any surprise that an unusually high percentage of exonerees have low IQs?

OK, we had a very hard time believing this as well, until one of the authors, Hattery, had an experience that replicated just a minor version of this type of interrogation. We have a neighbor who works in the Pentagon. She told us that regular citizens can take a tour of the Pentagon. That sounded pretty cool, so we filled out the requisite forms, submitted them online, and waited to be approved for our tour date. The day finally came, and as we prepared for the tour our neighbor suggested that after the formal tour was over, we could text her and she would meet us and give us the "behind the scenes tour," even eating lunch in the executive dining room, where we might spy a general or even Secretary of State Hillary Clinton. Who could turn this down? When the public tour ended, we texted our neighbor, and she met us at a security checkpoint not that different from what we routinely see at airports. Smith went through the checkpoint first, and things went just fine. Now he and the neighbor were waiting on the other side for Hattery. Well, Hattery approached the checkpoint, pulled out her driver's license, and was asked by a soldier holstering both a pistol and a rifle for her social security number. Hattery's mind went completely blank. He asked her if she wanted a piece of paper to write down her social security number in an attempt to jog her memory. As she looked at the piece of paper, all she could see were the snipers on the second floor and the man in front of her with the guns. She drew a complete blank, not even able to remember how many digits her social security number had. Attempting to write it down didn't help. Finally, after apologizing, after our neighbor vouched for Hattery, the soldier gave Hattery a stern scolding, telling her to "never do that again" and let her through. As soon as she passed through the gates, of course she remembered her social security number, all nine digits! We have reflected on this experience often. We are adults, both with PhDs; we are solidly in the professional class; we have testified in court as experts in intimate partner violence cases; and yet, in this moment that would rank as only a 1 on the intimidation scale compared to what many suspects experience—arrested "out of the blue," handcuffed, in an interrogation room, often for hours and hours with no food, no phone call, and in many cases with limited intellectual or educational capacity—and that was enough for Hattery to forget one of the most memorable parts of her identity. Think of how many times we spout off our social security numbers, at least the last four digits, to access banking, when we fill out our taxes, when we apply for jobs. If that minimally intimidating context can lead one with a great deal of privilege to forget something so simple, imagine what happens to an eighteen-year-old Black man, arrested for no reason he can identify, who didn't finish high school, who has been in the interrogation room for eight or ten hours without any food or a phone call, with no lawyer, who is told that his DNA was recovered at the scene, and if only he admits to it he can get some food and go home.

Based on the testimony of exonerees, both those whom we have interviewed and those whose accounts are captured in documentaries or case studies we've examined, another contributing factor to false confessions, especially those that are extracted in extreme and intimidating circumstances, is, sadly, the (false) belief that the criminal justice system is just. One thing all exonerees share in common is that they did not commit the crime. So solid is their belief in the fairness of the criminal justice system that they trusted that even if they gave a false confession in order to end the interrogation, get some food, call their parents, and go home, it would all be straightened out the next day when they had a lawyer and the police had more accurate information or evidence gleaned from their continued investigation of the crime. They never in a million years believed that the mistruths they told, unintentionally or after coercion, in the intimidating context of the interrogation room would ever lead to them facing charges, and certainly they never believed they would find themselves defending themselves in a court of law. And this is not so hard to believe, because for the vast majority of Americans who have never seen the criminal justice system up close, we have been told that the criminal justice system is just, that it is rooted in the pursuit of justice. Who of us would believe that any misunderstanding, a confession based entirely on a lie, on false information, on intimidation tactics, would not be cleared up the next day? The painful lessons that the thousands of wrongfully convicted have learned is that the criminal justice system is not designed to seek the truth, and once you "confess" to a crime, the most "believable" evidence a prosecutor can present, you might as well prepare for prison, because that is where you will be going. No juror will ever believe that your confession was false. Instead, you will be looked at as someone trying to backpedal and lie your way out of being guilty. Ironic, isn't it?

THE CASE OF THE CENTRAL PARK JOGGER

Sarah Burns's 2011 documentary *The Central Park Five*[10] captures the nuances of one of the most infamous cases that illustrates two of the leading contributors to wrongful convictions: prosecutors who break the law to get a conviction and false confessions that are coerced from defendants who are young, not particularly well educated, and interrogated for hours without food or the chance to call their parents.

On April 19, 1989, around nine o'clock at night in New York City's Central Park, Trisha Meili, a twenty-eight-year-old white female investment banker at the financial firm of Salomon Brothers was brutally beaten, raped, sodomized, and left for dead.

For several weeks after the assault, as Trisha Meili lay in a coma from a loss of blood, having her head bashed in, suffering from hypothermia, and having her left eye removed from the socket, New York City police conducted their investigation of the crime and initially identified six suspects (later reduced to five) who had been in the park on April 19.

Five teenagers—Antron McCray, Kevin Richardson, Raymond Santana, Kharey Wise, and Yusef Salaam—were arrested, and soon thereafter four, except for Salaam, *confessed to committing the crime*. The careful work of Sarah Burns's documentary reveals all of the patterns that we write about here. The young men, though they had been around Central Park that night, were nowhere near the actual scene of the crime, so their arrests seemed to them to come "out of the blue." These high school kids were detained and interrogated for hours. Hungry and eager to call their parents so that they could go home, and *believing* that all would be straightened out the next day, they succumbed to the strategies we described: they were coerced into making a confession. As documented on film, several of the young men sat with a detective who wrote out a possible scenario, asked the young men if it seemed like a reasonable explanation, and convinced them, by offering them food and a phone call to their parents, to sign what was later submitted in court as a confession.

Despite no concrete evidence connecting the youth to the crime, the emergence of doubts by those associated with the case, a lack of forensic evidence, and contradictory eyewitness accounts, the police and prosecutors continued to pursue the prosecution of these *innocent* young Black men.

Today, even journalists who were at the time convinced that the "wilding" taking place in Central Park on the night of April 19, 1989, was the prelude to the rape and attempted murder perpetrated by the hands of these Black and Hispanic youth, ultimately they changed their stories. Jim Dwyer of the *New York Times*, reflecting on the case, says, "Wish I had been more skeptical as a journalist. You know, a lot of people didn't do their jobs, reporters, police, prosecutors, defense lawyers. . . . This was a proxy war being fought, and these young men were the proxies for all kinds of other agendas. And the truth and the reality and justice were not part of it."[11]

Interesting. It sounds a bit like Ehrlichman's revelation, that the War on Drugs was really a War on Black people. Police and prosecutors in New York City bought into the stereotype that all Black and Hispanic young men were criminals in the making, and therefore, even if you convicted the wrong Black teenager in a particular case, you probably saved another person from becoming his next victim. Policing Black bodies.

And in the case of the Central Park jogger, much like the murder of Deborah Sykes in Winston-Salem, there was tremendous pressure on the police to make an arrest. Of lesser importance was getting it right.

Like most cases in which eyewitnesses misidentify suspects or in which prosecutors conduct their business in ways that are at best unprofessional and at worst unethical, the real perpetrators remain free to continue to ravage innocent people.

The real perpetrator, the lone rapist in the case of the Central Park jogger, remained free for several years. In 2002, while in prison for other unrelated crimes, convicted serial rapist and murderer Matias Reyes, a Puerto-Rican-born man serving a life sentence for other crimes, confessed to being the Central Park rapist.

Antron McCray, Kevin Richardson, Raymond Santana, Kharey Wise, and Yusef Salaam were exonerated in 2002.

Not long after Darryl Hunt was exonerated, another man, Joseph Abbott, was also exonerated from the same county, Forsyth County, North Carolina. A third man, Kalvin Michael Smith, who was convicted in the 1980s, also in Forsyth County, has been released from prison, though he has not yet been exonerated, and has a strong cadre of supporters who advocate that he was wrongfully incarcerated. What are the odds, we wondered, of three men being wrongfully convicted in a county of fewer

than a million people? The more we were able to confirm with data that
the practices that produce wrongful convictions occur in systemic patterns, we began to wonder if there were in fact corrupt prosecutors and
prosecutors' offices that routinely engaged in practices that produced a
disproportionate number of wrongful convictions. And so we decided to
focus our analysis on patterns of exonerations by geography.

THE GEOGRAPHY OF EXONERATION

We focused our analysis on the counties across the United States that had
the highest number of exonerations. Exonerations are in fact clustered, in
Cook County, Illinois, which leads the nation with slightly more than 6
percent of all exonerations, as well as in Dallas County, Texas; Harris
County, Texas; Kings County (Brooklyn), New York; Bronx, New York;
and Los Angeles County, California. It should be clear but it is worth
stating that not all of the top counties when it comes to exonerations fall
into the top counties in terms of population, so clearly this is not just a
"numbers game" in which the easy explanation is that more exonerations
take place where there are more people. It's more complicated than that,
and this is precisely what we set out to uncover.

When we examined that data from our database with specific attention
to geography, we found several telling patterns. Comparing the data from
each of the leading counties with respect to the data on all 1,358 exonerations, we found that not only do Black men comprise the majority of
exonerees, but in these counties Black men were significantly overrepresented among the exonerations.

Though Black men make up 46 percent of all people exonerated, in
Cook County, Illinois, seventy-five of the ninety-six (78 percent) of the
exonerations were of Black men. Not only are Black men in Cook County
exonerated at nearly *double the rate* of exonerations nationally, but Black
men in Cook County are also wrongfully convicted and exonerated disproportionately compared to their representation in the Cook County population, of which they make up only 25 percent. Put simply, Black men
are three times more likely to be wrongfully convicted and later exonerated than their representation in the Cook County population. Policing
Black bodies.

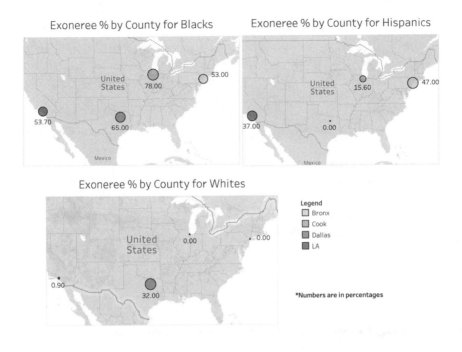

Exoneree % by County for Blacks

Exoneree % by County for Hispanics

Exoneree % by County for Whites

Legend
☐ Bronx
☐ Cook
☐ Dallas
☐ LA

*Numbers are in percentages

Exoneree Race by County

So, what produces the wrongful convictions that lead to exonerations in these counties? Prosecutorial misconduct is by far the largest contributor to wrongful convictions and exonerations. Though many cases involve several factors, the data reveal that *all cases of exoneration in these counties involved one or more forms of prosecutorial misconduct.* Eyewitness misidentification is the second-largest contributor to wrongful convictions, with an average of 40 percent of cases involving an eyewitness misidentification. Though there is very little difference across counties, Dallas County has a slightly lower rate of eyewitness misidentification as a contributing factor in cases of exoneration.

There is a fair amount of variance across counties when it comes to inadequate legal defense as a contributing factor to wrongful convictions and exonerations, with Dallas County and Harris County (both in Texas) having by far the highest percentage of cases explained in part by inadequate legal defense. Though we didn't discuss inadequate legal defense as a cause of wrongful conviction, suffice it to say that the stories of inadequate legal defense are, quite frankly, stunning. We've heard firsthand

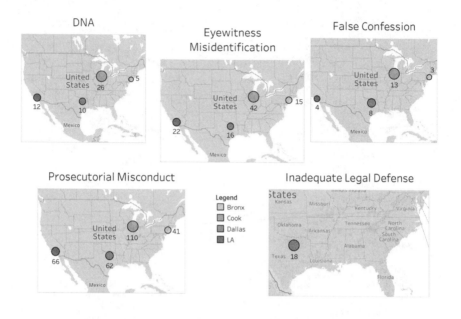

Contributing Factors to Wrongful Convictions in Top Four Counties

and read accounts of defense attorneys falling asleep during trials, coming to court visibly drunk or high, or never meeting one on one with their clients while "defending" men accused of rape or murder and facing significant sentences, including life in prison or the death penalty.

In sum, these patterns are disturbing but not terribly surprising given that most of the factors that lead to wrongful convictions are not the result of individual mistakes but of deeply entrenched patterns of behavior that are more or less utilized by different county police and sheriff's departments. For example, if lead prosecutors in a particular county generally condone and even endorse legal, but what we would argue are inappropriate and even unethical, interrogation strategies, then we would likely see these patterns across most or all cases in that particular county. Perhaps the best illustration is inadequate legal defense. It is not surprising that the two counties that are outliers in our data are both in the same state, which suggests that there may be issues with providing adequate defense in all or most Texas counties. Perhaps Texas has difficulty, for example, in staffing public defenders' offices with competent attorneys. If something this "simple" is the case, then, should real justice be a goal, the recommendations for achieving fairness are straightforward and relatively easy to implement.

Eyewitness misidentification presents an interesting case in that it can be exacerbated by police and prosecutorial misconduct, and it can also occur independently of the influence of law enforcement and prosecutor practices. This likely explains the fact that there is only minimal variation in this factor across the counties we examine here. Eyewitness misidentification has both individual and structural roots in wrongful conviction and exoneration.

When we began this research and discovered that just a small number of counties accounted for a disproportionate number of exonerations, we initially focused on what was transpiring in those counties: what the racial balance was, whether prosecutors were elected or appointed, and so forth. As we concluded this research, we began to focus on something different: exonerations illuminate not just a flawed criminal justice system but also the hard work and advocacy of reformers. It is therefore not surprising that approximately 125 exonerations have taken place in two counties with very active and long-standing local innocence projects that are housed in prestigious law schools: Northwestern University School of Law, adjacent to Cook County, and the Benjamin Cardoza School of Law in New York City, which birthed the first innocence project. Similarly, it is also not surprising that two of the counties leading the way in terms of exonerations are in Texas: Texas has an extraordinarily high rate of incarceration (602 per 100,000 residents), it has the most active executions, and it has long been a target for those advocating for the need to reform the criminal justice system.

THE COSTS OF EXONERATIONS

The most obvious costs of exoneration are the costs to the wrongfully convicted individual and his family. Darryl Hunt and the more than 1,500 exonerees to date have lost years of their lives that they can never get back. They can't get an education. They can't start a career and build a retirement fund. They can't start a family. Most can't find a job. They leave prison and move in with family, often their mothers, or, if they are lucky enough, their girlfriend or wife. Some will have children or reunite with children they fathered before they went to prison. Most will not.

Exonerees return to the "free world" like any other person released from prison, having spent decades locked in a cage. And they often have trouble readjusting to life on the outside. Kalvin Michael Smith spent twenty years in prison for a crime he didn't commit. He went to prison at age twenty-six, and when he finally came home, his innocence validated, he was forty-five years old.

> At his father's house, he laughs easily, but the frustration is there, close to the surface. The two joke sometimes about the things Smith still does that he picked up from prison. He wakes up early. Once, he left the room for something and his food was on the table. He told his father to watch his tray—he had been taught in prison never to leave his food unattended.
>
> Smith has scars. "It's harder to do the time," he said. "People don't understand. . . . It wasn't my fault I did 20 years for something I didn't do." He had trouble adjusting to prison. Now, he is having trouble adjusting to life outside prison walls.[12]

Exonerations have a cost. In addition to the costs to the exoneree, there are also economic costs and public safety costs.

The safety of the community is a common news story in twenty-first-century America. Starting in 2001 with the destruction of the New York City World Trade Center Towers and up through the Sandy Hook, Connecticut, elementary school shooting in 2012 as well as the shootings at the Pulse nightclub in Orlando, Florida, in 2016, at the time we were writing this book, public safety has become consuming for Americans and especially for law enforcement agencies.

Despite all of the attention and concern, many threats to public safety remain, and one is highlighted by exonerations: when we lock up the wrong person, the real perpetrators of serious crime like rape and murder continue to terrorize our communities.

Innocence Project researchers found that when the perpetrator of crimes is free—and the wrongfully convicted person is incarcerated—these actual perpetrators continue to perpetrate more violence, committing upward of two hundred additional crimes, including seventy-seven rapes, thirty-four murders, and thirty-five other violent crimes, before they are caught, all while the innocent man sits behind bars.[13] If you are not moved by any other argument in this chapter, we hope you are moved by this one. *You are less safe when the wrong person is convicted of a crime and the real perpetrator is allowed to continue to commit heinous crimes.* And the fact that in many cases the prosecutor knew he or she was likely putting away an innocent man and leaving the real rapist or murderer on the street is nearly impossible to comprehend. A real threat to our public safety is unethical policing and prosecutorial practices.

Exonerations also have financial costs. The greatest cost of all, without doubt, are the years that a wrongfully convicted person loses—years he can never get back—to get an education, to start a family, to build a life. That said, there are financial costs to the taxpayer as well. Compensation to exonerees varies. Some states mandate compensation, generally just a fraction of what an exoneree actually lost while incarcerated. Some exonerees, including Darryl Hunt, have been successful in suing the county or municipality in which they were wrongfully convicted. Lawsuits like these are paid by insurance policies that municipalities take out to cover malpractice of various sorts. All compensation and settlements from lawsuits are ultimately paid by us, the taxpayer.

In Illinois, and Cook County in particular, the leading county in exonerations is paying a hefty price for the entrenched and systematic policies and procedures that, to date, have yielded nearly one hundred exonerees. In a tally of payouts, the Center for Wrongful Convictions at Northwestern University estimated that between 1989 and 2011 upward of $300 million has been or will be paid by the state, with the bulk of the money coming from the city of Chicago. Unfortunately, in cities like Chicago, which are already hovering near bankruptcy, many exonerees, like Christopher Coleman who was finally released from prison in 2013 after serving twenty years, find out after the fact that their compensation has been indefinitely delayed simply because the city has run out of money. There is no time line as to when the compensation will be paid to Christopher Coleman and others like him. What? We understand tight finances, but a state, city, or municipality should not be allowed to default on compensation to those they so terribly wronged. Black bodies ripped out of their homes and communities, locked up for decades. Black bodies undervalued.

As many scholars have noted, and as we have discussed in our own research, one of the most contentious issues in the racial history of the United States is intimate relationships between whites and Blacks. Accusations of the rape of white women by Black men have been a cornerstone of race relations and the justice system for centuries. Activist Angela Davis documents the fact that the mere *accusation* of rape of a white woman would send vigilante mobs in search of a Black man to lynch, and tragically, tens of thousands of Black men were lynched between 1880 and 1930. Davis documents that only a handful of these tens of thousands of lynchings involved an *actual rape*, and a handful more involved consensual relations between white women and Black men. The rest, the overwhelming majority, were entirely false. Thus, we argue that the long-standing myth of the Black rapist and the lynching of tens of thousands of Black men, almost entirely without cause, provides the historical context, the backdrop if you will, for the way in which the police, the criminal justice system, and even the public deal with Black men accused of raping white women. Policing Black bodies, especially those that transgress the heavily surveilled boundary of intimate relationships.

Just as Susan Smith, who deliberately drove her car into a lake in South Carolina, killing her two young sons whom she had securely strapped in their car seats, blamed a "random" Black man and Charles Stuart, who fatally stabbed his pregnant wife as they left Lamaze class in Boston, told the police that a Black man had done the stabbing, when Black men are identified as rapists, there seems to be little concern about finding the *right* Black man; the goal is to simply find one, arrest him, and send him to prison. Just as it was during the height of the lynchings, it's as if all Black men are interchangeable. Someone needs to pay for the crime, and it's less important that the right Black man be identified than that *a Black man* pay for the crime. Evidence for this is found in public perceptions about exoneree Darryl Hunt. In the Winston-Salem community, it is often noted by whites that despite Mr. Hunt's innocence in Deborah Sykes's murder, he probably had done something or he wouldn't have been targeted by the police initially; he probably *deserved* the nearly twenty years he served for the other crimes he undoubtedly committed or was on a trajectory to commit, which by the way there has never been any evidence of. This perspective, of course, not only suggests the *perception* that all Black men are interchangeable but lessens the guilt associated with wrongful conviction and exoneration. If all Black men are or will engage in criminal behavior, much of which is probably undetected, then *time served is most likely time deserved*. These assumptions, which permeate whites' attitudes, including those of police officers, prosecutors, and judges, about race, are just another vestige of the system of racism at work in this country.

Unfortunately there are severe and harsh consequences for this approach to justice. Men like Darryl Hunt, Ronald Cotton, and nearly six hundred more whom we have identified have spent collectively between fifteen thousand and thirty thousand years in prison for raping or murdering white women, crimes that they of course never committed.

> What we have not been able to know, however, is whether there are systematic failures that cause wrongful convictions. Now that there have been so many DNA exonerations, we have a large body of errors to study. Did the first 250 DNA exonerations result from unfortunate but nevertheless unusual circumstances? Or were these errors the result of entrenched practices that criminal courts rely upon every day? Are there similarities among these exonerees? What can we learn from them? [14]

What we have learned, from reading the research of legal scholars, from working with exonerees and listening to their stories, and from examining cases that are documented by the Innocence Project and documentary filmmakers, is that exonerees are the canary in the mine. Their experiences represent the very worst of the criminal justice system, a system not built to deliver justice but one that devalues Black bodies, as defendants and as victims, and that will go to any lengths possible—including lying and cheating—to remove Black bodies from the "free world" and lock them away, invisible to mainstream America, where only a few dedicated souls are aware of their circumstances and work tirelessly for their release.

Exonerees, like anyone who has been locked in a cage for decades, return to the "free world" with all of the trauma they experienced in prison. In some ways the trauma may be even more severe because of their innocence. And even though some exonerees receive compensation for the time they were incarcerated, few if any receive the mental health care they need to heal their wounds and keep their fears at bay.

On March 16, 2016, just a few weeks more than ten years after he was exonerated, Darryl Hunt committed suicide. He spent twenty years in prison but was only able to survive ten years after his release. A year later, in April 2017, Phoebe Zerwick, the investigative journalist who broke the story that led to Darryl's exoneration, wrote a piece titled "The Last Days of Darryl Hunt," [15] in which she explored the challenges that Darryl faced and his decision to take his own life. Like many exonerees,

Darryl felt an intense sense of fear that he would be locked up again for a crime he didn't commit. That may seem odd to most of us, but for someone like Darryl, if it can happen once it can happen again. In order to deal with that fear, Darryl developed habits such as taking a few dollars out at an ATM at different times every day so that he would have an alibi for his time. Darryl was an incredibly humble man, and as a result, Zerwick writes that people expected Darryl to maintain that persona 100 percent of the time. She speculates that when he felt angry or depressed he had trouble finding ways to express those emotions because they contradicted people's expectations of him. Darryl was also very generous. He invested nearly every dollar he received in compensation back into his reentry project, the Darryl Hunt Project for Freedom and Justice. When we were with Darryl, we witnessed firsthand how difficult it was for him to say no to anyone who asked for help. Men returning from prison would come to Darryl's office needing help, and they would leave with a $20 bill to help them deal with their latest crisis, or get their next fix. Darryl died nearly broke. In the years after his release, he had begun using cocaine to "make himself numb." His wife recalls that he was afraid people would find out about his drug use and judge him. Even his attorney and friend of thirty years, Mark Rabil, didn't know of his drug use. "We wanted him to be what he seemed," Saundra Westervelt (a sociologist who worked with Darryl Hunt) said. "We didn't want him to fail. I think we have to own that."[16]

Zerwick concludes,

> It shouldn't surprise me that the facts have led me to such a complicated story and that so much is still unknown. I knew Hunt as a man of courage who inspired people by his dignity and his grace. Without his story, told in a film that reached audiences around the world, it's unlikely that we would have the criminal justice reforms that we have in North Carolina. Women adored him, but his personal life was a tangle of regret. His friends admired him, perhaps too much. He wanted a decent life but spent 19 years incarcerated for a crime he had nothing to do with and emerged a celebrity. Prison scarred him and I am almost certain that he used drugs to self-medicate. Some will think these facts diminish him. To me, they make him human.[17]

One final thought: sadly, both because of the way that exonerations work legally as well as because of the years that the wrongfully convicted are removed from mainstream culture, like any person with a *felony conviction* exiting prison and attempting to get their lives back on track, exonerees face the same barriers to reentry. Because they were convicted of a felony and they must "check the box," they can be denied access to social welfare and public housing. They were sent to prison wrongly because they had no access to resources, and this rarely changes by the time they are finally released. What kind of justice denies someone wrongfully convicted and exonerated the opportunity to reclaim their life? Only a society that believes blindly that justice is fair, that Black bodies have no value, and that Black men who have never been convicted of a crime aren't truly innocent; they just haven't committed a crime yet. But they will, just give it some time. Policing Black bodies.

10

INTERSECTIONALITY, COLOR-BLIND RACISM, AND A CALL TO ACTION

The killings of black men and women at the hands of the state with no justice to be had, is among the oldest and most familiar American stories.

—Nikole Hannah-Jones[1]

The Declaration of Independence begins with the statement that all [men] are created equal, that all [men] have a right to life, liberty and the pursuit of happiness.

We would hardly be the first to point out that the Declaration of Independence and the Constitution of the United States of America were penned by men with incredible privilege: white, slave owners, landed aristocrats, men who did not see their exclusion of Blacks or Native Americans or women or poor whites as in any way contradictory to their principles simply because they believed that Blacks and Native Americans and women and poor whites were socially, biologically, and morally inferior. They weren't left out. They simply weren't *entitled* to those rights promised in the Constitution.

Yet phrases like "all men are created equal" and the entitlement to "life, liberty and the pursuit of happiness" are thrown around by Americans, and those living in other countries as well, as if to profess that these are the core values of the United States, the aspirational goals of the founding fathers,[2] and that with some acknowledgment of the plight of the marginalized and oppressed, systems that formerly blocked access for

Blacks, Native Americans, women, and poor whites would simply break down and cease to exist, and the doors of opportunity would open for all.

The journey of this book has been to uncover and reveal the various mechanisms and strategies for policing Black bodies, practices that are systematic, codified into policy, and deliberate in nature. Black bodies have been policed since their arrival on this continent. Black bodies have been policed as a mechanism of social control as well as in order to limit the number of Black bodies that can gain access to sacred spaces, including boardrooms, the most elite colleges and universities, leadership in the military, and, of course, the White House.

Black bodies have been segregated. First into slave quarters, next by Jim Crow into "colored" waiting rooms and housing tracts, and today, as Michelle Alexander so eloquently describes, by the system of mass incarceration. Eugene Robinson[3] argues that poor Blacks have been removed so far away from mainstream life that they constitute a new social class: the "abandoned." The abandoned and those in prison, often one and the same group of poor Black people, are effectively removed, or cordoned off as Erik Olin Wright[4] argues, not only out of the way of capitalism, which has no use for their bodies and their labor, but literally and figuratively handcuffed in their ability to access the opportunity structure. The abandoned are not competing for seats at Harvard or Yale or even the University of Texas, regardless of what Abigail Fisher might think. The abandoned are not competing for jobs or scholarships or even to buy a home in an affluent neighborhood. They are not competing for access to any aspect of the American Dream. And how convenient for white people to have all of these bodies policed and conveniently removed from the competition for scarce resources.

Black bodies are policed simply for being Black or, more accurately, for being seen—for being seen in "white" spaces, for transgressing mainstream norms of behavior, for the mere possibility that they might engage in crime. As we were finishing up the first draft of this book in July 2016, the United States was under a "heat dome." Temperatures soared to nearly one hundred degrees day after day after day, from Arizona to New York to Maine. Black men's bodies were being murdered at a rapid pace in Baton Rouge, Louisiana, and Falcon Heights, Minnesota. A Black behavioral therapist, Charles Kinsey, was shot trying to administer help to an autistic man who had run away from a group home in Miami. The police, in a really interesting turn of fate, argued that they didn't mean to shoot the caregiver, who had his hands up, but rather the autistic man! What?

In a conversation with one of our colleagues, we were noting the fact that so many of the shootings of unarmed Black men happen in the summer. And think about it, it didn't just begin with Trayvon Martin or Mike Brown, but Emmett Till, who was murdered on August 28, 1955, and the civil rights workers James Chaney, Andrew Goodman, and Michael Schwerner, who were murdered on June 21, 1964, and whose bodies were dumped in the Tallahatchie River near Philadelphia, Mississippi. Why the summer?

There is a running debate among criminologists and law enforcement officials as to whether violent crime rises in the summer. Some speculate that violent crime rises in the summer because it is hot and tempers are shorter or because people are outside more often as daylight stretches to fifteen hours a day—this is a common theory with regard to stranger rape—or because summer holidays like Memorial Day when people gather and sometimes drink too much and tempers flare. And all of this may be true. But the policing of Black bodies is more insidious than the warm temperatures or too much alcohol.

Black bodies are policed in the summer simply because they are more visible in the summer, often in white spaces—because visibility is a form of transgression that is seen by whites and must be policed, not because Black bodies are behaving in ways that require policing, but simply because they exist, in white spaces, with Skittles and iced tea or selling cigarettes or CDs on the corner in neighborhoods where they live, or because they are transgender and are simply enjoying a walk in a park on a summer's afternoon.

The Universal Declaration of Human Rights guarantees, among many other things, in Article 3, the right to life, liberty, and security of person. The interrogation in this book has been about trying to connect the various ways in which policing Black bodies denies each of these rights, not to mention aspects of pretty much each of the articles ratified in the Universal Declaration of Human Rights, but that would be another book entirely. The deliberate and intentional policing of Black bodies, by police officers, in prisons and jails, in ghettos both rural and urban, in reproductive decisions, in seeking innocence, in the right to live one's gender identity free of violence and discrimination, individually and in combination categorically denies Black people the right to life, liberty, and security of person and significantly impairs the right to the pursuit of happiness guaranteed by the United States Constitution.

So how did it get to be this way? If we have accomplished nothing else in this book, what we have done is document a story that is rooted in history and persists today. Every policy and practice has been a deliberate and a direct response to Black bodies seeking justice, attempting to access the opportunity structure, and simply exercising the right to be. As the late Black historian John Hope Franklin put it, "from slavery to freedom."[5]

After the end of the Civil War, while Black people were focused on Reconstruction, white planters worked carefully and deliberately to develop plantation prisons that could be filled up with free Blacks so that their bodies could continue to provide the "free" labor that was critical to the success of the southern plantation economy. Black Codes restricted the movement of Black bodies and made it legal to lock up Black bodies for simply being in white spaces. Jim Crow segregation ushered in another era of policing that, among other things, was characterized by two key features: segregation and lynching. Segregation kept Black bodies in "appropriate" places, and lynching reminded Black people what and where those appropriate spaces were and that any transgression could be met with violence. Emmett Till was just a thirteen-year-old kid from Chicago, just being a kid in the hypersegregated South when he was murdered by grown white men in Mississippi, a state known for the murder of Blacks and for policing Black bodies.

After the end of the modern civil rights movement, as Black bodies demanded access and justice, President Nixon understood clearly, according to John Ehrlichman, Nixon's chief aid, that in addition to Vietnam, the biggest threat to the security of the United States was Black bodies. Unable to declare a war on Black people explicitly, he declared the now infamous War on Drugs that specifically and deliberately targeted Black bodies. We cannot overestimate the impact of the War on Drugs on Black bodies, Black families, and Black communities. As a result of the War on Drugs, millions of Black people, men and women and even children, have been incarcerated, for years, often for low-level drug possession. Many of these same bodies are incarcerated not for the crime they committed but for their inability to pay the fines and fees that are leveled as punishment.

As devastating as the War on Drugs is on its own, as Ehrlichman points out, it was also designed as an opportunity to generate and reinforce stereotypes of Black bodies as thugs and criminals. These stereotypes are a significant cause of two very dangerous practices: racial profiling and wrongful convictions. In a world in which every Black body, and every Black male body in particular, is dangerous, it means that every Black man should be suspected of a crime and that even when mistakes are made, as is the case in wrongful convictions, these mistakes, in the words of Jack Nicholson's character Colonel Jessup in the popular film *A Few Good Men*, "probably saved lives." All Black bodies need to be policed because all have the potential to threaten public safety. All Black bodies become interchangeable.

As sociologists, we are not satisfied with simply describing a problem; we are interested in analyzing it and understanding how it operates in a society steeped in inequalities that are structured by systems of race, class, and gender. The policing of Black bodies can only be understood through the lens provided by intersectional theory and by the frame of color-blind racism.

Recall the spiderweb we described in the opening chapter of the book. Intersectionality is a theoretical paradigm, and perhaps more important, an analytic tool that exposes systems of power that produce privilege and oppression. In the United States several systems of oppression have operated independently and in a reinforcing matrix of domination such that rewards and privileges are distributed and made available primarily to white, heterosexual, upper-middle-class men, and everyone else—including white women and Black men—is left to fight over the few scraps that fall from the table. Those without privilege experience oppression and a lack of access to the opportunity structure, such that over time disadvantages accrue to the members of these groups and their communities. A million Black men are in prison. Black men make up 60 to 70 percent of all those exonerated, not because they were lucky, but because they are disproportionately victims of police and prosecutorial misconduct that contributes to their wrongful conviction. Unarmed Black men are shot and killed by police offers sworn to protect them 2.5 times more often than white men. Black babies are ripped away from their mothers, whose only crime is an untreated drug addiction. Trans bodies are subjected to sexual and physical violence because they threaten our understanding of gender. Bans on every kind of social welfare make recovering from a mistake nearly impossible, the churning of the prison machine the destiny for nearly all Black men without a high school diploma.

Intersectionality is about power and power relations—the ability to determine whose bodies have value and whose can be discarded or locked away in prisons, their incarceration generating billions of dollars in revenue for private prison corporations and their grossly unpaid labor allowing corporations and state prison industries to post record profits. Intersectionality points clearly at the ways in which these interlocking systems of power, racism, patriarchy, and capitalism cordon off opportunities and access to the American Dream to wealthy white families, far away from everyone else. Equal opportunity is a farce. The deck is stacked in favor of white people, and especially wealthy whites, and it is deliberately stacked against Black bodies, even those that are middle class. The disproportionate percentage of subprime mortgages offered to middle- and even upper-middle-class Black families, even those with identical credit scores and histories to their white counterparts, is a case in point. And the probability of having one's body policed follows these same patterns.

Intersectionality is also about social justice. At its most basic level, the goal we set out to achieve in writing this book was to shine a light on a set of policies, practices, and lived realities that are often not seen as connected but which in fact, alone and in combination, deliberately create racial inequality, *specifically through the policing of Black bodies*. Only when we can describe and analyze a set of problems can we begin to design remedies and solutions. Intersectionality is just this type of analytical tool with the express goal of dismantling all forms of inequality and delivering the promises of the Declaration of Independence, the Constitution of the United States, and the United Nations Declaration of Human Rights.

So why doesn't everyone else simply see the matrix of domination? Why do we need to write a book that connects the race protests in Baltimore with mass incarceration and exoneration and the policing of Black women's sexuality? The ideology of color-blind racism is perhaps the most effective and well-designed tool for keeping racism intact. The ideology of color-blind racism has as its goal the ability to render racism invisible and to label those who claim to experience it as being overly sensitive, crazy, or even race baiters.

In writing this book we have explored a variety of ways in which color-blind racism serves as the cover under which the deliberate policing of Black bodies, and indeed the War on Black people, is allowed to go unchecked, even unrecognized, by even the most progressive whites. Our goal in writing this book is to lift the curtain, much like exposing the wizard in the *Wizard of Oz*. Our hope is that once those with a professed interest in dismantling racism and other forms of oppression are no longer blinded by color-blind racism, they will not only feel a call to action but will be armed with the information and facts they need to make the case clearly to others.

Writing this book during the summer of 2016 meant that we were also glued to our television watching both the Republican and Democratic National Conventions. Of particular interest for our analysis was the amount of color-blind racism rhetoric spewed during the Republican National Convention in Cleveland, Ohio. How often did speakers invoke phrases like the "human race" or "all Americans"?

Several notable politicians invoked a color-blind racism frame in order to make their arguments for electing Donald Trump. We quoted Rudy Giuliani as the epigram that opened our discussion of the shooting of unarmed Black men. But Giuliani wasn't the only Republican speaker making these kinds of color-blind racist statements. Many of the men and women who took the stage that hot week in July 2016 called for a return to "one America," an America that doesn't "see" race. Darryl Glenn, Republican nominee for the U.S. Senate seeking to represent the state of Colorado, and a Black man, said the following:

> This president ran to be commander in chief. Unfortunately, he's become "divider in chief." We're more racially divided today than before he ran. But there's more. The New Black Panthers, Jessie Jackson, and Al Sharpton don't speak for Black America. This is not about Black America, white America, or Brown America. This is about the United States of America.

Remarks like those of Darryl Glenn and Rudy Giuliani are examples of the "I don't see race" versions of color-blind racism. Our colleagues, including Eduardo Bonilla-Silva[6] and Tricia Rose, are quite clear about the damage that this type of belief does in advancing the racial project; specifically, claims that one doesn't see race render racism and racial inequality invisible. If people can't see racial inequality, then they are blinded to the need for race-based solutions that, if implemented successfully, would reduce the widespread and significant racial disparities we have detailed in this book. The policing of Black bodies.

But perhaps more insidious are the policies and practices we have focused on in this book that have the appearance of being race neutral but which are in fact race based. For example, as Michelle Alexander and Elizabeth Hinton describe, the War on Drugs, a policy that appears to be race neutral and appears to be in the best interests of all Americans, is in fact a racial law that targets Black bodies and has resulted in millions of Black bodies being incarcerated since it was conceived by Richard Nixon in the early 1970s. As Ehrlichman confirms, the War on Drugs was really a War on Black bodies. And Ehrlichman makes it clear that both he and Nixon clearly understood that a War on Black bodies would be offensive and thus could never be waged. But a War on Black bodies thinly disguised as a War on Drugs, which just happened to ensnare a disproportionate number of Black bodies, was morally and ethically acceptable. Or, as Dorothy Roberts so aptly illustrates, the war on drug-addicted mothers, which appeared, once again, to be race neutral and which was hard to oppose because it protected children, was in fact a set of policies and practices that specifically targeted Black women's bodies, and specifically Black women's sexuality. Or the stop-and-frisk laws, which once again appear to be race neutral but in fact targeted Black bodies in places like Manhattan and, as we discussed previously, were found to be racially discriminatory and subsequently overturned. Or the shooting of unarmed Black men by police officers, which might appear to be simply a matter of circumstance, a matter of the numbers. If more Black men are committing crime, then it stands to reason that more Black men will be shot by police officers simply trying to catch the bad guys and do their jobs to ensure public safety. And yet, as research has demonstrated, traffic stops that are nothing more than "fishing expeditions" not only target Black bodies—and though more men have been killed, it is important to acknowledge that women have also died as a result of these stops—but escalated into extreme violence and tragedy *specifically because they targeted Black bodies* who had not violated any significant traffic law.

Color-blind racism is the ideology that undergirds and rationalizes racism and racial inequality. If we have demonstrated nothing else in this book, it is this. And as we begin the hard work of identifying and proposing strategies for dismantling racism, we must acknowledge the role that color-blind racism plays in upholding the systematic nature of racial inequality and rendering it invisible. We cannot imagine any progress being made on the racial project without this acknowledgment.

So, how can we apply the analytical tools of intersectionality and color-blind racism specifically to the variety of ways that Black bodies are policed?

When it comes to the protests, those we focused on and others we chose to leave out, the factors that produce protests are remarkably similar to and consistent with every issue we explore in this book; the fundamental cause of riots is the policing of Black bodies. In some cases this policing is literally a result of police practices, for example, the racial profiling of cab driver Smith in Newark and the shooting of Michael Brown in Ferguson, and in other cases such as the Watts riots, the cause is a more complex mix of policing, including the policing of where Black bodies can live and work and go to school, the policing of their access to the American Dream.

An intersectional approach is useful in examining protests because it helps us to distinguish among protests that took place in the early parts of the twentieth century and those that have occurred in the last decade. As a result of rigid housing segregation laws that characterized the first half or more of the twentieth century, Black communities in places like Chicago were socioeconomically diverse. As a result of the passage of the Civil Rights Act of 1964 and the implementation of fair practices in housing— and lawsuits of course—in the words of *Washington Post* columnist Eugene Robinson, the Black community "disintegrated." The Black community began to be divided along lines of social class, which, as Robinson so eloquently argues, left poor Blacks concentrated in urban ghettos like Southeast D.C. and West Baltimore, while middle- and professional-class Blacks, as soon as changes in the laws paved the way, moved into predominantly white communities. With poverty and police brutality concentrated in the poor Black neighborhoods, the table was set for this most recent set of protests, ignited by the police beating or killing of unarmed Black men: Rodney King, Michael Brown, and Freddie Gray.

What is so interesting as we watched the protests unfold live on our flat-screen HD televisions and across the Internet and our Facebook and Twitter feeds was that color was everywhere: nearly all of the bodies that we saw, protesting or beaten or shot, were Black. The only exception to this was the police, those who beat and killed unarmed Black men, and for the most part those brought in to contain and control the protests. That said, except on "Black outlets" like the *Root*, what was notable was the *absence* of a discussion of color in the mainstream media. The only comments about "color" were focused on blaming Black people for "ruining" their own community or burning the only store in their neighborhood, or, as was the case in Baltimore, references were made to Black high school students as "thugs" with sagging pants, with nothing better to do than harass the police who had been sent, ostensibly, to protect them. How selfish. Rarely was there any mention of why there was only one store in the neighborhood or what it was like to have only one place to shop or what it felt like to be called a "thug" or why so many Black people had time to march day and night—because they experience extraordinarily high rates of unemployment.

Color-blind racism blurs the ways in which race and class shape communities so that they are either stable or unstable, likely to be able to withstand an injustice—on the rare event that one would take place in their community—or explode into violence, a release of decades of tension from having Black bodies and Black communities policed.

Just as there are structural explanations, primarily housing segregation, unemployment, and police brutality, that shape the likelihood of a community bursting into flames as members seek the only route they have access to protest their treatment, another strategy for policing Black bodies, mass incarceration, is not random. It is a direct result of policies and practices that are designed to segregate Black people from mainstream society. Employing the framework of color-blind racism is perhaps the only way to make sense of this, because otherwise it is pretty difficult to believe that mass incarceration is a direct result of a government war on Black bodies disguised as a "War on Drugs." The perspective provided by color-blind racism allows us to identify the ways in which the war on Black bodies was easy to disguise because it relied on our beliefs in meritocracy and a level playing field. The War on Drugs made sense if you believed that the intent was really to reduce drug use and increase public safety. It makes sense if you believe that all drug offenses were handled equally without regard to race. It makes sense if you believe that incarcerating someone for five to ten years for possessing an illegal substance would treat their addiction. It makes sense if you believe that it is appropriate for child molesters to get shorter sentences than people convicted of drug offenses. It makes sense if you believe that everyone gets a second chance.

In fact, none of these statements is true. As Marc Mauer, executive director of the Sentencing Project notes, locking up drug offenders, even drug dealers, while allowing child molesters and serial rapists to return to the "free world" after serving short sentences does not in fact contribute to public safety; in fact it inhibits public safety!

And that's the power and insidious nature of seemingly color-blind racist policies. It is written nowhere in the drug policies that Black bodies are to be differentially targeted. Instead, the policies criminalized drugs that were more commonly used in Black communities and assigned harsher mandatory minimum sentences to the possession of those drugs. And the fact that some white bodies got caught up in the War on Drugs didn't negate its intent, as Ehrlichman admitted: it was intended and designed as a war on Black people. Indeed, when white bodies got ensnared in the web of the War on Drugs, it provided confirmation that the drug laws were race neutral, and it is this belief that proves the most dangerous because it prevents us from seeing the truth.

An intersectional approach is critical to understanding anything about the criminal justice system, or truly any phenomenon in U.S. society, because all phenomena are constructed around interlocking systems of oppression. Not only did the War on Drugs target Black bodies and the bans on social welfare continue the policing of Black bodies long after sentences were served, but the mass incarceration of Black men served to remove unexploitable labor from the competitive market and cordon it off, in prisons and ghettos, so as not to clog up the well-oiled machine of capitalism. As Erik Olin Wright argued twenty years ago,

> In the case of labor power, a person can cease to have economic value in capitalism if it cannot be deployed productively. This is the essential condition of people in the "underclass." They are oppressed because they are denied access to various kinds of productive resources, above all the necessary means to acquire the skills needed to make their labor power saleable. As a result they are not consistently exploited. Understood this way, the underclass consists of human beings who are largely expendable from the point of view of the logic of capitalism. Like Native Americans who became a landless underclass in the nineteenth century, repression rather than incorporation is the central mode of social control directed toward them. Capitalism does not need the labor power of unemployed inner city youth. The material interests of the wealthy and privileged segments of American society would be better served if these people simply disappeared. However, unlike in the nineteenth century, the moral and political forces are such that

direct genocide is no longer a viable strategy. The alternative, then, is *to build prisons and cordon off the zones of cities in which the under-class lives.*[7]

As Ehrlichman's words reveal, the Nixon administration had no use for Black bodies; in fact it viewed them as the enemy. As Wright points out, practically speaking it might have been easier to simply declare an actual war on Black bodies and engage in genocide and/or massive "relocation." But by the second half of the twentieth century in the United States, this approach had become morally and ethically disdained. The real war was disguised as a race-neutral, morally grounded war that would remove drugs and drug users from our streets and "clean up" our inner cities—a brilliant strategy because it achieved just what Wright described, the re-moval or segregation of Black bodies into jails and prisons, systems of capitalism and racism working hand in hand.

As Wright so aptly points out, the unexploitable become a permanent "underclass," in large part because of the bans and barriers that citizens reentering the "free world" with a felony record face after they serve their time. These policies expand the policing of Black bodies by continuing to control their life chances as well as by continuing their segregation, away from the centers of economic prosperity and power, much like the cor-doning off of Native Americans to reservations, conveniently out of sight and out of mind. In his book *Disintegration: The Splintering of Black America, Washington Post* editor Eugene Robinson describes this group as the "abandoned." And he argues that the abandoned are so far out of sight, even for middle- and professional-class Blacks, that their interests no longer converge along race lines but rather are configured more tightly at the intersection of race and class lines, yet another illustration of the need for intersectional approaches. This phenomenon is further exacer-bated by the group of Blacks he terms the "transcendents," the Obamas and Tiger Woodses and Oprah Winfreys of the world who not only have access to power and privilege but in fact have more access than most white Americans. Their presence confirms and affirms whites' beliefs in color blindness, in a postracial society, and contributes to the incredible distance between the "abandoned" and the rest of society, conveniently cordoned off in places most Americans never have to travel: prisons and ghettos.

Though it may be difficult to argue that drafters of the Thirteenth Amendment were envisioning the continued "enslavement" of freed Blacks, many states implemented the "punishment" clause in just this way. For example, in the state in which we currently reside, the Commonwealth of Virginia, the Supreme Court of Virginia ruled in 1871 that prisoners were "slaves of the state." Perhaps it's not coincidental that laws like this were written into the books just a few years after the Black Codes came into effect. As we discussed in the first chapter, plantation economies in states dominated by agriculture would have fallen apart after the Civil War were there not some way to continue to exploit the labor of Black people, and Black men in particular. And thus laws were written by *former slaveholding white men* that criminalized certain activities of Black people (the Black Codes) and allowed the state to keep them enslaved during the periods of their incarceration. The irony cannot be overlooked.

In the second half of the twentieth century and especially in the post–civil rights era in which the Nixon administration launched a war against Black people neatly disguised as a "War on Drugs," the race-neutral language of the punishment clause of the Thirteenth Amendment no doubt was well understood by the business leaders who founded the companies that exploited prison labor. Just as it would have been morally and ethically abhorred to criminalize being Black, so too would it have been morally and ethically problematic to exploit *Black* labor through the mechanisms of prison labor practices, yet it was perfectly acceptable and *legal*, thanks to the Thirteenth Amendment, to pay slave wages to incarcerated people, 50 percent of whom *just happened to be Black.*

The prison-industrial complex and its attendant "prison industries" mimic the slave mode of production, such that in the end, wealthy whites (primarily men) are profiting by not paying a living wage to Black inmates (also primarily men). Thus corporations are engaging in an exploitive labor practice, termed by Marx as the extraction of surplus value. By not paying what the labor is worth when inmates are working on farms, building furniture, or assembling products for giant multinational corporations like Microsoft and McDonald's, prison industries make enormous profits. And when prison industries engage in this practice, they also receive an unfair advantage over their competitors. The whole scene is reminiscent of the "plantation economy" of seventeenth-, eighteenth-, and nineteenth-century America. The enslaved were Black chattel. They had no rights, and they were a captive labor force. *All of the above* is the same for today's incarcerated people, including the captive nature of this new labor force.

What we find most fascinating in deconstructing this rarely visible, mysterious system of prison industries is that inmates have suddenly been identified and reconstituted as the latest, greatest group whose labor can be exploited. Prisons provide a "captive" population, one that is highly vulnerable, and one that has increasingly been exploited for its labor. We extract from Wright's quote again:

> In the case of labor power, a person can cease to have economic value in capitalism if it cannot be deployed productively. . . . As a result they are not consistently exploited. Understood this way, the underclass consists of human beings who are largely expendable *from the point of view of the logic of capitalism.* The alternative, then, is *to build prisons and cordon off the zones of cities in which the underclass lives.*[8]

We argue that while Wright was astute in his observation that prisons provided a mechanism for removing the "unexploitable" labor from society, what is fascinating about the prison-industrial complex is the phenomenon that this formerly "unexploitable" class of Americans has now been redefined as highly exploitable by national and multinational corporations. This is in fact a shocking turn of events. How can a group of people whose labor is deemed so utterly unexploitable when they live in Crenshaw or Lawndale or West Baltimore suddenly be transformed, inside prison walls, into the ideal labor? Not only for the labor-intensive work of raising catfish or hoeing okra or even building furniture, but also for making circuit boards for IBM or answering customer service calls for the New York Department of Transportation?

There is no other way to understand the prison-industrial complex than by employing the intersectional and color-blind racism frameworks. Though Wright's discussion focuses on class and not explicitly on race, it is not coincidental that the population of people whose labor is judged unexploitable when they live in the "free world" are primarily Black. Centuries of denying Blacks access to education and skill building, together with the accumulation of all forms of racist policies, result not accidentally in a profile of the Black community that is characterized by high unemployment, low levels of education, and high levels of poverty, all of which lead to the conclusion Wright draws that certain labor is deemed by capitalists as unexploitable. These factors as well as others, including centuries of housing segregation, all deliberately enacted, result in Black people being disproportionately vulnerable to having their bodies policed and their labor deemed worse than expendable; it is, in fact, useless. That is, until these same Black bodies are behind prison walls, locked in cages, often for decades.

The policies and practices that allow prison industries to make a profit by incarcerating Black bodies and exploiting their labor during their period of incarceration, and which allow for even more wealth to accumulate to white business owners, are at face value race neutral. Even the incarceration clause in the Thirteenth Amendment does not explicitly target Black people. Thus, a color-blind racism framework is a powerful tool that allows us to render visible the racist intent and outcome of legalizing the slave labor of incarcerated people. As Ehrlichman said, Nixon understood that you could not make it illegal to be Black, and the Thirteenth Amendment made it illegal to enslave Black people. But it left open a gaping hole that made it legal to enslave people who are incarcerated. Race neutral on the face of it but racialized and racist in the application.

As with every strategy for policing Black bodies that we explore in this book, the school-to-prison pipeline is best understood by applying an intersectional framework and the lens of color-blind racism. It would be nice to believe that the people who commit crime and pose the biggest threat to public safety are the people whom we incarcerate. In fact, as we have demonstrated in our discussions of mass incarceration and the prison-industrial complex, Black bodies are policed and incarcerated at significantly greater rates and in significantly different ways. And this racialized policing is always problematic, and Black bodies pay a significant price. What can be more tragic than applying these racist policies and practices to children—Black children—who are hauled off in handcuffs for being accused of stealing a sixty-five-cent carton of milk and beaten and raped when they are incarcerated? Sadly, thousands are left to die in prison, serving life without the possibility of parole.

In fact, as the theory of color-blind racism makes clear, there is no meritocracy at work when it comes to policing the bodies of boys and girls. The policing of Black boys and girls is nothing short of labeling the same acts that when performed by white boys and girls are considered mischief as crimes when they are committed by Black youth and dealing with this misbehavior with incarceration rather than intervention. The

data are clear, when white boys and girls are truant or get caught shoplifting or smoke small amounts of pot, they are *many times less likely* to be
arrested, detained, and incarcerated than Black kids engaged in the same
behavior.

And the results of this differential treatment, though they may seem
minimal at first glance, are in fact monumental. White kids have their
parents called, and they will likely be referred to substance abuse treatment, counseling, or perhaps a stay in a mental health facility depending
on the severity and cause of the behavior. With this kind of help and
intervention, most of these kids will get their lives together and, even if
they take longer than their peers, will ultimately access the American
Dream, perhaps going to college, getting a good job, and raising a family.
In contrast, Black boys and girls who have engaged in the same kind of
misbehavior are *many times more likely*—depending on the offense—to
be arrested, charged with a crime, convicted, and sentenced, often confined to a jail, a detention center, or even an adult prison. At the mild end,
Black boys and girls will be convicted of a misdemeanor or two, as was
Kuntrell Jackson. The misdemeanor itself might not seem so bad on the
face of it until the youth is arrested for another act of misbehavior; the
original misdemeanor is then transformed into a "prior," and the likelihood of incarceration for each subsequent act increases, until as was the
case with Kuntrell Jackson, a child under the age of eighteen will be
sentenced to decades, if not life, in prison. The simple act of stealing a
sixty-five-cent carton of milk can launch the school-to-prison pipeline.

When we fail to see the systematic and racialized nature of our labeling of and response to childhood misbehavior and deviance, we fall into
the trap of blaming the individual for making poor decisions rather than
the system for failing our children.

The power of applying an intersectional lens to an analysis of the
school-to-prison pipeline is that it allows us to see the ways in which the
systematic application of racialized policing of youth contributes to the
accumulation of privileges among whites and the accumulation of disadvantages among Blacks. The simple example above, the accumulation (or
not) of convictions, impacts, in very real ways, the likelihood that an
individual will eventually serve time in jail or prison. The very act of
being incarcerated (or not) will impact one's life forever. Those who are
incarcerated will for the rest of their lives face barriers to finding employ-

ment, getting an education, and even voting, whereas those disadvantages will not accrue to those who are never convicted or incarcerated.

Perhaps there is no better example of policing Black bodies than the treatment of women in the criminal justice system for illustrating the power of applying an intersectional lens. Though women make up only about 10 percent of the incarcerated population, this does not mean that their experiences are not worthy of interrogation. And in order to adequately understand not only the racial but also the gender differences in their experiences, we must employ an intersectional lens.

Though many of the issues facing Black women are the same as those facing Black men, some are unique. Most notable is the fact that the bodies of Black women and girls are sexualized, and it is their sexuality that is policed, through abuse, through the criminalizing of pregnancy, and via archaic approaches to the treatment of pregnant inmates.

All women, regardless of race, find themselves incarcerated for reasons that are unique to their gender; the majority of women who are incarcerated were convicted of drug felonies or financial crimes. The vast majority of women who are incarcerated were victims of sexual and/or intimate partner violence before they entered prison. Many suffered from mental health issues. Interviews like the ones we conducted revealed quite clearly the relationship between victimization and incarceration—the sexual-abuse-to-prison pipeline, if you will. Most girls and women who end up in prison were engaging in behaviors that were an attempt either to self-medicate or to escape the violence in their lives or both. Women and girls go to prison because they are abandoned by our society, their experiences with victimization rendered invisible and defined as individual rather than structural in nature. And, not surprisingly, Black women's bodies are policed more often than white women's by sexual and intimate partner violence, and they are simultaneously less likely, because of both race and social class, to be able to access the services they need to heal and escape from the violence.

And for a million children in the United States, the failures to address the impact of the victimization their mothers experience results in them being left behind while their mothers do time. Tens of thousands of children, including some of our own students, were "born in prison," ripped away from the human being who incubated them as soon as they are born and whisked away within hours to a waiting relative or grandmother if all goes well, and directly into foster care if things go poorly.

And Black children are nine times more likely to live the reality of a mother in prison than children of other racial and ethnic backgrounds. We can only speculate and barely imagine the impact this has on their futures. What we do know is that children of incarcerated parents are significantly more likely to wind up in prison themselves. The intergenerational policing of Black bodies.

The theory of color-blind racism is really the only "logical" way to make sense of what seems to be such an irrational set of policies and practices that unnecessarily police Black women's bodies and harm Black children. Perhaps the most obvious and egregious example is the criminalizing of pregnancy. A clear outgrowth of the War on Drugs, the criminalization of drug-using pregnant bodies is a clear attempt to police Black women's bodies and Black women's sexuality in particular. As with all drug policies, they appear on the surface to be color blind, they don't specifically target one group of pregnant bodies or another. Yet when we examine the data, an entirely different picture emerges. There are very few cases we can find, for example, that involve criminalizing pregnant alcohol users, though we know that fetal alcohol syndrome is a real thing. We never see images of a pregnant mother using Oxycontin in handcuffs. She is sent to rehab instead, which illustrates just the patterns the data show: when pregnant Black women are discovered to be using drugs, they are arrested; when pregnant white women's drug use is discovered, they are sent to rehab.

Similarly, the bans on social welfare appear to be race neutral. Nowhere in the law does it state that only Black women can be denied access to public housing or food stamps. And yet, in reality, these policies and practices are racialized precisely because Black women are far more likely to be poor before being incarcerated than white women are. In fact, 50 percent of all Black children live in poverty. It's obvious, then, that a ban that seems race neutral on the face of it is racist in practice. As long as we continue to believe that welfare policies and drug policies are race neutral, and as long as we continue to render all victims of sexual and intimate partner violence invisible and deny them access to the support and services they need to heal, we will continue to see a rise in the incarceration of women, and disproportionately Black women, Black mothers, whose children are left behind facing the intergenerational cycle of policing Black bodies.

The policing of trans bodies, and Black trans bodies in particular, clearly illustrates the ways in which both intersections of identity or positionality and structural systems of oppression and privilege produce differential outcomes for people occupying different social locations.

At the individual level, trans people experience discrimination at work, they sometimes find it difficult to find a job, they experience harassment, they are more likely to be fired from a job, and as a result they report higher rates of unemployment. And, as with every phenomenon we analyze, all of these experiences are exacerbated for Black trans folks. Many trans people experience homelessness as a result of both housing discrimination and being kicked out by unsympathetic family and friends. For a variety of reasons, including employment and housing discrimination, many trans people are forced to work in the illegitimate economy, most often selling drugs and engaging in sex work. All of these factors contribute to the fact that trans people experience extraordinarily high rates of violence, both in the streets and, as we have explored in this book, in prison, with Black trans women experiencing the highest rates of both physical and sexual violence.

Much like the spiderweb we described in chapter 1, though one experience alone, such as unemployment or insecure housing, can leave trans people vulnerable to violence, it is the intersection of identities or positionalities that results in the exponential rise in risk that trans people experience. Deborah King refers to this as "double jeopardy," multiple marginal identities resulting in multiplicative, rather than simply additive, disadvantages, oppressions, and risks.[9]

At the structural level, trans people are at risk for having their bodies policed for a variety of systematic reasons, including laws (or their absence) and policies. The simple fact that gender identity is not a protected category by the Office of Civil Rights means that it is legal to discriminate against trans people when it comes to housing, education, and employment, all of which results in precarity, or extreme vulnerability, for trans people. Despite the fact that racial discrimination and gender discrimination are illegal, discrimination against women and people of color remains common and systematic. Thus, Black trans women will find themselves at the very middle of the spiderweb, with multiple, entrenched systems of oppression blocking their access to the opportunity structure, to jobs, to housing, and to education.

The North Carolina bathroom policy is a mechanism by which trans people's bodies are policed in public, in regular spaces by regular people. And because housing in prisons is essentially an extension of the bathroom policy, requiring that inmates be incarcerated based on the presence or absence of certain anatomy, trans people are at significant risk for having their very bodies, their very beings, policed through extreme physical and sexual violence. And because Black people are incarcerated at significantly higher rates than members of other racial and ethnic groups, a pattern that extends to the trans community, Black trans bodies, and Black trans women in particular, are subjected to policing both formally and informally.

The spark that ignited the sometimes controversial but always compelling Black Lives Matter movement was the shooting of an unarmed Black man, Trayvon Martin, by police surrogate George Zimmerman. As we have argued throughout this book, the Black Lives Matter movement, though sparked by the murder of Trayvon Martin, had in fact been a long time brewing. Activists spurred into action by the Black Lives Matter movement were in fact reacting to the centuries-long policing of Black bodies that they, their families, their ancestors, and their communities had experienced. And, as with every strategy for policing the Black body that we interrogate in this book, from the school-to-prison pipeline to mass incarceration to exoneration, though there are white men killed by police officers, and though Black police officers kill unarmed Black men, these tragedies follow a remarkably similar pattern: unarmed Black men, often young but not always, are disproportionately the victims in police killings. And though Black men of all socioeconomic classes find themselves unfairly profiled and even stopped and frisked, many of the Black men killed by police were poor or lower-middle class, living in communities in which police officers often believe that any Black man they see is up to no good, is the next criminal who will rob the local convenience store, or, as in the cases of Eric Garner and Alton Sterling, Black men who are just trying to eke out an existence in an economic system that offers them few options.

But unarmed Black men aren't murdered by police officers just because of perceptions; they are also murdered as a direct result of "killology." As long as the government is at war with Black bodies, as proclaimed by Nixon in 1972, then police officers will be justified in killing them, an act of state-sanctioned violence, for which they will be praised rather than held accountable in any meaningful way. Police officer Timothy Loehmann, who killed twelve-year-old Tamir Rice,

> would tell investigators that he had no choice. . . . He told the grand jury he was scared . . . many police officers see themselves as combatants in a war zone, besieged and surrounded, operating in enemy territory, one wrong move away from sudden death. And here's the thing. It's not an act. I'm sure Timothy Loehmann was indeed terrified. That fear, the fear of the occupying soldier, is the entire problem. [10]

The spiderweb of intersectionality provides the framework for understanding the distribution of these police killings, not just of (mostly) young Black men, but also geographically, in the very same communities in which Blacks have previously protested in response to the policing of their bodies, the very communities in which there have long been accusations of police brutality, the same communities in which 50 to 70 percent of men will be incarcerated in their lifetimes. We found it quite interesting, for example, that the police chief of Dallas, David Brown, was lauded for employing best practices, while simultaneously Dallas County has one of the highest rates of wrongful convictions and incarceration of Black men. All must not be going well if the Dallas police and prosecutors have been locking up the wrong men. In fact, it was precisely these kinds of connections that led us to write this book, the observation that the communities where police were ravaging the bodies of (young) Black men were the same communities where exonerations were taking place and where protests had occurred. We knew that it could not be a coincidence but rather must be part of the analysis and ultimate explanation. In places where Black bodies are policed more aggressively, all kinds of related policing of Black bodies coexist. This is yet another example of intersectionality: the intersection of body and place.

The lens of color-blind racism is also useful in making sense of these otherwise senseless tragedies. Though many police chiefs would have us believe that all people, if they were in the wrong place at the wrong time, could become the victim of a police shooting, this argument is quite simply absurd. Reflecting back on the data provided by the research of Epp, Maynard-Moody, and Haider-Markel, it is quite clear that Black bodies, and Black men in particular, are subjected to unwarranted traffic stops, fishing expeditions, significantly more often than are white people, and when stopped, these fishing expeditions are far more likely to escalate quickly and result in a police officer, usually though not always white, killing an unarmed Black man.

Color-blind racism also renders invisible the stereotypes that Black and white officers hold about Black men: that they are up to no good, that they will likely commit a crime if given enough time, and that they are not only hypermasculine but prone to violence. These same stereotypes were invoked in the majority of the tens of thousands of lynchings that took place in the southern regions of the United States in the period between Reconstruction and approximately 1940.

Stereotypes of angry, hypermasculine, violent Black men are so powerful that they invade even the lives of highly educated, professional Black men who are doctors, lawyers, or college professors. In her research on the invisibility of Blackness, Adia Harvey Wingfield shares the insights of Black professionals whom she interviewed:

> I was coming off the elevator, and this female partner, who's on my floor—who's freaking two doors down from me—was getting off the elevator. I allowed her to get off the elevator first, which I always do, and I was coming behind her to get in the door on our floor, and she waved her badge and she literally tried to close the door to keep me from getting in. And I had to show her my badge, like with my picture on it that [shows] I work here, for her to let me in. . . . First of all, I had on a suit. I didn't have on a tie, but I had on a suit. I mean, what do you think I am? Let's assume you thought I was the copy guy; still, why are you—she's acting like a—she's literally closing the door! Maybe she thought I was going to hurt her. I don't know what she was thinking. But that kind of stuff, those types of things happen, and you have to be mindful. Every day, I have to think, okay, well, how's this person perceiving me? They haven't seen me in court. They haven't seen any of the briefs I've written. They haven't seen me interact with a client. So, they don't know my abilities as a lawyer. All they see is the black bald guy who, if he was stuck in traffic that morning, has an angry face or—so I don't know what it's going to be. So those types of things make it uniquely hard for black men. And so when you don't have people that look like you who've been around for a while, [but] they know that white men are lawyers, it's kind of hard.[11]

The point that the lawyer is making is that Black men are simultaneously both invisible and stereotyped as violent. Being rendered invisible, his female, white colleague doesn't really *see* him and therefore can't distinguish him from other Black male bodies that she encounters at work or on public transportation or walking through the local park. In the encounter he describes, the fact that she has never really *seen* him results in her lumping him in with all of the other images of Black men she *has seen*, and of course most of those images portray Black men as violent. Images of Black men as violent are not only long-standing and widespread, but as Ehrlichman so aptly noted in his discussion of the War on Drugs, this "war" allowed whites to parade violent, drug-addicted Black faces across the nightly news, every night these images flooding the living rooms of all Americans of all races. If a Black man dressed in a suit, who works on the same floor as a female colleague, can be misperceived as a threat, what chance does a young Black man riding through any community in the United States have that a police officer won't see him as a threat? Just as Jonathan Ferrell, the former football player who sought help after a car accident, was perceived by not only the police but first by the woman who called 911 as a criminal; or Trayvon Martin, whom George Zimmerman described as being "huge"; or Michael Brown, who Officer Darren Wilson described as being much bigger than him, even though they were the same height; or Terence Crutcher, shot in Tulsa because the officer perceived him as a "zombie," a monster; or Prince Jones, who sat in his car not troubling anyone.

When it comes to interrogating wrongful convictions and exonerations, really there is no other explanation for the patterns that we identified than the lens provided by intersectional theory. Not only are exonerations gendered and racialized, but they most commonly occur in a particular circumstance: the rape or murder of a white woman by a Black man, a crime that is simultaneously extremely rare and the most common crime in which wrongful convictions are handed down. Only intersectional theory can explain a phenomenon as disproportionate as this, and only intersectional theory provides the historical context in which to understand wrongfully accusing Black men of raping white women, an accusation that many Black feminists argue led to the lynching of tens of thousands of Black men in the nineteenth and twentieth centuries. An intersectional lens further illuminates the value assigned to Black bodies. Not only do the majority of wrongful convictions and exonerations rest on the false accusation of a Black man raping a white woman, but they almost never occur when the perpetrator is white and the victim is Black. We work harder to get it right when white men are accused, especially if they are accused of harming a Black body. The worst miscarriage of justice in a racist system like ours would be to wrongly incarcerate a white body, something of such great value, for injuring a Black body, something of such little value.

As we've said over and over, it's impossible to know how many people are rotting in prison for crimes they did not commit, but if the wrongfully convicted generally represent the most marginalized incarcerated people, those with the fewest resources to defend themselves, those with the least capacity to understand the system they are ensnared in, we can safely assume that social class is another important intersecting identity and social structure that shapes wrongful convictions and exonerations. We cannot conclude this discussion without looping back to our discussion of mass incarceration: what better way to remove the marginalized, those who are defined as having very little to contribute to the complex economy in which we live, than to lock them up, guilty or not? Policing Black bodies.

Unique to our discussion of wrongful convictions and exonerations are three other "status" variables: age, intellectual capacity, and education. As we have demonstrated, it's much easier to coerce a false confession out of the most vulnerable: teenagers, those who have not graduated from high school, and those with low IQs. But it's not just as simple as targeting poor, uneducated Black teenagers. Thinking back to our discussion of the protests in Baltimore, the talking heads labeling the young Black men protesting as "thugs," it seems clear that when police officers and prosecutors see Black teenage boys, they see thugs. This makes it much easier for them to believe that they must be guilty, if not of this crime then of something, and they are simply doing their jobs and contributing to public safety by locking up Black bodies that will commit crimes if they haven't already.

Though we believe that all of our discussions in this book disrupt our widely held beliefs that the criminal justice system is fair, exonerations may be the most powerful tool in this regard. For most of us, it is beyond the realm of possibility to imagine what happened to Darryl Hunt or Ronald Cotton, or the 1,500 exonerees who have returned to our society, thousands of years lost, never to be regained. It is only a color-blind belief in the criminal justice system that allows us to continue to lock up people for crimes they never committed. Only the belief in a color-blind Lady Justice allows this to happen, allows us to believe that those who are wrongfully convicted must have done something. To think otherwise is unfathomable. Ask Justice Scalia or Justice Thomas, who believed so fiercely that the criminal justice system is fair that they ruled in a case argued in front of the United States Supreme Court that people convicted of crimes, even those facing the death penalty, *did not have a constitutional right to have their DNA tested, even if such a test had the possibility of exoneration.* Only a color-blind lens would lead one to have so much faith in our criminal justice system.

So, what is to be done?

First and foremost we must end the war on Black bodies. Period.

Practically speaking, there are many steps that could be taken that would lessen the impact of policing Black bodies. *Let us be clear, none of these changes would dismantle the racist criminal justice system.* As we and many others have argued, the War on Drugs is a major strategy for policing Black bodies. Repealing the complex web of drug laws, eliminating mandatory minimums as well as the sentencing disparities with regard to crack and cocaine, and repealing the three-strikes laws would go a long way toward addressing the nearly half a million Black men in prison on drug felony convictions. But that's just the beginning. In addition, we must pass laws that prohibit making money off of policing. That includes dismantling the private prison system and prohibiting the exploitation of prison labor by prison industries, but it also means prohibiting municipalities from operating what amount to payday lending services for minor traffic violations. No one should be policed for no other reason than to fill the city coffers with fees generated from moving violations. And no one should see their fines doubled and tripled or taxed with interest when the court operates on such a limited schedule that citizens just trying to pay their fines are turned away, as is the case in Ferguson. No one should be incarcerated for the inability to pay fines and fees, and this is especially the case when payment is the only sentence levied on the defendant. Policies should prohibit the seizing of drug forfeitures. Police should be encouraged to focus their energies on building relations with the community rather than being charged with generating revenue. All felony disenfranchisement laws must be immediately repealed. Reenfranchising the Black community promises at least a chance that Black folk can have a voice in who governs their bodies. Every jail and prison must have appropriate, nonsolitary options for housing trans inmates in accordance with their gender identity. We must not only prohibit but discontinue the practice of shackling women in labor and delivery and develop humane policies for managing child custody and care when mothers and fathers are incarcerated. When it comes to wrongful convictions, we recommend a policy similar to medical practice: attorneys should be required to hold malpractice insurance, and those wrongfully convicted should have the right to sue for damages, just as they can if the surgeon cuts off the wrong leg or replaces the wrong knee. Money talks, and if attorneys were financially responsible for their mistakes, we can bet they would make fewer of them. And while we're at it, every single ruling by the United States Supreme Court that denies innocent defendants and those wrongly convicted of pursuing every avenue to ensure their acquittal must be overturned immediately. DNA tests must be constitutionally guaranteed and available for all of those facing criminal charges. We call for abolishing, immediately, the death penalty and solitary confinement. Both are inhumane and violate not only civil but also human rights. Juveniles, no matter what, should never face a *sentence of life without the possibility of parole*. Ever. And no child should be incarcerated unless there is absolutely no other alternative. The vast majority of incarcerated children need social workers and mental health care, not prison. And no child should ever be handcuffed and hauled off to prison for "stealing" a sixty-five-cent carton of milk. All law enforcement agencies should be required to supply data on the race and gender of everyone they stop and the outcome of that stop. And any departments that show a statistically significant racial disparity will be put on probation and monitored by the Office of Civil Rights and the U.S. Department of Justice. All of these and many more changes in policy and procedure would provide some relief for the two million Americans incarcerated in the United States today.

These changes would be a good start, but if we want to seriously address the systematic policing of Black bodies, we will need to do more than change policies. We will need to completely rewire the racial ideology and racist structures of the United States and replace them, 100 percent, with principles of equality. For all. For starters, we must be completely honest and transparent in acknowledging the unique racial history of the United States. Regardless of what we all learned in school history and civics classes, the United States was not in fact founded on principles of equality and opportunity for all. It was founded on principles of equality and opportunity for only those people defined as fully human: heterosexual, landed white men. Thus, the very notion that we would *not* see racial inequality in every aspect of social, economic, educational, and carceral life is simply preposterous. Once one accepts this premise, it will come as no surprise that Black bodies are policed in every corner of our society, not only in prisons and low-income Black neighborhoods but in women's health clinics, in schools, and on the streets of every community. White bodies have never been so thoroughly policed. Ever.

The second step is rejecting the powerful and almost intoxicating—at least for white people—ideology of color-blind racism. To proclaim that one does not see color is to ignore, and worse yet, render invisible, racist policies and practices, embedded in our very Constitution, that have structured every aspect of life in the United States from the moment the colonists arrived on the continent in 1620 all the way up until today. As Patricia Hill Collins reminds us in her 2016 book *Intersectionality*, systems of oppression are relational; they are a two-way street on which one group benefits by the oppression of another group. The persistence of racist policies and practices results in a continued widening of the racial gap as access to the American Dream and advantages such as homeownership, educational access, and gainful employment continue to accrue to whites, whereas the opposite, disadvantages, accrue to Blacks. It is this cumulation, which has a multiplicative effect, that produces a racial gap that widens with each subsequent generation. In other words, despite a possible narrowing of the racial gap in the immediate period after the civil rights movement, if policies are not put into place that reverse the policing of Black bodies, the racial gap will continue to increase in every aspect of life for every future generation.

The third step, based on the revelations of the first two, requires us to interrogate systematically and critically every single policy and practice, especially those that appear on the surface to be "race neutral." Be it the War on Drugs or the criminalization of pregnancy or the school-to-prison pipeline, each of these policies and thousands of others must be deconstructed and critically examined, first to illuminate their real intent and second so that they can be dismantled.

We are not so naive as to believe that any of this is easy. Color-blind racism is so deeply embedded in our collective consciousness that to unseat its grasp will take deliberate effort. And it will require white people to take a backseat and listen to our Black citizens, something we have never really done before.

Even if all of these steps are accomplished and the system of racial domination comes tumbling down, there are at least two other steps that must be taken. First and foremost, we must critically examine the United States as a carceral state, and we must be honest about the primary function of this carceral state. We are not addicted to incarceration. We use the system of incarceration to police Black bodies and remove them from mainstream society, not just for the period of their sentence, but we police their bodies long after they leave the prison walls so that their chances of successfully reentering society are almost entirely blocked. The United States is way out of bounds with regard to policing and incarcerating our citizenry, and the United States can only remain relevant in the next century if we dismantle our system of mass incarceration and invest in the potential of all bodies. The United States cannot continue to develop as a strong economy if we continue to allow the human capital of millions of our young people to decay for decades in prison.

Lastly, we must develop a plan for closing the racial gap. It is not enough to dismantle racism and believe that what would emerge is a level playing field.

What policies and practices can be designed and implemented that acknowledge the four hundred plus years of racism and create a level playing field, not simply by eradicating racism [12] but by honestly and fairly addressing the four-hundred-year accumulation of advantage and

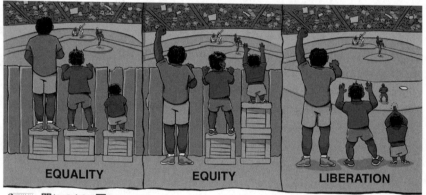

Equality, Equity, and Liberation
Source: **Center for Story-Based Strategy and Interaction Institute for Social Change. Artist: Angus Maguire.**

disadvantage? This is perhaps the greatest challenge we face as a society and a nation. It's not as simple as building the kinds of ladders or stools depicted in the image of equality and equity. Because all systems of oppression, including racism, are relational and based fundamentally in power relations, there is no solution that does not involve the redistribution of power and privilege and also of resources and opportunities. This would require even more redistribution than a socialist approach because it will demand redress for four hundred plus years of systematic, deliberate oppression. Resources will have to be redistributed from those who have accumulated advantage to those who have accumulated disadvantage. Whole communities will have to be reorganized. Nearly every social institution, from schools to the economy to politics to incarceration, will have to be dismantled entirely and reconfigured from scratch based on a new model, one that truly values all lives equally and distributes power and resources in the same manner.

This sounds like a nearly impossible task, and it is indeed overwhelming. But there are things we can do in our daily lives to combat the policing of Black bodies. In addition to the ideas we recommend here, we include in appendix B a list of organizations you can volunteer with or that you can follow on Facebook or Twitter so that you can stay current on issues related to the carceral state in the United States and abroad.

Boycott companies that exploit prison labor. But don't just simply stop buying their products or services; call or e-mail their national headquarters and tell them why. If you own a small business, consider hiring someone with a felony record who is trying to get their life back on track. You can still perform a background check and employ practices to safeguard yourself, but take a chance. If you have legal skills, volunteer at an innocence project in your community. Even if you don't have legal skills, you can still contribute by opening and sorting the thousands and thousands of letters that arrive from incarcerated people desperate to prove their innocence. Go online and find an inmate looking for a pen pal. Being locked up twenty-three hours a day makes one hungry for any kind of human contact. Donate your gently used books to a jail or prison library. Reading can help pass the time. Call and write your congresspeople when bills are introduced that will impact drug laws or sentencing disparities. Volunteer to help reenfranchise citizens who have had their right to vote taken away because they were convicted of a felony. This gives power back to those who so desperately need it. Volunteer with young people in juvenile detention centers, homeless shelters, or low-resourced schools. Preventing the school-to-prison pipeline prevents not only future crime but also mass incarceration. Start a book club and choose our book. And after you read our book, choose another of the books we recommend here. If you do nothing else, talk about what you have read about in this book. So few people understand the enormity or depth of the issue and its impact on our society. We believe that the more people are aware, the more inclined they will be to act.

What other choice do we have? What if we can't figure this out? Where do we go as a society if we continue to exacerbate racial inequalities and police Black bodies? We will implode. We simply won't survive into the next century. We must take on this mantle and Make America Equitable for All Its Citizens, not again, but literally for the first time since the founding of America!

APPENDIX A

High-Profile Police Shootings of Black Men and the Outcomes

Sean Bell—On November 25, 2006, this twenty-three-year-old Black man was out with friends celebrating his upcoming wedding. As they were leaving the party, Bell and his friends were ambushed by a team of New York City police officers who fired fifty shots at the car they were sitting in at a parking lot outside the club where they had been celebrating. Bell was shot thirty-one times and died as a result. The Bell family settled with the city of New York for approximately $7 million.

Outcome: None of the officers were convicted. The officers received a settlement.

Mike Brown—An eighteen-year-old Black man shot and killed on August 9, 2014, in Ferguson, Missouri (his body lay in the street for five hours).

Outcome: Officer Darren Wilson was not indicted for shooting Michael Brown. Many people question whether justice was done.

Philando Castile—July 6, 2016, fatally shot seven times at point-blank range in front of his girlfriend and her four-year-old daughter by Jeronimo Yanez, a St. Anthony, Minnesota, police officer.

Outcome: Yanez acquitted of the killing.

Jamar Clark—November 15, 2015, Jamar Clark, a twenty-four-year-old Black man, was shot by Minneapolis Police in Minneapolis, Minnesota.

Outcome—no charges filed.

Amadou Diallo—On February 4, 1999, twenty-three-year-old unarmed Diallo was shot and killed after four New York City officers fired forty-one shots at him in the doorway of his Bronx apartment building. He was doing nothing wrong.

Outcome: The officers were charged but acquitted of all charges. His family settled with the city of New York for $3 million. The officers received a pension.[1]

Samuel DuBose—On July 19, 2015, in Cincinnati, Ohio, DuBose, an unarmed Black man, was fatally shot by Ray Tensing, a University of Cincinnati police officer.

Outcome: A second trial ended in a mistrial on June 23, 2016.

Jonathan Ferrell—Once an athlete playing for the Florida A&M football team, a once storied historical Black college (HBCU), the twenty-four-year-old Ferrell crashed his car and went for help, stopping at a nearby home. The white woman who lived at the house where he sought help called the police. Two officers responded and have testified that they believed Ferrell was going to take away their guns, despite the fact that there was never any other evidence of this. The woman who called the police likely communicated that she was afraid he was going to break into her house when all he was attempting to do was get help after the accident. On September 14, 2013, police shot him ten times, killing him.

Outcome: The officers received a settlement.[2]

Dontre Hamilton—On April 30, 2014, a police officer, Christopher Manney, shot and killed Dontre Hamilton at Red Arrow Park in Milwaukee, Wisconsin.

Outcome: No charges were ever brought against Officer Manney.

Trayvon Martin—February 26, 2012, seventeen-year-old Trayvon Martin was fatally shot in Sanford, Florida, by George Zimmerman.

Outcome: Zimmerman acquitted of second-degree murder and of manslaughter charges.

Laquan McDonald—Shot and killed on October 20, 2014, in Chicago, Illinois. He was shot sixteen times in fourteen seconds.

Outcome: This case marks the first time in nearly thirty-five years that a Chicago police officer (Jason D. Van Dyke) has been charged with first-degree murder for an on-duty fatality—pending.

Tamir Rice—A twelve-year-old Black youth, shot and killed on November 22, 2014, in Cleveland, Ohio. He was shot twice within two seconds of Officer Loehmann's arrival on the scene.

Outcome: Ohio grand jury decided *not to indict* Officers Timothy Loehmann and Frank Garmback.

Keith Lamont Scott—Forty-three-year-old Black man, fatally shot on September 20, 2016, in Charlotte, North Carolina, by Brentley Vinson, a Black city police officer.

Outcome—In November 2016, county prosecutors decided not to charge Vinson, concluding that the shooting was justified.

Alton Sterling—A thirty-seven-year-old Black man, shot several times at close range on June 5, 2016, while held down on the ground by two white Baton Rouge police officers.

Outcome: The Justice Department has decided not to bring charges against the officers involved in the death of Alton Sterling.

David Lee Turner—Turner, a former NFL player, was shot and killed on July 10, 2011. He played for the Cincinnati Bengals. Accounts have it that Turner, his son, and a friend were walking away from a convenience store with two cans of beer when they were approached by a police patrol car. The officers told Turner to put down his package, which he did. After he understood that the police had completed their investigation, Turner, his son, and the friend started to walk away. One of the two police shot and killed Turner.[3]

APPENDIX B

Resources

Prison Legal News

A monthly print publication covering criminal justice issues, a project of the Human Rights Defense Center, a 501(c)(3) nonprofit organization.

https://www.prisonlegalnews.org

Corrections Today

The professional membership publication of the American Correctional Association (ACA). The magazine is published six times a year.

http://bit.ly/2uxqlda

The Marshall Project

A nonprofit, nonpartisan online journalism organization focusing on issues related to criminal justice in the United States.

http://bit.ly/2tTe7hc

National Association of Police Organizations (NAPO)

A coalition of police unions and associations from across the United States.

http://www.napo.org

Prison Policy Initiative

A criminal justice–oriented American public policy think tank.
http://bit.ly/2uxwndP

Urgency of Intersectionality

Professor Kimberly Crenshaw, TED Talk
http://bit.ly/2swOI9p

Eight Deadliest Race Riots in U.S. History

Nick Chiles in the *Atlanta Black Star* (November 19, 2014) chronicles
the history of race riots.
http://bit.ly/2sUrTw1

Mass Incarceration

John Phaff, *Locked In: The True Causes of Mass Incarceration—and
How to Achieve Real Reform* (New York: Basic Books, 2017).
http://amzn.to/2sUJDqV

School-to-Prison Pipeline

American Civil Liberties Union is committed to challenging the
"school-to-prison pipeline," a disturbing national trend wherein
children are funneled out of public schools and into the juvenile
and criminal justice systems.
http://bit.ly/2toTj0p

Prison-Industrial Complex

Descriptive term describing the overlapping interests of government
and industry that use surveillance, policing, and imprisonment as
solutions to economic, social, and political problems.
http://bit.ly/2uSuw2L

Black Women's Bodies Are Constantly Policed and Hypersexualized

Historically, Black women's bodies have constantly been policed and
sexualized.
Hazel V. Carby, "Policing the Black Woman's Body in an Urban
Context," *Critical Inquiry* 18 (1992): 738–55.
https://doi.org/10.1086/448654

Black Trans Bodies Are Under Attack

Spotlight on the violence and discrimination faced by transgender women of color.
http://bit.ly/2ty6P0g

Shooting Unarmed Black Men

Angela J. Davis, *Policing the Black Man: Arrest, Prosecution, and Imprisonment* (New York: Pantheon, 2017).
http://amzn.to/2sx3MUQ

Exonerating the Innocent

The Innocence Project is a nonprofit legal organization that is committed to exonerating wrongly convicted people through the use of DNA testing.
https://www.innocenceproject.org

Bureau of Justice Statistics

The bureau collects, analyzes, and publishes data relating to crime in the United States.
https://www.bjs.gov

Pew

The Pew Charitable Trusts uses evidence-based, nonpartisan analysis to solve today's challenges.
http://www.pewtrusts.org

Prison Talk

Online community with an interest in prisoner support.
http://www.prisontalk.com

Recommended Films

13th (directed by Ava DuVernay, 2016)
The House I Live In (directed by Eugene Jarecki, 2012)

NOTES

1. SETTING THE STAGE

1. Chris Hayes, *A Colony in a Nation* (New York: Norton, 2017), 16–22.

2. The Movement for Black Lives Platform, https://policy.m4bl.org/platform.

3. All were acquitted July 27, 2016.

4. By "policing of Black bodies," we mean the term to be read more widely than just actual police interacting with Black people. We mean "policing" to cover housing segregation, redlining, resegregation of schools, and sentencing for powder and crack cocaine. We must not forget the issue of naming and how "ethnic-"sounding names receive fewer callbacks for jobs.

5. Robert Staples, "White Racism, Black Crime, and American Justice: An Application of the Colonial Model to Explain Crime and Race," *Phylon* 36, no. 1 (1975): 14–22.

6. Patricia Hill Collins, *Black Feminist Thought: Knowledge, Consciousness and the Politics of Empowerment* (Boston: Unwin Hyman, 1990).

7. Joan Acker, "Inequality Regimes: Gender, Class, and Race in Organizations," *Gender & Society* 20 (2006): 441–64, doi:10.1177/0891243206289499.

8. Craig Steven Wilder, *Ebony & Ivy: Race, Slavery, and the Troubled History of America's Universities* (New York: St. Martin's, 2014).

9. Marilyn Frye, *The Politics of Reality: Essays in Feminist Theory* (Freedom, CA: Crossing Press, 1983), 2.

10. Frantz Fanon, *Black Skin, White Masks* (New York: Grove Press, 1952).

11. Eduardo Bonilla-Silva, "Rethinking Racism: Toward a Structural Interpretation," *American Sociological Review* 62, no. 3 (1997): 465–80, 472, http://www.jstor.org/stable/2657316.

12. W. I. Thomas and Dorothy Thomas, *The Child in America: Behavior Problems and Programs* (New York: Knopf, 1928), 571.

13. Eduardo Bonilla-Silva, "The Structure of Racism in Color-Blind, 'Post-Racial' America," *American Behavioral Scientist* 59, no. 11 (2015): 1358–76, 1360.

14. A lecture given by Professor Tricia Rose at George Mason University, April 4, 2016.

15. Frantz Fanon, *The Wretched of the Earth*, trans. Richard Philox (New York: Grove, 1984), 187, Kindle.

16. National Urban League, *40 Years: The State of Black America, 1976–2016*, 2016, http://soba.iamempowered.com/node/191.

17. Charles Murray, *Coming Apart: The State of White America, 1960–2010* (New York: Crown, 2013).

18. No coincidence this is happening in the state of Mississippi, http://wapo.st/1smuTB4.

2. URBAN RIOTS AND PROTEST, OR A LOGICAL RESPONSE TO POLICING BLACK BODIES

1. Ta-Nehisi Coates, "The Clock Didn't Start with the Riots: Black People in Baltimore Are Subjected to Violence All the Time," *Atlantic*, April 30, 2015, http://www.theatlantic.com/politics/archive/2015/04/ta-nehisi-coates-johns-hopkins-baltimore/391904.

2. Chris M. Messer, Krystal Beamon, and Patricia A. Bell, "The Tulsa Riot of 1921: Collective Violence and Racial Frames," *Western Journal of Black Studies* 37, no. 1 (2013): 50–59.

3. John Hope Franklin, "Tulsa Still Hasn't Faced the Truth about the Race Riot of 1921," delivered before the House Judiciary Committee, Subcommittee on the Constitution, Civil Rights, and Civil Liberties, April 28, 2007, http://bit.ly/2seTec7.

4. John Hope Franklin, "Tulsa Still Hasn't Faced the Truth about the Race Riot of 1921," delivered before the House Judiciary Committee, Subcommittee on the Constitution, Civil Rights, and Civil Liberties, April 28, 2007, http://bit.ly/2seTec7.

5. Allan Spear, *Black Chicago: The Making of a Negro Ghetto, 1890–1920* (Chicago: University of Chicago Press, 1967). See also the *New York Times* for full coverage of the riot—with a list of the deceased—and an accounting of who was involved: http://nyti.ms/1U5TkvN.

6. Chicago Commission on Race Relations, *The Negro in Chicago: A Study of Race Relations and a Race Riot* (Chicago: University of Chicago Press, 1922).

7. Janet L. Abu-Lughod, *Race, Space, and Riots in Chicago, New York, and Los Angeles* (New York: Oxford University Press, 2007).

8. Fred C. Shapiro and James W. Sullivan, *Race Riots, New York, 1964* (New York: Crowell, 1964).

9. Charles Brooks, "Harlemworld: Doing Race and Class in Contemporary Black America," *Black Issues Book Review*, March–April 2002.

10. The most famous record of this period is by the Black philosopher and Rhodes Scholar Dr. Alain Locke. See, especially, *The New Negro: An Interpretation* (New York: Albert and Charles Boni, 1925).

11. Jeffery Stewart, "Harlem Renaissance," Online NewsHour Forum, PBS, February 20, 1998.

12. Martin Luther King Jr., "Beyond the Los Angeles Riots: Next Step, the North," *Saturday Review*, November 13, 1965, 33–35, 105.

13. McCone Commission Report, California, *Governor's Commission on the Los Angeles Riots: Plus One Hundred Four Shocking Photos of the Most Terrifying Riot in History*. Los Angeles: Kimtex, 1965.

14. Elizabeth Hinton, *From the War on Poverty to the War on Crime: The Making of Mass Incarceration in America* (Cambridge, MA: Harvard University Press, 2016), 299.

15. Denise Kersten Wills, "'People Were Out of Control': Remembering the 1968 Riots," *Washingtonian*, April 2008.

16. Michael Alison Chandler, "One in 10 D.C. Students Score 'College Ready' on New High School Math Test," *Washington Post*, October 27, 2015, http://wapo.st/1Wg2kgH.

17. John Fiske, *Media Matters: Race and Gender in U.S. Politics* (Minneapolis: University of Minnesota Press, 1996), 188.

18. Rich Connell and Richard Serrano, "L.A. Is Warned of New Unrest: Webster Report Urges Swift Action in City Plagued by Hostility, Rage and Resentment in Many Areas. Budget Crisis and Politicking Could Delay Reforms," *Los Angeles Times*, October, 22, 1992, http://lat.ms/22IuPrX.

19. Snejana Farberov, "Caught on Camera: Police Shooting of Teenager Which Has Shocked America and Left City of Ferguson on the Brink as Officers Face Protests over 'Racism and Brutality' and Looters Go on Rampage," *Daily Mail*, August 15, 2014, http://dailym.ai/1YbihsD.

20. Justin Sink, "Obama Calls for Calm after 'Disturbing' Events in Ferguson," *The Hill*, August 14, 2014, http://thehill.com/homenews/administration/215152-obama-calls-for-calm-after-disturbing-events-in-ferguson.

21. http://brennerbrief.com/list-ferguson-businesses-destroyed.

22. Department of Justice Report, "Investigation of the Ferguson Police Department," March 2015, 1.

23. Department of Justice Report, "Investigation of the Ferguson Police Department," March 2015, 55.

24. David A. Graham, "The Mysterious Death of Freddie Gray," *Atlantic*, April 22, 2015, http://theatln.tc/24YO7ZQ.

25. Emily Badger, "The Long, Painful and Repetitive History of How Baltimore Became Baltimore," *Washington Post*, April 29, 2015, http://wapo.st/1VQkLd8.

26. Luke Broadwater, "Wells Fargo Agrees to Pay $175M Settlement in Pricing Discrimination Suit," *Baltimore Sun*, July 12, 2012, http://bit.ly/28IuKQX.

27. Conor Friedersdorf, "The Brutality of Police Culture in Baltimore," *Atlantic*, April 22, 2015, http://theatln.tc/28ItPz0.

28. Doug Donovan and Jean Marbella. "Dismissed: Tenants Lose and Landlords Win in Baltimore's Rent Court," *Baltimore Sun*, April 26, 2017, http://data.baltimoresun.com/news/dismissed.

3. MASS INCARCERATION

1. Chris Hayes, *A Colony in a Nation* (New York: Norton, 2017).

2. A. N. LeBlanc, "Prison Is a Member of Their Family," *New York Times Magazine*, January 12, 2003. Emphasis ours.

3. Joshua Aiken, "The Downstream Effect of 35 Years of Jail Growth? A State Prison Boom," *Prison Policy Initiative*, June 4, 2017, https://www.prisonpolicy.org/blog/2017/06/14/downstream.

4. Chris Hayes, *A Colony in a Nation* (New York: Norton).

5. Maya Schenwar, "The Quiet Horrors of House Arrest, Electronic Monitoring, and Other Alternative Forms of Incarceration: How Imprisonment Extends beyond the Jailhouse into Every Arena of American Life," *Mother Jones*, January 22, 2015, http://www.motherjones.com/politics/2015/01/house-arrest-surveillance-state-prisons.

6. Maya Schenwar, "The Quiet Horrors of House Arrest, Electronic Monitoring, and Other Alternative Forms of Incarceration: How Imprisonment Extends beyond the Jailhouse into Every Arena of American Life," *Mother Jones*, January 22, 2015, http://www.motherjones.com/politics/2015/01/house-arrest-surveillance-state-prisons.

7. Patrick Langan, *Race of Prisoners Admitted to State and Federal Institutions, 1926–86*, NCJ-125618 (Washington, D.C.: U.S. Department of Justice, 1991), https://www.ncjrs.gov/pdffiles1/nij/125618.pdf.

8. M. R. Durose, and Patrick A. Langan, *State Court Sentencing of Convicted Felons, 1998 Statistical Tables* (Washington, DC: U.S. Department of Justice, 2001).

9. C. C. Spohn, *Thirty Years of Sentencing Reform: The Quest for a Racially Neutral Sentencing Process* (Washington, DC: National Institute of Justice, 2000).

10. E. A. Carson and E. Anderson, *Prisoners in 2015* (Washington, DC: Bureau of Justice Statistics, 2016); D. J. James, *Profile of Jail Inmates, 2002* (Washington, DC: Bureau of Justice Statistics, 2004); M. Mauer and R. King, *A 25-Year Quagmire: The War on Drugs and Its Impact on American Society* (Washington, DC: Sentencing Project, 2007); T. D. Minton and Z. Zeng, *Jail Inmates in 2015* (Washington, DC: Bureau of Justice Statistics, 2016).

11. (ONDCP) Information Clearinghouse, http://www.whitehousedrugpolicy. gov/publications/factsht/druguse.

12. Dan Baum. "Legalize It All: How to Win the War on Drugs," *Harper's Bazaar*, April 2016, http://harpers.org/archive/2016/04/legalize-it-all.

13. Elizabeth Hinton, *From the War on Poverty to the War on Crime: The Making of Mass Incarceration in America* (Cambridge, MA: Harvard University Press, 2016), 312.

14. Dorothy Roberts, *Killing the Black Body: Race, Reproduction, and the Meaning of Liberty* (New York: Vintage, 1999), 155.

15. http://www.drugpolicy.org/drugwar/mandatorymin/crackpowder.cfm.

16. Elizabeth Hinton, *From the War on Poverty to the War on Crime: The Making of Mass Incarceration in America* (Cambridge, MA: Harvard University Press, 2016), 312.

17. Elizabeth Hinton, *From the War on Poverty to the War on Crime: The Making of Mass Incarceration in America* (Cambridge, MA: Harvard University Press, 2016), 313.

18. Chris Hayes, *A Colony in a Nation* (New York: Norton, 2017), 84.

19. Council of Economic Advisors, *Fines, Fees, and Bail Payments in the Criminal Justice System That Disproportionately Impact the Poor*, 2, https:// www.whitehouse.gov/sites/default/files/page/files/1215_cea_fine_fee_bail_ issue_brief.pdf.

20. Chris Hayes, *A Colony in a Nation* (New York: Norton, 2017), 84–85.

21. Alexes Harris, *A Pound of Flesh: Monetary Sanctions as a Punishment for the Poor* (New York: Russell Sage).

22. Chris Serres, "Homeless and Penniless, Minnesota Sex Offender Is Sent Back to Jail Because He Can't Afford Treatment," *Minneapolis Star-Tribune*, May 4, 2016, http://www.startribune.com/homeless-and-penniless-minnesota- sex-offender-is-sent-back-to-jail-because-he-can-t-afford-treatment/378045171.

23. Devah Pager, "The Mark of a Criminal Record," *American Journal of Sociology* 108 (2003): 937–75.

24. D. Mukamal, "After Prisons: Roadblocks to Reentry; A Report on State Legal Barriers Facing People with Criminal Records" (New York: Legal Action Center, 2004).

25. D. Mukamal, "After Prisons: Roadblocks to Reentry; A Report on State Legal Barriers Facing People with Criminal Records" (New York: Legal Action Center, 2004).

4. SCHOOL-TO-PRISON PIPELINE

1. Beth Schwartzapfel, "Sentenced Young: The Story of Life without Parole for Juvenile Offenders," *Aljazeera America*, February 1, 2014, http://america. aljazeera.com/features/2014/1/sentenced-young-thestoryoflifewithoutparoleforjuvenileoffenders.html.

2. "K–12 Education: Better Use of Information Could Help Agencies Identify Disparities and Address Racial Discrimination," GAO-16-345, Government Accountability Office, April 21, 2016, http://gao.gov/products/GAO-16-345.

3. See Angela J. Hattery and Earl Smith, *African American Families: Myths and Realities* (Lanham, MD: Rowman & Littlefield, 2014), chapter 5, for a lengthy discussion.

4. Melissa S. Kearney and Benjamin H. Harris, "Ten Economic Facts about Crime and Incarceration in the United States," Brookings Institute, May 1, 2014, http://www.brookings.edu/research/reports/2014/05/10-crime-facts.

5. Elizabeth Hinton, *From the War on Poverty to the War on Crime: The Making of Mass Incarceration in America* (Cambridge, MA: Harvard University Press, 2016), 33–34.

6. Tony Fabelo, Michael D. Thompson, Martha Plotkin, Dottie Carmichael, Miner P. Marchbanks III, and Eric A. Booth, *Breaking Schools' Rules: A Statewide Study of How School Discipline Relates to Students' Success and Juvenile Justice Involvement* (Public Policy Research Institute, 2011).

7. Tony Fabelo, Michael D. Thompson, Martha Plotkin, Dottie Carmichael, Miner P. Marchbanks III, and Eric A. Booth, *Breaking School's Rules: A Statewide Study of How School Discipline Relates to Students' Success and Juvenile Justice Involvement* (Public Policy Research Institute, 2011).

8. Nancy A. Heitzeg, *The School-to-Prison Pipeline: Education, Discipline, and Racialized Double Standards* (New York: Praeger, 2016), 7.

9. Sheila Burke, "Arrest of Tennessee Children Exposes Flawed Juvenile Justice," ABC News, May 13, 2016, http://abcnews.go.com/US/wireStory/arrest-tennessee-children-exposes-flawed-juvenile-justice-39084653.

10. Roz Plater, "Prince William Student Handcuffed, Suspended over 'Stolen' $0.65 Milk Carton," ABC7, May 20, 2016, http://wjla.com/news/local/prince-william-student-handcuffed-suspended-over-stolen-065-milk-carton.

11. U.S. Department of Justice, http://www.ojjdp.gov.

12. Joshua Rovner, "Disproportionate Minority Contact in the Juvenile Justice System," Sentencing Project, 2014, http://sentencingproject.org/wp-content/uploads/2015/11/Disproportionate-Minority-Contact-in-the-Juvenile-Justice-System.pdf.

13. Carimah Townes, "Black People Twice as Likely to Be Arrested for Pot in Colorado and Washington—Where It's Legal," *Think Progress*, March 21, 2016, http://thinkprogress.org/justice/2016/03/21/3761973/black-people-still-more-likely-to-face-marijuana-arrests.

14. Annie E. Casey Foundation, "Maltreatment of Youth in U.S. Juvenile Corrections Facilities: An Update," 2015, 7, http://www.aecf.org/resources/maltreatment-of-youth-in-us-juvenile-corrections-facilities.

15. Ben Montgomery and Waveney Ann Moore, "For Their Own Good: A St. Petersburg Times Special Report on Child Abuse at the Florida School for Boys," *Tampa Bay Times*, April 17, 2009, http://www.tampabay.com/specials/2009/reports/marianna.

16. Michael Schwirtz and Michael Winerip, "Kalief Browder, Held at Rikers Island for 3 Years without Trial, Commits Suicide," *New York Times*, June 8, 2015, http://nyti.ms/1rROE3l.

17. Allen J. Beck, David Cantor, John Hartge, and Tim Smith, *Sexual Victimization in Juvenile Facilities, Reported by Youth 2012* (Washington, DC: Bureau of Justice Statistics, 2013).

18. http://archive.tennessean.com/article/20100207/NEWS0205/2070362/Sex-abuse-allegations-plague-TN-juvenile-detention-center.

19. Allen J. Beck, David Cantor, John Hartge, and Tim Smith, *Sexual Victimization in Juvenile Facilities, Reported by Youth 2012* (Washington, DC: Bureau of Justice Statistics, 2013).

20. Ashley Nellis, "The Lives of Juvenile Lifers: Findings from a National Survey," Sentencing Project, 2012, http://sentencingproject.org/wp-content/uploads/2016/01/The-Lives-of-Juvenile-Lifers.pdf.

21. Ashley Nellis, "The Lives of Juvenile Lifers: Findings from a National Survey, Sentencing Project, 2012, http://sentencingproject.org/wp-content/uploads/2016/01/The-Lives-of-Juvenile-Lifers.pdf.

22. Ashley Nellis, "The Lives of Juvenile Lifers: Findings from a National Survey," Sentencing Project, 2012, http://sentencingproject.org/wp-content/uploads/2016/01/The-Lives-of-Juvenile-Lifers.pdf.

23. Michelle Alexander, *The New Jim Crow* (New York: New Press, 2010), 207–8.

5. THE PRISON-INDUSTRIAL COMPLEX

1. UNICOR website: http://www.unicor.gov/About_FPI_Programs.aspx.

2. Corrections Corporations of America, a private prison company, reported revenues of $1.2 billion in 2005.

3. Clayton Mosher and Gregory Hooks, "Don't Build It Here Revisited (or 'There Is No Economic Salvation through Incarceration')—Prisons Do Not Create Jobs," *Prison Legal News*, January 15, 2010, http://bit.ly/292zPEp; Gregory Hooks, "The Prison Industry: Carceral Expansion and Employment in U.S. Counties, 1969–1994," *Social Science Quarterly* 85, no. 1 (2004): 38–57.

4. Elizabeth Hinton, *From the War on Poverty to the War on Crime: The Making of Mass Incarceration in America* (Cambridge, MA: Harvard University Press), 321.

5. Wendy Sawyer, "How Much Do Incarcerated People Earn in Each State?" *Prison Policy Initiative*, April 10, 2017, https://www.prisonpolicy.org/blog/2017/04/10/wages.

6. Harvey Yoder, "Va. Faces a Worsening Prison Crisis," *News Leader*, June 1, 2015, http://www.newsleader.com/story/opinion/columnists/2015/06/01/va-faces-worsening-prison-crisis/28256983.

7. Derek Gilna, "Businesses, Members of Congress, Not Happy with UNICOR," *Prison Legal News*, March 15, 2014, https://www.prisonlegalnews.org/news/2014/mar/15/businesses-members-of-congress-not-happy-with-unicor.

8. Linda Thieman, "Fallon Requests Info on Jobs Lost to Prison Labor, Clarifies 'Gulag' Remark," *Blog for Iowa* [blog], June 30, 2004, http://www.blogforiowa.com/blog.

9. A visit to their website (http://prisonblues.com) reveals that they not only market denim products for sale to consumers in the United States but also to customers in Japan! So, Japanese can now buy Prison Blues garments, manufactured by inmates in the Eastern Oregon Correctional Institution, over the Internet! We note that the proliferation and popularization of prison life as demonstrated by this garment line is pervasive in the music industry, made popular by hip-hop artists like 50 Cent and Snoop Dog.

10. Catfish farming was once one of Mississippi's top agricultural commodities, grossing approximately $255 million annually. Now all of this has changed. As Hugh Warren, executive vice president of the Catfish Farmers of America (CFA), put it, "We are struggling right now." The catfish farmers who used to get seventy-five cents per pound are now down to approximately sixty cents per pound. See "Profitability Remains Elusive for Mississippi Catfish Farmers," *Mississippi Business Journal*, August 2, 2004.

11. Clayton Mosher and Gregory Hooks, "Don't Build It Here Revisited (or 'There Is No Economic Salvation through Incarceration')—Prisons Do Not Create Jobs," *Prison Legal News*, January 15, 2010, http://bit.ly/292zPEp.

12. "Inside the Secret Industry of Inmate-Staffed Call Centers," NBC News, January 12, 2012, http://usnews.nbcnews.com/_news/2012/01/12/10140493-inside-the-secret-industry-of-inmate-staffed-call-centers.

13. Erica Barnett, "Prison Coffee: Starbucks Admits Its Contractor Uses Prison Labor," *Michigan Citizen* 24 (2002): A7. Emphasis ours.

14. Erica Barnett, "Prison Coffee: Starbucks Admits Its Contractor Uses Prison Labor," *Michigan Citizen* 24 (2002): A7. Emphasis ours.

15. Kamal Ghali, "No Slavery Except as a Punishment for Crime: The Punishment Clause and Sexual Slavery," *UCLA Law Review* 55 (2008): 607.

16. Angela Y. Davis, "Masked Racism: Reflections on the Prison Industrial Complex," *Colorlines Magazine*, 1998.

17. Shane Bauer, "My Four Months as a Private Prison Guard: A Mother Jones Investigation," *Mother Jones*, July/August 2016, http://bit.ly/28TZwIP.

6. POLICING BLACK WOMEN'S BODIES

1. Manuel Villa, "The Mental Health Crisis Facing Women in Prison," *San Antonio Express*, June 22, 2017, http://bit.ly/2tYlaCa.

2. Names of people we interviewed have been changed to protect their identities.

3. Malika Saada Saar, Rebecca Epstein, Lindsay Rosenthal, and Yasmin Vafa, *The Sexual Abuse to Prison Pipeline: The Girls' Story* (Washington, DC: Center for Poverty and Inequality, Georgetown University Law Center, 2015), 7, http://bit.ly/1DqeScy. Emphasis ours.

4. Dorothy Roberts, *Killing the Black Body: Race, Reproduction, and the Meaning of Liberty* (New York: Vintage, 1999), 150–51.

5. Dorothy Roberts, *Killing the Black Body: Race, Reproduction, and the Meaning of Liberty* (New York: Vintage, 1999), 157. Emphasis ours.

6. D. R. Neuspiel, "Racism and Perinatal Addiction," *Ethnicity and Disease* 6 (1996): 47–55.

7. Nancy Sokoloff, "The Impact of the Prison Industrial Complex on African American Women," *SOULS* 5 (2003): 31–46, 35.

8. B. E. Richie, "Challenges Incarcerated Women Face as They Return to Their Communities: Findings from Life History Interviews," *Crime and Delinquency* 47 (2001): 368–89, 381–82.

7. POLICING TRANS BODIES

1. Deborah Sontag, "Transgender Woman Cites Attacks and Abuse in Men's Prison," *New York Times*, April 5, 2015, http://www.nytimes.com/2015/04/06/us/ashley-diamond-transgender-inmate-cites-attacks-and-abuse-in-mens-prison.html. Emphasis ours.

2. Betsy Lucal, "What It Means to Be Gendered Me: Life on the Boundaries of a Dichotomous Gender System," *Gender & Society* 13 (1999): 781–97, 786–88, doi:10.1177/089124399013006006.

3. Jaime M. Grant, Lisa A. Mottet, Justin Tanis, Jack Harrison, Jody L. Herman, and Mara Keisling, *Injustice at Every Turn: A Report of the National Transgender Discrimination Survey* (Washington, DC: National Center for Transgender Equality and National Gay and Lesbian Task Force, 2011).

4. *A Blueprint for Equality: A Federal Agenda for Transgender People*, National Center for Transgender Equality, 2015, chapter 13, http://www.transequality.org/sites/default/files/docs/resources/NCTE_Blueprint_2015_Prisons.pdf.

5. Jaime M. Grant, Lisa A. Mottet, Justin Tanis, Jack Harrison, Jody L. Herman, and Mara Keisling, *Injustice at Every Turn: A Report of the National Transgender Discrimination Survey* (Washington, DC: National Center for Transgender Equality and National Gay and Lesbian Task Force, 2011).

6. Jaime M. Grant, Lisa A. Mottet, Justin Tanis, Jack Harrison, Jody L. Herman, and Mara Keisling, *Injustice at Every Turn: A Report of the National Transgender Discrimination Survey* (Washington, DC: National Center for Transgender Equality and National Gay and Lesbian Task Force, 2011).

7. Valerie Jenness, Cheryl L. Maxson, Kristy N. Matsuda, and Jennifer Macy Sumner, *Violence in California Correctional Facilities: An Empirical Examination of Sexual Assault* (Irvine: Center for Evidence-Based Corrections, University of California, 2007).

8. Jaime M. Grant, Lisa A. Mottet, Justin Tanis, Jack Harrison, Jody L. Herman, and Mara Keisling, *Injustice at Every Turn: A Report of the National Transgender Discrimination Survey* (Washington, DC: National Center for Transgender Equality and National Gay and Lesbian Task Force, 2011).

9. George Brown and Everett McDuffie, "Health Care Policies Addressing Transgender Inmates in Prison Systems in the United States," *Journal of Correctional Health Care* 15, no. 4 (2009): 280–91.

10. Jaime M. Grant, Lisa A. Mottet, Justin Tanis, Jack Harrison, Jody L. Herman, and Mara Keisling, *Injustice at Every Turn: A Report of the National Transgender Discrimination Survey* (Washington, DC: National Center for Transgender Equality and National Gay and Lesbian Task Force, 2011).

11. Jaime M. Grant, Lisa A. Mottet, Justin Tanis, Jack Harrison, Jody L. Herman, and Mara Keisling, *Injustice at Every Turn: A Report of the National Transgender Discrimination Survey* (Washington, DC: National Center for Transgender Equality and National Gay and Lesbian Task Force, 2011).

12. Sabrina Rubin Erdley, "The Transgender Crucible," *Rolling Stone*, July 30, 2014, http://www.rollingstone.com/culture/news/the-transgender-crucible-20140730#ixzz49bNbBmBK.

13. Valerie Jenness and Sarah Fenstermaker, "Forty Years after *Brownmiller*: Prisons for Men, Transgender Inmates, and the Rape of the Feminine," *Gender and Society* 30, no. 1: 16.

8. POLICE KILLINGS OF UNARMED BLACK MEN

1. Chris Hayes, *A Colony in a Nation* (New York: Norton, 2017), 76. Emphasis ours.

2. Radley Balko, *Rise of the Warrior Cop: The Militarization of America's Police Forces* (New York: PublicAffairs Books, 2013).

3. James D. Walsh, "The Bullet, the Cop, the Boy," *New York Magazine*, June 14, 2017, http://nym.ag/2sDkuVm.

4. Description from the PublicAffairs Books website: http://www.publicaffairsbooks.com/book/rise-of-the-warrior-cop/9781610394574.

5. Steve Featherstone, "Professor Carnage," *New Republic*, April 17, 2017, https://newrepublic.com/article/141675/professor-carnage-dave-grossman-police-warrior-philosophy.

6. John Paul Wilson, Kurt Hugenberg, and Nicholas O. Rule, "Racial Bias in Judgments of Physical Size and Formidability: From Size to Threat," *Journal of Personality and Social Psychology* 113, no. 1 (2017): 59–80, http://psycnet.apa.org/psycinfo/2017-11085-001.

7. Bill Whitaker, "Officer Betty Shelby on Terence Crutcher Shooting," CBS News, April 2, 2017, http://cbsn.ws/2rExSJi.

8. Chris Hayes, *A Colony in a Nation* (New York: Norton, 2017), 38–39.

9. The US Police Shootings Database (USPSD), https://us-police-shootings-database.silk.co; *Washington Post*, http://wapo.st/1J4wTor; *The Guardian*, http://bit.ly/1Ey6d8u.

10. A comprehensive overview of the barriers to accessing information is provided by Cody T. Ross, "A Multi-Level Bayesian Analysis of Racial Bias in Police Shootings at the County-Level in the United States, 2011–2014," *PLoS One* 10, no. 11 (2015), https://doi.org/10.1371/journal.pone.0141854.

11. Charles R. Epp, Steven Maynard-Moody, and Donald P. Haider-Markel, *Pulled Over: How Police Stops Define Race and Citizenship* (Chicago: University of Chicago Press, 2014).

12. History.com Staff, "Emmett Till Murderers Make Magazine Confession," 2009, http://bit.ly/295Kkqq.

13. Adam Ferrise, "Timothy Russell's Family Upset with Michael Brelo Verdict, but 'It Wasn't All Brelo's Fault,'" Cleveland.com, May 23, 2015, http://bit.ly/28VY1dk.

14. Ruben Castaneda, "Officer Liable in Student's Killing," *Washington Post*, January 20, 2006, http://wapo.st/2alrZcw.

15. Ta-Nehisi Coates, *Between the World and Me* (New York: Spiegel & Grau, 2015), 80.

16. "You Never Read This Headline: 'Black Cop Shoots White Cop,'" *New York Daily News*, May 29, 2009, http://nydn.us/1kqEYru.

17. Rocco Parascandola, "NYPD Officer Andrew Dunton, Who Shot and Killed Off-Duty Cop Omar Edwards in Terrible Friendly-Fire Incident in 2009, Will Be Promoted to Sergeant," *New York Daily News*, September 28, 2012, http://nydn.us/2sPg2Rb.

18. Trace Cowen, "Black Off-Duty Cop Shot by White Officer While Trying to Help with Stolen Car Incident," *Complex*, June 23, 2017, http://bit.ly/2t4Vmad.

19. Department of Justice Report, "Investigation of the Baltimore City Police Department," 2016, https://www.justice.gov/opa/file/883366/download.

20. Redditt Hudson, "I'm a Black Ex-Cop, and This Is the Real Truth about Race and Policing," *Vox*, July 7, 2016, https://www.vox.com/2015/5/28/8661977/race-police-officer.

9. THE ULTIMATE FAILURE: EXONERATION

1. Phoebe Zerwick, "Murder, Race, Justice: The State vs. Darryl Hunt," *Winston-Salem Journal*, 2003, http://darrylhunt.journalnow.com.

2. Brandon L. Garrett, "Judging Innocence," *Columbia Law Review* 108 (2008): 55–142.

3. David Schaper, "Chicago Crime Spikes as Police Avoid Becoming the Next Viral Video," March 11, 2016, http://n.pr/1nD5Jv7.

4. Samuel R. Gross, Barbara O'Brien, Chen Hu, and Edward H. Kennedy, "Rate of False Conviction of Criminal Defendants Who Are Sentenced to Death," *Proceedings of the National Academy of Sciences of the United States of America* 111, no. 20 (2014), http://www.pnas.org/content/111/20/7230.abstract.

5. Innocence Project, http://www.innocenceproject.org.

6. National Registry of Exonerations, http://bit.ly/LI3yEk.

7. Gary L. Wells, N. Steblay, and J. Dysart, "Double-Blind Photo-Lineups Using Actual Eyewitnesses: An Experimental Test of a Sequential versus Simultaneous Lineup Procedure," *Law and Human Behavior* 39 (2015): 1–14.

8. Elizabeth Loftus, *Eyewitness Testimony* (Cambridge, MA: Harvard University Press, 1996).

9. https://www.innocenceproject.org/causes/false-confessions-admissions.

10. http://www.pbs.org/kenburns/centralparkfive.

11. Cynthia Fuchs, "When Truth and Reality Collide: 'The Central Park Five' and 'West of Memphis,'" *PopMatters*, November 14, 2012, http://www.popmatters.com/pm/review/165435-doc-nyc-2012-the-central-park-five-and-west-of-memphis.

12. Michael Hewlett, "Kalvin Michael Smith Is Out of Prison but He's Still Not Free," *Winston-Salem Journal*, June 4, 2017, http://www.journalnow.com/news/local/kalvin-michael-smith-is-out-of-prison-but-he-s/article_8408cccf-8ccb-598d-8adc-3aa240fa76c0.html.

13. The Innocence Project, http://bit.ly/1Rorhat.

14. Brandon L. Garrett, "Judging Innocence," *Columbia Law Review* 108 (2008): 55–142.

15. https://lastdays.atavist.com/the-last-days-of-darryl-hunt.

16. https://lastdays.atavist.com/the-last-days-of-darryl-hunt.

17. https://lastdays.atavist.com/the-last-days-of-darryl-hunt.

10. INTERSECTIONALITY, COLOR-BLIND RACISM, AND A CALL TO ACTION

1. Nikole Hannah-Jones, "The Grief That White Americans Can't Share," *New York Times Magazine*, June 22, 2016, http://nyti.ms/2a2BEkf.

2. Many showed up at the Constitutional Convention in Philadelphia in May 1787 with their slaves. The list is long and includes George Washington and James Madison.

3. Eugene Robinson, *Disintegration: The Splintering of Black America* (New York: Anchor, 2011).

4. Erik Wright, *Class Counts: Comparative Studies in Class Analysis* (New York: Cambridge University Press, 1997).

5. John Hope Franklin, *From Slavery to Freedom* (New York: Knopf, 1947).

6. Eduardo Bonilla-Silva, "The Structure of Racism in Color-Blind, 'Post-Racial' America," *American Behavioral Scientist* 59, no. 11 (2015), http://bit.ly/21M1FJs.

7. Erik Wright, *Class Counts: Comparative Studies in Class Analysis* (New York: Cambridge University Press, 1997). Emphasis ours.

8. Erik Wright, *Class Counts: Comparative Studies in Class Analysis* (New York: Cambridge University Press, 1997). Emphasis ours.

9. Deborah King, "Multiple Jeopardy, Multiple Consciousness: The Context of a Black Feminist Ideology," *Signs* 14, no. 1 (Autumn 1988): 42–72.

10. Chris Hayes, *A Colony in a Nation* (New York: Norton, 2017), 84.

11. Adia Harvey Wingfield, *No More Invisible Man: Race and Gender in Men's Work* (Philadelphia: Temple University Press, 2013), 116.

12. Tim McGettigan and Earl Smith, *A Formula for Eradicating Racism* (New York: Palgrave Macmillan, 2015).

APPENDIX A

1. Michael Cooper, "Officers in Bronx Fire 41 Shots, and an Unarmed Man Is Killed," *New York Times*, February 5, 1999, http://nyti.ms/28VUwF4.

2. Alex Johnson, "Officer in Jonathan Ferrell Killing: 'He Kept Trying to Get My Gun,'" NBC News, August 13, 2015, http://nbcnews.to/28WLO97.

3. Robert Littal, "Former Bengals RB David Lee 'Deacon' Turner Shot & Killed by Cops," Black Sports Online, July 11, 2011, http://bit.ly/2am5FPD.

BIBLIOGRAPHY

A Blueprint for Equality: A Federal Agenda for Transgender People. National Center for Transgender Equality, 2015, chapter 13. http://www.transequality.org/sites/default/files/docs/resources/NCTE_Blueprint_2015_Prisons.pdf.

Abu-Lughod, Janet L. *Race, Space, and Riots in Chicago, New York, and Los Angeles.* New York: Oxford University Press, 2007.

Acker, Joan. "Inequality Regimes: Gender, Class, and Race in Organizations." *Gender & Society* 20 (2006): 441–64. doi:10.1177/0891243206289499.

Aiken, Joshua. "The Downstream Effect of 35 Years of Jail Growth? A State Prison Boom." *Prison Policy Initiative*, June 4, 2017. https://www.prisonpolicy.org/blog/2017/06/14/downstream.

Alexander, Michelle. *The New Jim Crow.* New York: New Press, 2010.

Annie E. Casey Foundation. "Maltreatment of Youth in U.S. Juvenile Corrections Facilities: An Update." 2015. http://www.aecf.org/resources/maltreatment-of-youth-in-us-juvenile-corrections-facilities.

Badger, Emily. "The Long, Painful and Repetitive History of How Baltimore Became Baltimore." *Washington Post*, April 29, 2015. http://wapo.st/1VQkLd8.

Balko, Radley. *Rise of the Warrior Cop: The Militarization of America's Police Forces.* New York: PublicAffairs Books, 2013.

Barnett, Erica. "Prison Coffee: Starbucks Admits Its Contractor Uses Prison Labor." *Michigan Citizen* 24 (2002): A7.

Bauer, Shane. "My Four Months as a Private Prison Guard: A Mother Jones Investigation." *Mother Jones*, July/August 2016. http://bit.ly/28TZwIP.

Baum, Dan. "Legalize It All: How to Win the War on Drugs." *Harper's Bazaar*, April 2016. http://harpers.org/archive/2016/04/legalize-it-all.

Beck, Allen J., David Cantor, John Hartge, and Tim Smith. *Sexual Victimization in Juvenile Facilities, Reported by Youth 2012.* Washington, D.C.: Bureau of Justice Statistics, 2013.

Bonilla-Silva, Eduardo. "Rethinking Racism: Toward a Structural Interpretation." *American Sociological Review* 62, no. 3 (1997): 465–80. http://www.jstor.org/stable/2657316.

———. "The Structure of Racism in Color-Blind, 'Post-Racial America.'" *American Behavioral Scientist* 59, no. 11 (2015): 1358–76. http://bit.ly/21M1FJs.

Broadwater, Luke. "Wells Fargo Agrees to Pay $175M Settlement in Pricing Discrimination Suit." *Baltimore Sun*, July 12, 2012. http://bit.ly/28IuKQX.

Brooks, Charles. "Harlemworld: Doing Race and Class in Contemporary Black America." Book review. *Black Issues Book Review*, March–April 2002.

Brown, George, and Everett McDuffie. "Health Care Policies Addressing Transgender Inmates in Prison Systems in the United States." *Journal of Correctional Health Care* 15, no. 4 (2009): 280–91.

Burke, Shelia. "Arrest of Tennessee Children Exposes Flawed Juvenile Justice." ABC News, May 13, 2016. http://abcnews.go.com/US/wireStory/arrest-tennessee-children-exposes-flawed-juvenile-justice-39084653.

Carson, E. A., and E. Anderson. *Prisoners in 2015*. Washington, D.C.: Bureau of Justice Statistics, 2016.

Castaneda, Ruben. "Officer Liable in Student's Killing." *Washington Post*, January 20, 2006. http://wapo.st/2alrZcw.

Chandler, Michael Alison. "One in 10 D.C. Students Score 'College Ready' on New High School Math Test." *Washington Post*, October 27, 2015. http://wapo.st/2scHRRQ.

Chicago Commission on Race Relations. *The Negro in Chicago: A Study of Race Relations and a Race Riot*. Chicago: University of Chicago Press, 1922.

Coates, Ta-Nehisi. *Between the World and Me*. New York: Spiegel & Grau, 2015.

———. "The Clock Didn't Start with the Riots: Black People in Baltimore Are Subjected to Violence All the Time." *Atlantic*, April 30, 2015. http://www.theatlantic.com/politics/archive/2015/04/ta-nehisi-coates-johns-hopkins-baltimore/391904.

Collins, Patricia Hill. *Black Feminist Thought: Knowledge, Consciousness and the Politics of Empowerment*. Boston: Unwin Hyman, 1990.

Connell, Rich, and Richard Serrano. "L.A. Is Warned of New Unrest: Webster Report Urges Swift Action in City Plagued by Hostility, Rage and Resentment in Many Areas. Budget Crisis and Politicking Could Delay Reforms." *Los Angeles Times*, October 22, 1992. http://lat.ms/22IuPrX.

Cooper, Michael. "Officers in Bronx Fire 41 Shots, and an Unarmed Man Is Killed." *New York Times*, February 5, 1999. http://nyti.ms/28VUwF4.

Council of Economic Advisors. *Fines, Fees, and Bail Payments in the Criminal Justice System That Disproportionately Impact the Poor*. 2015. https://www.whitehouse.gov/sites/default/files/page/files/1215_cea_fine_fee_bail_issue_brief.pdf.

Cowen, Trace. "Black Off-Duty Cop Shot by White Officer While Trying to Help with Stolen Car Incident." Complex, June 23, 2017. http://bit.ly/2t4Vmad.

Davis, Angela Y. "Masked Racism: Reflections on the Prison Industrial Complex." *Colorlines Magazine*, 1998.

Department of Justice Report. "Investigation of the Baltimore City Police Department." 2016. https://www.justice.gov/opa/file/883366/download.

Department of Justice Report. "Investigation of the Ferguson Police Department." March 2015. http://bit.ly/2sSGUjg.

Donovan, Doug, and Jean Marbella. "Dismissed: Tenants Lose and Landlords Win in Baltimore's Rent Court." *Baltimore Sun*, April 26, 2017. http://data.baltimoresun.com/news/dismissed.

Durose, M. R., and Patrick A. Langan. *State Court Sentencing of Convicted Felons, 1998 Statistical Tables*. Washington, D.C.: U.S. Department of Justice, 2001.

Epp, Charles R., Steven Maynard-Moody, and Donald Haider-Markel. *Pulled Over: How Police Stops Define Race and Citizenship*. Chicago: University of Chicago Press, 2014.

Equal Justice Initiative. "EJI Wins New Sentencing for 14-Year-Old Who Was Sentenced to Die in Prison." April 26, 2013. http://www.eji.org/node/767.

Fabelo, Tony, Michael D. Thompson, Martha Plotkin, Dottie Carmichael, Miner P. Marchbanks III, and Eric A. Booth. *Breaking Schools' Rules: A Statewide Study of How School Discipline Relates to Students' Success and Juvenile Justice Involvement*. Public Policy Research Institute, 2011.

Fanon, Frantz. *Black Skin, White Masks*. New York: Grove Press, 1952.

———. *The Wretched of the Earth*. Translated by Richard Philox. New York: Grove Press, 1984.

Farberov, Snejana. "Caught on Camera: Police Shooting of Teenager Which Has Shocked America and Left City of Ferguson on the Brink as Officers Face Protests over 'Racism and

Brutality' and Looters Go on Rampage." *Daily Mail*, August 15, 2014. http://dailym.ai/1YbihsD.

Featherstone, Steve. "Professor Carnage." *New Republic*, April 17, 2017. https://newrepublic.com/article/141675/professor-carnage-dave-grossman-police-warrior-philosophy.

Ferrise, Adam. "Timothy Russell's Family Upset with Michael Brelo Verdict, but 'It Wasn't All Brelo's Fault.'" Cleveland.com, May 23, 2015. http://bit.ly/28VY1dk.

Fiske, John. *Media Matters: Race and Gender in U.S. Politics*. Minneapolis: University of Minnesota Press, 1996.

Franklin, John Hope. *From Slavery to Freedom*. New York: Knopf, 1947.

———. "Tulsa Still Hasn't Faced the Truth about the Race Riot of 1921." Delivered before the House Judiciary Committee, Subcommittee on Constitution, Civil Rights, and Civil Liberties, April 28, 2007. http://bit.ly/2seTec7.

Friedersdorf, Conor. "The Brutality of Police Culture in Baltimore." *Atlantic*, April 22, 2015. http://theatln.tc/28ItPz0.

Frye, Marilyn. *The Politics of Reality: Essays in Feminist Theory*. Freedom, CA: Crossing Press, 1983.

Fuchs, Cynthia. "When Truth and Reality Collide: 'The Central Park Five' and 'West of Memphis.'" *PopMatters*, November 14, 2012. http://www.popmatters.com/pm/review/165435-doc-nyc-2012-the-central-park-five-and-west-of-memphis.

Garrett, Brandon L. "Judging Innocence." *Columbia Law Review* 108 (2008): 55–142.

Ghali, Kamal. "No Slavery Except as a Punishment for Crime: The Punishment Clause and Sexual Slavery." *UCLA Law Review* 55 (2008): 607.

Gilna, Derek. "Businesses, Members of Congress, Not Happy with UNICOR." *Prison Legal News*, March 15, 2014. https://www.prisonlegalnews.org/news/2014/mar/15/businesses-members-of-congress-not-happy-with-unicor.

Graham, David A. "The Mysterious Death of Freddie Gray." *Atlantic*, April 22, 2015. http://theatln.tc/24YO7ZQ.

Grant, Jaime M., Lisa A. Mottet, Justin Tanis, Jack Harrison, Jody L. Herman, and Mara Keisling. *Injustice at Every Turn: A Report of the National Transgender Discrimination Survey*. Washington, D.C.: National Center for Transgender Equality and National Gay and Lesbian Task Force, 2011.

Gross, Samuel R., Barbara O'Brien, Chen Hu, and Edward H. Kennedy. "Rate of False Conviction of Criminal Defendants Who Are Sentenced to Death." *Proceedings of the National Academy of Sciences of the United States of America* 111, no. 20 (2014). http://www.pnas.org/content/111/20/7230.abstract.

Guardian. Police Shooting Data Base. http://bit.ly/1Ey6d8u.

Hannah-Jones, Nikole. "The Grief That White Americans Can't Share." *New York Times Magazine*, June 22, 2016. http://nyti.ms/2a2BEkf.

Harris, Alexes. *A Pound of Flesh: Monetary Sanctions as a Punishment for the Poor*. New York: Russell Sage, 2016.

Hattery, Angela J., and Earl Smith. *African American Families: Myths and Realities*. Lanham, MD: Rowman & Littlefield, 2014.

Hayes, Chris. *A Colony in a Nation*. New York: Norton, 2017.

Heitzeg, Nancy A. *The School-to-Prison Pipeline: Education, Discipline, and Racialized Double Standards*. New York: Praeger, 2016.

Hewlett, Michael. "Kalvin Michael Smith Is Out of Prison but He's Still Not Free." *Winston-Salem Journal*, June 4, 2017. http://www.journalnow.com/news/local/kalvin-michael-smith-is-out-of-prison-but-he-s/article_8408cccf-8ccb-598d-8adc-3aa240fa76c0.html.

Hinton, Elizabeth. *From the War on Poverty to the War on Crime: The Making of Mass Incarceration in America*. Cambridge, MA: Harvard University Press, 2016.

History.com Staff. "Emmett Till Murderers Make Magazine Confession." 2009. http://bit.ly/295Kkqq.

Hooks, Gregory. "The Prison Industry: Carceral Expansion and Employment in U.S. Counties, 1969–1994." *Social Science Quarterly* 85, no. 1 (2004): 38–57.

Hudson, Redditt. "I'm a Black Ex-Cop, and This Is the Real Truth about Race and Policing." Vox, July 7, 2016. http://www.vox.com/2015/5/28/8661977/race-police-officer.

Innocence Project. "DNA Exonerations in the United States." http://bit.ly/1Rorhat.
"Inside the Secret Industry of Inmate-Staffed Call Centers." NBC News, January 12, 2012. http://usnews.nbcnews.com/_news/2012/01/12/10140493-inside-the-secret-industry-of-inmate-staffed-call-centers.
James, D. J. Profile of Jail Inmates, 2002. Washington, D.C.: Bureau of Justice Statistics, 2004.
Jenness, Valerie, and Sarah Fenstermaker. "Forty Years after Brownmiller: Prisons for Men, Transgender Inmates, and the Rape of the Feminine." Gender and Society 30, no. 1 (February 2016): 14–29.
Jenness, Valerie, Cheryl L. Maxson, Kristy N. Matsuda, and Jennifer Macy Sumner. Violence in California Correctional Facilities: An Empirical Examination of Sexual Assault. Irvine: Center for Evidence-Based Corrections, University of California, 2007.
Johnson, Alex. "Officer in Jonathan Ferrell Killing: 'He Kept Trying to Get My Gun.'" NBC News, August 13, 2015. http://nbcnews.to/28WLO97.
"K–12 Education: Better Use of Information Could Help Agencies Identify Disparities and Address Racial Discrimination." GAO-16-345. Government Accountability Office, April 21, 2016. http://gao.gov/products/GAO-16-345.
Kearney, Melissa S., and Benjamin H. Harris. "Ten Economic Facts about Crime and Incarceration in the United States." Brookings Institute, May 1, 2014. http://www.brookings.edu/research/reports/2014/05/10-crime-facts.
King, Deborah. "Multiple Jeopardy, Multiple Consciousness: The Context of a Black Feminist Ideology." Signs 14, no. 1 (Autumn 1988): 42–72.
King, Martin Luther, Jr. "Beyond the Los Angeles Riots: Next Step, the North." Saturday Review, November 13, 1965, 33–35, 105.
Langan, Patrick. Race of Prisoners Admitted to State and Federal Institutions, 1926–86. NCJ-125618. Washington, D.C.: U.S. Department of Justice, 1991. https://www.ncjrs.gov/pdffiles1/nij/125618.pdf.
Law, Victoria. "Giving Birth While Shackled May Be Illegal, but Mothers Still Have to Endure It." Guardian, February 13, 2015. https://www.theguardian.com/us-news/2015/feb/13/mothers-prison-illegal-shackled-while-giving-birth.
LeBlanc, A. N. "Prison Is a Member of Their Family." New York Times Magazine, January 12, 2003.
Littal, Robert. "Former Bengals RB David Lee 'Deacon' Turner Shot & Killed by Cops." Black Sports Online, July 11, 2011. http://bit.ly/2am5FPD.
Locke, Alain. The New Negro: An Interpretation. New York: Albert and Charles Boni, 1925.
Loftus, Elizabeth. Eyewitness Testimony. Cambridge, MA: Harvard University Press, 1996.
Lucal, Betsy. "What It Means to Be Gendered Me: Life on the Boundaries of a Dichotomous Gender System." Gender & Society 13 (1999): 781–97. doi:10.1177/089124399013006006.
Mauer, M., and R. King. A 25-Year Quagmire: The War on Drugs and Its Impact on American Society. Washington, D.C.: Sentencing Project, 2007.
McCone Commission Report, California. Governor's Commission on the Los Angeles Riots: Plus One Hundred Four Shocking Photos of the Most Terrifying Riot in History. Los Angeles: Kimtex, 1965.
McGettigan, Timothy, and Earl Smith. A Formula for Eradicating Racism. New York: Palgrave Macmillan, 2015.
Messer, Chris M., Krystal Beamon, and Patricia A. Bell. "The Tulsa Riot of 1921: Collective Violence and Racial Frames." Western Journal of Black Studies 37, no. 1 (2013): 50–59.
Minton, Todd, and Zhen Zeng. Jail Inmates in 2015. Washington, D.C.: Bureau of Justice Statistics, 2016.
Montgomery, Ben, and Waveney Ann Moore. "For Their Own Good: A St. Petersburg Times Special Report on Child Abuse at the Florida School for Boys." Tampa Bay Times, April 17, 2009. http://www.tampabay.com/specials/2009/reports/marianna.
Mosher, Clayton, and Gregory Hooks. "Don't Build It Here Revisited (or 'There Is No Economic Salvation through Incarceration')—Prisons Do Not Create Jobs." Prison Legal News, January 15, 2010. http://bit.ly/292zPEp.
Mukamal, D. "After Prisons: Roadblocks to Reentry; A Report on State Legal Barriers Facing People with Criminal Records." New York: Legal Action Center, 2004.

Murray, Charles. *Coming Apart: The State of White America, 1960–2010*. New York: Crown, 2013.

National Registry of Exonerations. http://bit.ly/LI3yEk.

National Urban League. *40 Years: The State of Black America, 1976–2016*. 2016. http://soba. iamempowered.com/node/191.

Nellis, Ashley. "The Lives of Juvenile Lifers: Findings from a National Survey." Sentencing Project, 2012. http://sentencingproject.org/wp-content/uploads/2016/01/The-Lives-of-Juvenile-Lifers.pdf.

Neuspiel, D. R. "Racism and Perinatal Addiction." *Ethnicity and Disease* 6 (1996): 47–55.

Pager, Devah. "The Mark of a Criminal Record." *American Journal of Sociology* 108 (2003): 937–75.

Parascandola, Rocco. "NYPD Officer Andrew Dunton, Who Shot and Killed Off-Duty Cop Omar Edwards in Terrible Friendly-Fire Incident in 2009, Will Be Promoted to Sergeant." *New York Daily News*, September 28, 2012. http://nydn.us/2sPg2Rb.

Plater, Roz. "Prince William Student Handcuffed, Suspended over 'Stolen' $0.65 Milk Carton." ABC7, May 20, 2016. http://wjla.com/news/local/prince-william-student-handcuffed-suspended-over-stolen-065-milk-carton.

"Profitability Remains Elusive for Mississippi Catfish Farmers." *Mississippi Business Journal*, August 2, 2004.

Richie, Beth E. "Challenges Incarcerated Women Face as They Return to Their Communities: Findings from Life History Interviews." *Crime and Delinquency* 47 (2001): 368–89.

Roberts, Dorothy. *Killing the Black Body: Race, Reproduction, and the Meaning of Liberty*. New York: Vintage, 1999.

Robinson, Eugene. *Disintegration: The Splintering of Black America*. New York: Anchor, 2011.

Ross, Cody T. "A Multi-Level Bayesian Analysis of Racial Bias in Police Shootings at the County-Level in the United States, 2011–2014." *PLoS One* 10, no. 11 (2016): e0141854. https://doi.org/10.1371/journal.pone.0141854.

Rovner, Joshua. "Disproportionate Minority Contact in the Juvenile Justice System." Sentencing Project, 2014. http://sentencingproject.org/wp-content/uploads/2015/11/Disproportionate-Minority-Contact-in-the-Juvenile-Justice-System.pdf.

Rubin Erdley, Sabrina. "The Transgender Crucible." *Rolling Stone*, July 30, 2014. http://www.rollingstone.com/culture/news/the-transgender-crucible-20140730#ixzz49bNbBmBK.

Saar, Malika Saada, Rebecca Epstein, Lindsay Rosenthal, and Yasmin Vafa. *The Sexual Abuse to Prison Pipeline: The Girls' Story*. Washington, D.C.: Center for Poverty and Inequality, Georgetown University Law Center, 2015. http://bit.ly/1DqeScy.

Sawyer, Wendy. "How Much Do Incarcerated People Earn in Each State? *Prison Policy Initiative*. April 10, 2017. https://www.prisonpolicy.org/blog/2017/04/10/wages.

Schaper, David. "Chicago Crime Spikes as Police Avoid Becoming the Next Viral Video." March 11, 2016. http://n.pr/1nD5Jv7.

Schenwar, Maya. "The Quiet Horrors of House Arrest, Electronic Monitoring, and Other Alternative Forms of Incarceration: How Imprisonment Extends beyond the Jailhouse into Every Arena of American Life." *Mother Jones*, January 22, 2015. http://www.motherjones.com/politics/2015/01/house-arrest-surveillance-state-prisons.

Schwartzapfel, Beth. "Sentenced Young: The Story of Life without Parole for Juvenile Offenders." *Aljazeera America*, February 1, 2014, http://america.aljazeera.com/features/2014/1/sentenced-young-thestoryoflifewithoutparoleforjuvenileoffenders.html.

Schwirtz, Michael, and Michael Winerip. "Kalief Browder, Held at Rikers Island for 3 Years without Trial, Commits Suicide." *New York Times*, June 8, 2015. http://nyti.ms/1rROE3l.

Serres, Chris. "Homeless and Penniless, Minnesota Sex Offender Is Sent Back to Jail because He Can't Afford Treatment." *Minneapolis Star-Tribune*, May 4, 2016. http://www.startribune.com/homeless-and-penniless-minnesota-sex-offender-is-sent-back-to-jail-because-he-can-t-afford-treatment/378045171.

Shapiro, Fred C., and James W. Sullivan. *Race Riots: New York, 1964*. New York: Crowell, 1964.

Sink, Justin. "Obama Calls for Calm after 'Disturbing' Events in Ferguson." *The Hill*, August 14, 2014, http://thehill.com/homenews/administration/215152-obama-calls-for-calm-after-disturbing-events-in-ferguson.

Sokoloff, Nancy. "The Impact of the Prison Industrial Complex on African American Women." *SOULS* 5 (2003): 31–46.

Somashekhar, Sandhya, Wesley Lowery, Keith L. Alexander, Kimberly Kindy, and Julie Tate. "Black and Unarmed." *Washington Post*, August 8, 2015. http://wapo.st/1J4wTor.

Sontag, Deborah. "Transgender Woman Cites Attacks and Abuse in Men's Prison." *New York Times*, April 5, 2015. http://www.nytimes.com/2015/04/06/us/ashley-diamond-transgender-inmate-cites-attacks-and-abuse-in-mens-prison.html.

Spear, Allan. *Black Chicago: The Making of a Negro Ghetto, 1890–1920*. Chicago: University of Chicago Press, 1967.

Spohn, C. C. *Thirty Years of Sentencing Reform: The Quest for a Racially Neutral Sentencing Process*. Washington, D.C.: National Institute of Justice, 2000.

Staples, Robert. "White Racism, Black Crime, and American Justice: An Application of the Colonial Model to Explain Crime and Race." *Phylon* 36, no. 1 (1975): 14–22.

Stewart, Jeffrey. "Harlem Renaissance." Online NewsHour Forum, PBS, February 20, 1998.

Thieman, Linda. "Fallon Requests Info on Jobs Lost to Prison Labor, Clarifies 'Gulag' Remark," *Blog for Iowa* [blog], June 30, 2004, http://www.blogforiowa.com/blog.

Thomas, W. I., and Dorothy Thomas. *The Child in America: Behavior Problems and Programs*. New York: Knopf, 1928.

Townes, Carimah. "Black People Twice as Likely to Be Arrested for Pot in Colorado and Washington—Where It's Legal." *Think Progress*, March 21, 2016. http://thinkprogress.org/justice/2016/03/21/3761973/black-people-still-more-likely-to-face-marijuana-arrests.

US Police Shootings Database (USPSD). https://us-police-shootings-database.silk.co.

Villa, Manuel. "The Mental Health Crisis Facing Women in Prison." *San Antonio Express*, June 22, 2017. http://bit.ly/2tYlaCa.

Wagner, Peter. "Tracking State Prison Growth in 50 States." *Prison Policy Initiative*. 2014. http://www.prisonpolicy.org/reports/overtime.html.

Walsh, James D. "The Bullet, the Cop, the Boy." *New York Magazine*, June 14, 2017. http://nym.ag/2sDkuVm.

Wells, Gary L., N. Steblay, and J. Dysart. "Double-Blind Photo Lineups Using Actual Eyewitnesses: An Experimental Test of a Sequential versus Simultaneous Lineup Procedure." *Law and Human Behavior* 39 (2015): 1–14.

Whitaker, Bill. "Officer Betty Shelby on Terence Crutcher Shooting." CBS News, April 2, 2017. http://cbsn.ws/2rExSJi.

Wilder, Craig. *Ebony & Ivy: Race, Slavery, and the Troubled History of America's Universities*. New York: St. Martin's, 2014.

Wills, Denise Kersten. "'People Were Out of Control': Remembering the 1968 Riots." *Washingtonian*, April 2008.

Wilson, John Paul, Kurt Hugenberg, and Nicholas O. Rule. "Racial Bias in Judgments of Physical Size and Formidability: From Size to Threat." *Journal of Personality and Social Psychology* 113, no. 1 (2017): 59–80. http://psycnet.apa.org/psycinfo/2017-11085-001.

Wingfield, Adia Harvey. *No More Invisible Man: Race and Gender in Men's Work*. Philadelphia: Temple University Press, 2013.

Wright, Erik. *Class Counts: Comparative Studies in Class Analysis*. New York: Cambridge University Press, 1997.

Yoder, Harvey. "Va. Faces a Worsening Prison Crisis." *News Leader*, June 1, 2015. http://www.newsleader.com/story/opinion/columnists/2015/06/01/va-faces-worsening-prison-crisis/28256983.

"You Never Read This Headline: 'Black Cop Shoots White Cop.'" *New York Daily News*, May 29, 2009. http://nydn.us/1kqEYru.

Zerwick, Phoebe. "Murder, Race, Justice: The State vs. Darryl Hunt." *Winston-Salem Journal*, 2003. http://darrylhunt.journalnow.com.

INDEX